THE GREAT APPROACH

New Light and Life for Humanity

BENJAMIN CREME

SHARE INTERNATIONAL FOUNDATION

Amsterdam, London, Los Angeles

First Edition, June 2001
Second printing, March 2002

*The cover picture is reproduced from a painting by Benjamin Creme, entitled **Oracle** (1964-1984). "The Oracle is the prophet or soothsayer, one who knows what others do not know and who is thus consulted about future events." (from **The Esoteric Art of Benjamin Creme**)*

This book is dedicated
to my revered Master.
His limitless wisdom and knowledge
are its inspiration.

CONTENTS

PART TWO

THE GREAT APPROACH

PART THREE

THE COMING OF A NEW LIGHT

QUESTIONS AND ANSWERS

PREFACE

The Great Approach: New Light and Life for Humanity is about the coming into the world of the Masters of Wisdom, with Their leader Maitreya, the Christ, as World Teacher; and about the implications for humanity, as well as for the Masters Themselves, of this great event.

The book is divided into three independent but related parts. It includes articles from my Master, my own edited talks, and a very wide range of questions and answers arising from these talks.

Part One, 'Life Ahead for Humanity', provides an overview of the background and history of the Masters and Their return to the everyday world. In particular, it focuses on the events leading to the gradual emergence of Maitreya and to the Day of His Declaration. This will be an extraordinary 'Pentecostal' experience for humanity, and the start of the gradual transformation of all our structures and institutions. Part One continues with a series of questions and answers which point to ways of recognizing Maitreya before His true identity is revealed; His appearances to fundamentalists worldwide, and the creation of healing wells. This section also deals with market forces and commercialization, and through Maitreya's influence the creation of a just economic order. The environment and pollution are underlined as major priorities and the various activities of 'extraterrestrials' in ameliorating this crisis are revealed. It also covers His concerns for the problems of humanity, such as the divisions in the world, especially the plight of millions in developing countries, and it puts forward His proposals for solving these problems.

Part Two, 'The Great Approach', which lends its title to the book as a whole, deals with that most extraordinary event, the externalization of the work of the Spiritual Hierarchy onto the physical plane for the first time in 98,000 years in Their role as teachers. This is a climactic event for the Masters Themselves, as well as for humanity: They return to physical-plane activity, only now in group formation, in order to re-enact Their *own* life expression in preparation for the Way of the Higher Evolution. This is part of the long-term plan of the coming together of the Masters and humanity, and the evolution of Hierarchy Itself as a centre on this planet. In Their relation to humanity, the Masters, with Maitreya at Their head, have provided a blueprint for the future of a brilliant, transformed world free from want and war.

The Ways of the Higher Evolution are so far beyond humanity's consciousness that we cannot conceive what might lie ahead for the Masters. For this reason, I have elected, unusually, but hopefully not irreverently, to treat this section of the book from a humorous stance, underlining how far beyond our knowledge that future is.

Topics arising from the article on the Great Approach include ways in which Masters actually work, both individually and as a group, and more on the work of preparation and its implications for those involved.

Part Three begins with my commentary on an article by my Master, 'Let there be Light', which was previously published in *Share International* magazine (December 1983). It deals with Light from the esoteric point of view, including the Light of Knowledge, the Christ Principle, Cosmic Electricity and the new Science of Light, which will transform our future. An extraordinary vista opens before us of awareness and discovery.

I describe our long evolutionary journey, and how each incarnation adds a modicum of light to the matter of our vehicles — physical, emotional and mental. The different aspects of light are discussed, and the Christ Principle introduced as the first Master, through the soul. The Light of Knowledge is released into the world by the Masters, so bringing us into the initiatory experience. This esoteric process is shown as *the* method by which we expand our consciousness to work intelligently with the Plan of evolution, and eventually to become a Master.

The Atlantean civilization is shown not as myth but as a reality of the human evolution. The great war between the forces of Light (the Masters of the Spiritual Hierarchy) and of Darkness (the Lords of Materiality) brought it to a premature end. This interrupted the evolutionary Plan, and led the Masters of the time to retreat to the mountains and deserts of the world, seemingly leaving humanity to cope on its own. Now, after 98,000 years, They begin Their return.

One important aspect of the reappearance work which this book does not cover is Transmission Meditation. This crucial part of the work was introduced by my Master in March 1974, when the first Transmission Meditation group was formed in London. Transmission Meditation is fully covered in *Transmission: A Meditation for the New Age* as well as *Maitreya's Mission Volumes One, Two* and *Three* (Share International Foundation).

Acknowledgements: I would like to express my gratitude to the many people in London and San Francisco whose time and effort have contributed to this book. Their devotion to the tasks of transcribing, inputting and proof-reading, cheerfully and efficiently undertaken, have made its publication possible. In particular, I would like to express my gratitude, once again, to Michiko Ishikawa for her invaluable work in organizing the copious material into readable form.

Editors Note: Most of the articles and questions and answers contained in this book were published originally in the monthly magazine, *Share International,* during the period March 1997 to February 2001. Some are from Benjamin Creme's public lectures. The date of first publication or the lectures is given at the end of each question.

PART ONE

LIFE AHEAD FOR HUMANITY

The World Teacher for the New Age

The following article is an edited version of a talk by Benjamin Creme given on 18 July 2000 at the Masonic Auditorium in San Francisco, USA.

This information is about the total transformation of every aspect of our lives: political, economic, religious, social, scientific, cultural, educational and personal. If what I say is true, the current ways of thinking, living, relating and expressing our inner selves will be fundamentally altered in the time ahead. If this is your first acquaintance with this information, you may find it difficult to accept and believe, especially if you are approaching it from an orthodox religious or philosophical background. If you find it impossible to believe, please be assured that I shall not be the slightest bit offended or even disappointed.

Of course, I do believe that what I say is true. Otherwise I would not spend my time traipsing around the world making it known; there are many things I could be doing. For myself, I am totally convinced that these are the true happenings of our time; that, even as I write, these events are unfolding. As they further unfold, I believe they will prove to your fullest satisfaction that this is the true condition of our present time in history.

My conviction is the result of my study, over many years, of the Ageless Wisdom Teachings. This body of teachings was

1

given to the world by the Masters of Wisdom, in particular that phase of them which was released to the world by the Tibetan Master, Djwhal Khul, through an English disciple, Alice A.Bailey, between 1919 and 1949. This forms the philosophical background from which I speak, a body of teachings which follows sequentially on those given through Madame Helena Petrovna Blavatsky, founder of the Theosophical Society, between 1875 and 1889.

The Theosophical teachings were the preparatory phase of the Ageless Wisdom Teachings, given for our time, and the Alice Bailey teachings the intermediary phase. The Tibetan Master, through Alice Bailey, predicted a further, revelatory, phase which He said would emerge worldwide over the medium of the radio, and presumably now television, some time after 1975. This phase of the teachings involved revelations coming from the Masters, and above all from the Master of all the Masters, the Lord Maitreya, Who embodies the Christ Principle and is, therefore, the Christ on our planet.

Probably more importantly, my conviction is based on my own personal experiences and contacts. But having said that, I would like to assure you that what I say I present to you for your consideration only, not as dogma. If it appears to you to be right, logical, if it has the ring of truth, if events in the outer world tend to point in the same direction, then by all means accept it, but otherwise not. I shall be perfectly content if people approach this information with an open mind. That is all I ask. At the same time, I know that it is almost an impossibility.

We all imagine that we have an open mind. In my not too little experience, I have found a truly open mind to be about the rarest of all human attributes. To every new idea, no matter how lofty, how noble, how true, we bring our conditioning from the very cradle. As we listen to the speaker, we relate what the speaker is saying to what we already believe — and therefore think we know — about the subject. When these two things coincide, we accept what the speaker is saying because he is agreeing with us. When they do not coincide, we tend to reject what we hear. I believe this is one of the major reasons why it has taken humanity so long to evolve to the point where we are today. Some people may put that at a few million years at most but the Masters of our Spiritual Hierarchy, Who ought to know the age of humanity, put it at 18½ million years.

Eighteen-and-a-half million years is a very long time. None of us remembers it, but our unwritten history is there. One day the history of humanity going back to those times will be written and known, and even shown on television.

Over the ages, if we had had a more open attitude to knowledge, to change of consciousness, to change of perception of the possibilities of life and the nature of the reality in which we live, people like Galileo or Copernicus would have had altogether easier lives. They would not have been forced, as in the case of Galileo, to recant their fundamental, intelligent, brilliant analysis of the nature of our solar system, showing that the world was not flat, that in fact it moved around the sun as do all the planets. To us it seems so obvious, so natural because we were taught it at school, and because as children we are much more open-minded. If what I am saying were taught to the children of the world (not that I advise that especially), they would probably take it in much more easily and readily than their elders.

I am not, therefore, asking you to believe what I write. Just in making it known, my work is being done, and I really do not mind whether you believe it or not. If you do believe it, then watch out! If you truly believe it, and wish, therefore, to do something about it, because you will come to know it as the most important thing you could be doing in this world, you will be galvanized into action in a way which you had never thought

3

possible. It will demand your utmost in time, energy and commitment, but will leave you deeply, profoundly, spiritually satisfied because you will have helped to prepare the way for the Great Teacher Who, to my certain knowledge, is in the world; in this way you will be preparing the world for His full, open emergence, entering into our lives in the deepest possible way. At the very least, if this information gives you renewed hope for the future, for the future of your children and your children's children, I shall be satisfied.

Entering a New Age

It is a very difficult time for humanity. A large majority of people, especially in the less developed areas, the so-called Third World, have a very painful existence indeed. We in the developed West have our problems, of course. The problems are real, but usually quickly solvable. The major problems of the world, those which cause problems for everyone, are perfectly solvable, according to the Masters. We have the solution in our grasp if we did but know it and use it.

Most people know that we are entering a new era, a new cosmic cycle, the Age of Aquarius. This is not some fanciful astrological prognostication thought up by New Age groups. It is a hard astronomical fact that you can verify by a visit to any observatory. It is the result of the movement of our solar system around the heavens in relation to the constellations of the zodiac. This journey takes about 25,000 to 26,000 years to complete. Approximately every 2,150 years, therefore, our sun comes into an alignment, an energetic relationship, with each of the constellations in turn. When our sun is in that alignment, we say we are in the Age of that particular constellation.

For the last 2,000-plus years, that relationship has been with the constellation Pisces. We have been in the Age of Pisces, which was inaugurated by Jesus in Palestine 2,000 years ago. All the close disciples of Jesus knew the true purpose of His

4

mission was to inaugurate the Age of Pisces, set in motion the ideas and energies which, as humanity responded to them, would create the civilization which is now coming to an end. We are living at the end of the civilization of Pisces, at the very difficult transitional period between the Age of Pisces and the Age of Aquarius. The early Christian iconography has the fish as its symbol. This dominates the entire gospel story. It was common knowledge among the early Christians that the Age of Pisces was being inaugurated, and they were in at the start, so to speak. The symbol of the fish is the age-old symbol for Pisces.

The Age of Pisces has come to an end, and the new age has begun. The energies of Pisces began to recede in 1625 and the energies of Aquarius began to come in and affect our planet in 1675. For the last 300-plus years we have been in the Age of Aquarius, responding each day a little more to these incoming energies, which have a very different effect on humanity from those of Pisces.

As we have responded to them, the energies of Pisces have created the world we see, with all its divisions, the world which is now fast fading as these energies recede, as the sun moves away from the sphere of influence of Pisces, and as the institutions, therefore, fall apart. They have become crystallized, bereft of energy, and so are crumbling away before our very eyes.

This is very painful for many people because it leaves them insecure. All that they have held dear throughout their lives (in the plural) is slipping away. They feel that the world is turned upside down, that they have no real place in it, that the political and economic certainties on which they have relied from infancy no longer have meaning. The institutions are barely discernible as those in which they could believe for so long.

These people make up the conservative and reactionary forces in the world. They hold onto the old, resisting change with all their might, not because they are evil but because they love the past. The younger members of society are inevitably responding more to the new Aquarian energies which daily are mounting in potency. The energy of Pisces and the energy of Aquarius are now roughly equal — and that is our problem. If one or the other dominated, life would be simpler. Because of their equality of tension, they present humanity with major decisions. Do we hold on to the old selfish, individualistic ways of the past, with all the self-seeking and greed that represents? Or do we look for new ways to live and relate that will better express the quality of the incoming energy of Aquarius which is synthesis? This is easier for younger people, and much more difficult for those who are older, and who, if they are in a favourable position in social life, like what life has given them so far and are fearful of losing it. So they resist change.

The world is divided, therefore, into two groups — the conservative, reactionary groups holding on, fighting a last ditch stand against change, and the newer, younger, progressive groups responding more to the quality and energy of Aquarius. That confrontation can be seen in political, economic, religious and social spheres in every country of the world.

It leaves humanity with great decisions to make because the world is in a very perilous state. Politically, there are enormous tensions that could devastate the world, erupt into nuclear war and destroy all life on the planet which we can now do many times over. Economically, there are structures which are so unjust and negative in their effects on the majority of people that we should be rid of them immediately. Religiously, there are oppositions and confrontations which belie the fact that all religions stem from the same spiritual source: the Masters of Wisdom and the Lords of Compassion, the Spiritual Hierarchy of our planet.

Elder Brothers of humanity

This group of perfected men has stood behind the scenes of life from the earliest time and beneficently guided, protected and stimulated humanity in its long evolutionary journey from early animal man and woman up to the present time. Sometimes They have worked more openly, but for the last 98,000 years, with very few exceptions, They have lived in the remote mountain and desert areas of the world, such as the Himalayas, the Andes, the Rockies, the Cascades, the Carpathians, the Urals, the Atlas, and the Gobi and other deserts.

From these mountain and desert areas, working mainly through Their disciples, men and women in the world, They have beneficently overseen our evolution. With the total, unconditional love and service which They alone can display, They have brought humanity to the readiness of a new revelation, a revelation about the nature of the reality in which we live, which we call God, and the resonance of That in ourselves, so we shall know more about the reality of divinity and our own divine nature. A tremendous revelation is about to be given to humanity by the only One Who can do so.

At the start of every new age, from the beginning of time, a Teacher has come into the world to inaugurate the age, set in motion the ideas which would uplift and galvanize humanity, bringing it forward in its evolution, and creating conditions in which this could be done. We know some of these teachers as Hercules, Hermes, Rama, Mithra, Vyasa, Confucius, Zoroaster, Krishna, Shankaracharya, the Buddha, the Christ and Mohammed. These are all names of great Teachers Who have come to bring the message of the Masters, the Elder Brothers of humanity. The Masters are Those Who have gone ahead of us in evolution, Who, as ordinary men and women, have completed the evolutionary journey and need no further incarnation on planet Earth, for Whom this Earth is simply a field of service.

7

The Masters take upon Themselves the duty and role of serving humanity. They are our guides and teachers, the inspirers of those who are ready for that inspiration. They are the protectors of humanity, the shield, as Maitreya calls it, and from the earliest time have never left humanity without guidance. The extraordinary thing is that humanity has never been alone. Never in all our history have we been without help from behind the scenes or quite openly. Our entire evolution, over these millions of years, has taken place step by step, without infringing our free will (so it has tended to be slow), with the help of such a group of perfected men, and, of course, Their predecessors.

For over 500 years the Masters, living in these remote mountain and desert retreats, have known that sooner or later They would be required to return to the everyday world. This pertains to Their own evolution, called the Way of the Higher Evolution, about which we can know little or nothing. Theirs is not the acme of all perfectionment. The Masters see stretching ahead of Them vistas of Being and knowing which we cannot begin to imagine. For Them it is a relative perfection, but from our point of view They are perfect. There is nothing that this planet can give Them except a field of service. A great many of the Masters take up that service, and we should be more than grateful that They do.

The evolutionary path, humanity will come to understand, is a scientific one. It does not take place haphazardly. It is open to everyone, and we are all evolving at somewhat different rates. That is why some become Masters ahead of others. Our last few incarnations are marked off by certain great expansions of consciousness, five in number. These constitute the five major planetary initiations. Each one gives to the initiate a deeper insight into the plan of evolution, into the mind of the great cosmic Being, the Planetary Logos, Who ensouls this planet.

This planet itself is a living, breathing, incarnating entity. It does not incarnate in exactly the same way as we do, but does so in relation to the Plan of our Solar Logos. Our Planetary Logos relates the evolution of this planet to the Plan for the solar system as a whole. All proceeds according to plan.

Since there is a Plan, there are custodians of the Plan. The Masters of Wisdom and the Lords of Compassion make up the Spiritual Hierarchy, our esoteric Hierarchy, Who are now beginning to return to the outer world. Until relatively recently, it was thought that that would probably be in about 1,200 or 1,300 years from now. But so fast has been the recent evolution of humanity, and in particular so dramatic and changing to the Plan has been the experience of the two world wars of the 20th century, that humanity has taken a great leap forward and become ready for a new revelation. It has also allowed the Masters — not all of Them but a large number — to come into the everyday world.

The first group of Masters, the vanguard, came in 1975 — one into New York, one into London, one into Geneva, one into Darjeeling, and one into Tokyo. They were followed by one in Moscow and another in Rome. The one in Rome is probably the best known of all the Masters, the Master Jesus. The disciple Jesus, as He was in Palestine, was overshadowed[1] by Maitreya, the Master of all the Masters. Maitreya embodies what we call the Christ Principle, the energy of love. He is the Lord of Love, as His brother the Buddha was the Lord of Wisdom. Six hundred years before Jesus, the Buddha overshadowed and worked through His disciple the Prince Gautama, and the Prince Gautama became Gautama Buddha. The Buddha showed the Wisdom of God in its perfection in a man for the first time. Six hundred years later, Maitreya, the Lord of Love, overshadowed His disciple, Jesus[2], who was not yet a Master but very near it, and showed the Love of God in its perfection in a man for the first time. In so doing, He inaugurated the Age of Pisces, which is now coming to an end.

Energies of Pisces

The energies of Pisces have given to humanity two great qualities. One is individuality. In the 2,000 years since Jesus's time, humanity has come out of the herd, become potent individuals in their own right. This is a tremendous step forward in evolution. Without individuality, which is the very nature of the soul (we are souls in incarnation), the distinctiveness of each individual cannot be expressed.

The other is idealism, or devotion to an ideal. However, it has been a very abstract type of devotion. It is not devotion or idealism that demanded the actual precipitation of the ideal onto the physical plane. If people are idealistic and can imagine something, they tend to believe that that is all you need to do, that the ideal is then manifest in the world. Of course, it is not.

For example, the brotherhood of man has been an ideal for hundreds of years but there is no brotherhood of man in the world today. It was mooted as an ideal in the French Revolution: equality, fraternity and liberty. But where is the true equality? Where the fraternity, the true liberty? They do not exist except as potent ideas in the mind of humanity.

Now must be the time when these ideals are fixed in the world, actually grounded and anchored on the physical plane through the political, economic and social changes which will bring them into being. Otherwise there would be no future for the race; we would destroy ourselves. At this very moment, we are dashing headlong towards the edge of a precipice which would mean the end of all life on this planet. I personally believe that will not happen. But unless we change direction, we would, through the Law of Cause and Effect, destroy all life, human and sub-human, on Earth. Very shortly we will be faced by Maitreya with a choice. We are already faced with it, but the vast majority of people do not even consider it something to take seriously.

The announcement

In June 1945, at the end of the Second World War, Maitreya, Who holds the office of World Teacher in the Hierarchy of Masters, made an extraordinary announcement. He said that if humanity, of its own free will, took the first steps to change, put its house in order, then He would come, not by overshadowing a disciple as He did in Palestine, but Himself, and at the earliest possible moment. He said He would come not alone but at the head of a large group of His disciples, the Masters of Wisdom.

(From the point of view of the Masters, the two world wars were really one war which began in 1914, went underground in 1918, came above ground again in 1939 and ended with the defeat of the Axis powers by the Allies, behind whom stood the spiritual Hierarchy of Masters and initiates.)

It was 98,000 years ago, in the late Atlantean era, that the Masters last worked openly in the world. With the end of the war that devastated the Atlantean civilization and part of the continent of which North and South America are remnants, the Masters retreated into the mountains and deserts where They have remained ever since. A few have been more open, but very few. They are beginning to take up Their places in the world in ways that will allow us to know and recognize Them as the Masters, the Teachers, the Guides of the race. This is the most extraordinary event which you could contemplate and it is happening now.

Maitreya said, in June 1945, that He would come when a measure of peace had been restored, when the principle of sharing was beginning to govern economic affairs, and when the religious and political groups were cleaning house, setting their affairs in order. As soon as our minds were moving in these directions, He said He would come without fail at the earliest possible time. It was hoped that it would be in about five years. It was hoped in 1945 that the pain and suffering, the ghastly conditions of the war, would have chastened us and led to a change of direction. But not all the nations had suffered, and not equally, and the great powers quickly went back to the old greedy, selfish, competitive, nationalistic ways of Pisces, the ways of the past.

The energies of Pisces have divided humanity because we have over-emphasized the individuality that the Piscean experience has given us. Our idealism has been very narrow and self-directed, so we have become fanatical believers in our own ideal — whether democracy, fascism or communism. Everyone believes that their ideal is given by God as a gift above all others. Likewise, nationalistic individuals believe their country is the best of all possible countries, God's gift to the world. These beliefs create the divisions and separations, the unnecessary antagonisms, the blinkers that people adopt to keep their eyes from seeing the values and qualities of other people. We have to live and interact with other people, and we can do it through co-operation or through competition.

Spiritual crisis

Until now, the vast majority of humanity has decided that competition is the only way forward. That belief is driving us to a totally untenable position. Today the major expression of that tension is in the political and economic fields. Humanity is going through a great spiritual crisis which is focused through these areas of activity and must be resolved in them. If it is not so resolved, we will destroy all life on the planet. This is the most important thing that humanity could recognize. It is a spiritual problem focused through political and economic structures.

The way forward for humanity is the realization of who and what we are. Few know who they are. No one knows why we are here, where we are going, where we have come from, what is the aim and purpose of life. So how can we live correctly? How can we relate to each other correctly if we do not even know who we are? It has been the role of religions to teach humanity that its nature is spiritual, divine. But the churches have been eminently unsuccessful in teaching humanity. They have failed humanity.

The purpose of the churches was to teach and to heal. To my mind, they have taught badly and healed practically not at all. Instead of healing and teaching, they have given us a set of rules, man-made dogmas and doctrines which they have called the word of God, words which God, I am sure, would be very unhappy to accept as His. These dogmas and doctrines are the very things which keep humanity apart, keep religious people apart, and separate religious people from political or economic or scientific people. There should be no separation. There is no separation in life.

Life gives you political and economic problems and situations. It also gives you spiritual problems and dilemmas. We live in a spiritual world; the nature of life is spiritual. It could not be otherwise because each one of us is the divine spark of God, the Self, which reflects itself as the human soul. The individualized human soul reflects itself at a lower level of vibration as the human personality, who in any particular life is a man or woman. So all men have been women and all women have been men. In this way, human progress from early animal man and woman has been brought forward to this time for the revelation of our true nature. Few at any time know these truths, and few indeed today question the reality of the political and economic structures that we are forced to use.

Humanity has been given a ridiculous choice: you can either be free or have justice. If you live in America or Europe, in the main you opt for freedom. Americans in particular love the idea of freedom but there is little justice in America and not much more in Europe. If you lived in the Soviet bloc (which no longer exists as a bloc but the consciousness is still there), you opted for justice but had no freedom. This choice is totally absurd. Both freedom and justice are divine, and divinity is indivisible. You cannot have freedom without justice, or justice without freedom.

You cannot give humanity a choice and say: "If you vote for me, I will give you freedom, forget about the justice," or: "If you vote for us, we will give you justice, forget about the freedom." Both are essential because both are part of the human, and therefore divine, nature. They come from the soul. If the soul is manifesting through an individual, that person will want both freedom and justice for everyone. They are essentially the same. They cannot be separated because spirit is not separable. Divinity is a whole and needs the wholeness of its expression. It is about unity, and unity results only from the fusion of justice and freedom.

When Maitreya makes Himself known and enunciates the concept of unity, you will find that the idea of anyone wanting freedom without justice or justice without freedom is ridiculous. It cannot be done. Yet this is what the political structures of today offer in the West and the Soviet bloc, which has collapsed and is seeking a measure of freedom to overlay the measure of justice which it already had. Because of the market-forces orientation which it has been forced to adhere to, that justice and freedom are slow to come.

Maitreya calls market forces the forces of evil because they have in-built inequality in them. Yet the market-forces economy saturates the entire world, even the erstwhile Soviet bloc. It benefits the few at the expense of the many. That is why it is evil. Its mechanism is commercialization, and Maitreya calls commercialization more dangerous to humanity than an atomic bomb because it is insidious. We do not even see it happening. Yet the tentacles of commercialization now penetrate the whole of our existence.

In the USA, if you do not have medical insurance and are poor you cannot get new teeth; you cannot have an operation if you need one. This is the most unjust medical system in US history. If you are not rich enough to take out insurance or pay the bills, you have to suffer. You have to limp. You cannot have your heart transplant or pacemaker or other necessary medical care. Medical care is a service that all nations should provide for their people. It is an essential part of human life like food, shelter and education.

These are the fundamentals, the services that all people in all nations need. Yet at the moment there is no country in the world, not even the USA, probably the richest in the world, in which all of these pertain as universal rights. They should be universal rights but if you look at the world as it is, as Maitreya sees it, you see two worlds.

Two worlds

You see the developed world, the G8 nations and a few more, usurp and waste three-quarters of the world's food and 83 per cent of all other resources, so that the developing world has to make do with the rest. They have more than two-thirds of the world's population, but have to make do with a quarter of the world's food and 17 per cent of the other resources. As a result, they die in their millions.

One-fifth of the world's population, around 1,200 million people in the developing world, are living in official, absolute poverty. That means they live on less than $1 a day. They live miserable, stunted lives, deprived of all we take for granted. More than 30 million of them are actually dying of starvation in a world in which there is no shortage of food, a world with a huge surplus per capita. That is the reality for the people of the developing world.

We are so complacent that we do not even take it seriously. We think it is normal. We think that we can get on: "We're all right, Jack." Our stock exchange is climbing high. Nothing to worry us. We are saving up, and will get what we want, more of what we want, and more and more of what we think the world needs to give us. What about the people of the developing world? The majority of humanity live in the developing world, and they have almost nothing.

We have everything there is and more, and we do not share it with those who have nothing. Greed, selfishness and complacency cause the starving millions of the world. If there is a drought, inevitably, millions die. If there were a drought in the US or Europe no one would die. We would import enough food for all because we can afford to pay for it. There is no shortage of food. There is food rotting away in the storehouses of the developed world, eaten by rats.

This is the reality in the developing world. Many have nothing to eat, no house, no work, no way of making any money. They may have to walk 10 miles for bits of wood to make a fire to cook some fibres. They have to walk 10 miles for brackish water which poisons their children. They do not know where the next meal is coming from. Maybe they had a meal last week. We wonder what we will have for dinner tonight. We think about this at lunch time. They think: "Is it possible that in one or two weeks' time aid will come and my children will be able to eat something?"

That is the day-to-day reality for millions of people, and we shut our eyes to it. Maitreya says: "How can you watch these people die before your eyes and call yourselves men?" [Message 11(3)] He says: "The problems of mankind are real but solvable.

The solution lies within your grasp. Take your brother's need as the measure for your action and solve the problems of the world. There is no other course." [Message 52] We have a solution that is so easy. Maitreya says we must see ourselves as one, brothers and sisters of one humanity under the one God. Therefore, the food, raw materials, energy and science of the world belong to everyone, and should be redistributed more equitably around the world.

We think we give aid to the developing world. We give them aid with a string attached — the interest on the aid. More money flows from the developing world to the developed world in repayment of the loans, plus the interest, than flows from the developed world to the developing world in actual loans. It is not aid. It is usury. We have the developing world 'over a barrel', and there is nothing they can do about it. We dominate the economic structures of the world. Globalization is a reality but a terrible one for them. We force them, in receipt of aid, to restructure their economy to provide us with cheap commodities like coffee and tea that we buy in bulk at the lowest possible price, while they cannot live because their land is growing tea and coffee for export to the developed world. This is a reality to which people are blind because the media networks do not emphasize it. We have to see it; otherwise we will destroy all life on the planet. We are really up against it and do not have long to make up our minds.

The coming of Maitreya, the World Teacher

To make sure that we take the right steps and change, Maitreya and His group have come into the world actually ahead of schedule. They thought it might be in 1,200 years, but the emergency is so great that They have come now. Maitreya hoped it would be in about five years from 1945, but it was not until July 1977 that He was able to descend from His mountain. He said then, I am coming whether they are ready or not. "All

17

else failing, I shall emerge into a world ready but unprepared."
[Message 61] The changes have taken place just enough to come
within the law. He descended from His mountain retreat, about
17,500 feet up in the Himalayas, and came down to the plains of
Pakistan. Maitreya stayed there for some days to acclimatize
Himself, and on 19 July 1977 He entered London, England. He
remains in the Asian community of that city, which He calls His
'point of focus' in the modern world.

From there He directs His energies to all parts of the world
in a highly scientific fashion which only He is able to do. He is
awaiting an opportunity to come forward and declare Himself
openly to the world as the World Teacher — not as the Christ,
not as Maitreya Buddha, not as the Imam Mahdi as He is
awaited by Muslims, nor as Krishna as Hindus await Him or the
Messiah as He is awaited by Jews. These are all names for the
same individual, the head and leader of our Spiritual Hierarchy,
Who, age after age, has presented humanity with this link with
the spiritual kingdom.

The Hierarchy is the kingdom of souls or the spiritual
kingdom, in Christian terms the kingdom of God. These men are
not Gods, but they are God-like men. Everyone has the total
potential of divinity within them. The Masters are not different
from us. The only difference between the Masters and ourselves,
between the Christ, the Buddha or Krishna and ourselves, is that
They have *demonstrated* the divinity at a level which astounds
and inspires, while we are way down the ladder of evolution
awaiting the time when we can do the same thing. It does not
happen by waiting — only by actually doing it. All of us,
whether we know it or not, are engaged on a path of evolution
which eventually will make everyone a Master. It is inevitable.
It is part of our destiny as human beings.

The next destined step for humanity is the creation of right
human relationships. That means the demonstration of our

ability to live in peace. If we cannot live in peace, we cannot live at all because a war today on a major scale would destroy all life. So the first step into right human relations is the creation of conditions of peace. Maitreya says this is simple but there is only one way in which we can produce peace: that is to create justice in the world. Without justice there will never be peace and without peace there will be no world. How then do we get justice? We share the resources. There are more than enough resources for all the people in the world. When we share, Maitreya says, we take the first step into our divinity. Sharing, He says, is divine, freedom is divine, justice is divine. These are all divine aspects. "To manifest his divinity, man must embrace these three." [Message 81]

Sharing, justice and freedom

Sharing, justice and freedom are the well-springs of our life. We must demonstrate them in the world, not just as ideals on the astral plane that we can feel good about. We have to manifest them. We see everywhere, if we care to look, the pain and anguish of countless millions of people who have nothing to eat, nothing to give their children. Can you imagine if you had no money to buy food for your children, and you saw them wasting away, starving to death in front of your eyes? It is an appalling thought, but that is the day-to-day experience of millions of people.

Every day 24,000 children die of starvation, and we do little or nothing about it. We put our hands in our pockets, give a few pounds or dollars to Oxfam when there is a special need. There is a special need all the time. This is a day-to-day problem, not something that can be solved now and again with a few dollars of aid. It needs the complete transformation of our political and economic structures. It is a question of political will to carry it out. Most people would be less complacent if they understood the circumstances, if they really saw what was happening and

19

how it related to them. They would give, because most people have the Christ Principle beginning to work in them. They are full of desire for good, but they do not know how to manifest it or do not see the urgency of the need.

Compared to the developing world, almost everyone in the developed world is living not only in affluence and abundance, but in what I call 'cloud cuckoo land'. We think we can go on like this for ever. We cannot. Do we really imagine that the people of the developing world will put up with this state of affairs for ever? Do we think they do not know what is actually taking place, what other people have, how they live, the waste? They are beginning to demand their rights.

The people of the world are beginning to make their needs known and are pulling down the Berlin Wall, and the Berlin Walls of all the developed nations, demanding their right to eat, to work, to bring up their children in peace and in decent circumstances. These demands will grow. Maitreya will emerge and stimulate and potentize these demands of the people until there is no government on Earth which can stand against these demands for freedom, justice and right relationship. If the next destined step is for right human relations it has to be brought about. It can only be brought about when people make it happen. It is not an idea which automatically takes place.

Maitreya says: "Nothing happens by itself. Man must act and implement his will." [Message 31] The vague, idealistic individual thinks if we have the ideal it is already there. It is not. There is little liberty, equality and fraternity in the world. They are only ideals, and until we make those ideals factual on the political and economic level we have failed ourselves and our brothers and sisters. We have failed our time. And the time for this change has come.

The Emergence

Maitreya is emerging forthwith. As soon as the stock market crash He has predicted for several years truly begins to grip, Maitreya will emerge openly. He will begin to teach but not as Maitreya, or the World Teacher, not as the Christ or the Imam Mahdi or the Messiah, which He could claim to be because that indeed is how we see Him. He wishes only to be called the Teacher, because He says: "If I am the Christ to Christians, what about the Jews, Hindus, Muslims and Buddhists? If I am Maitreya Buddha to the Buddhists, what about the Christians, the Jews and the others?"

These are man-made terms, and they confuse, blind and cause dissension. He says: "Do not run after Me. Do not try to claim Me and put Me in your pocket; otherwise you will lose Me." He does not come for individual religious groups. In fact, He is not a religious teacher *per se*. He is a spiritual teacher, an educator in the broadest sense of that word. He has come to educate humanity about its own nature, to show us that we are divine, that in every single person is the divine spark which connects us with all cosmos. This is the inner reality. He comes to inspire humanity to reveal that reality and to become like the Masters, not only potentially but actually divine.

The Masters have gone ahead and are a guarantee for us. They were men and women who have fought and wrestled Their way to express that divinity and have achieved it. They are men without fault, and know that the same potential rests in us. Their return means the beginning of the creation of a truly spiritual civilization, the restoration of the nature and quality of the civilizations of Atlantis many thousands of years ago.

The Atlantean civilizations lasted 12 million years. Some had a science far greater than anything we have today. They could do things which we cannot even begin to do. In the reasonably near future we will take these powers seriously again

21

and begin to demonstrate some fully reasonable human potentials, such as the ability to come into telepathic rapport at will over any distance. Telepathy is a natural human trait which the Masters use all the time. Most people have lost the ability. The Masters do not talk; They simply think to each other. That will become the norm, so it will become impossible to tell a lie. Can you imagine how difficult that will be for us?

How do we develop these divine qualities? Maitreya says we are already divine. We are an immortal Being, the immortal Self, He calls it. The Self equates with God, the Divine Spark, the Monad in Theosophical terminology. Our difficulty is that we identify with everything and anything other than that Self. We do not even know who we are, so how could we possibly live together properly? So we live according to certain ancient precepts of competition, greed and selfishness as the norm. But they are not normal. We are neurotics living abnormal lives at the end of the civilization of Pisces, in ways which could destroy all life.

That will not happen because Maitreya and a group of His Masters, 14 so far, are in the world. They believe (and They ought to know) that we are ready to change. To make it sure, through the Law of Cause and Effect, we are bringing about the events that will drive us to change and accept the principle of sharing, because we will have no alternative.

World stock market crash

The stock markets of the world have been going through a dizzying, yo-yo-like effect over the last few years. We have seen a rise in the Dow Jones index to about 11,000. It goes down 600 points one day and a few days later it comes up 400 points. Then it drops another 200 and then up 300, and so on. This is happening in different bourses around the world, and creates a yo-yo effect which is so unstable that no government, country or economy is unaffected.

To justify the level at which the Dow Index currently stands, the US economic growth rate would need to be about 10 per cent per annum. In fact, it is nowhere near that, so a bubble is being created. That bubble will burst and with it will come plunging down the stock markets of the US and the world. All the factors that were there in 1929 are in place today.

In 1988-1991 Maitreya issued a series of prophecies which have come to pass with uncanny accuracy. One was that there would be a world stock market crash which He said would begin in Japan. Japan then was at the height of its economic power. The Nikkei Average stood at 40,000 points. Within a year the collapse began to take place. He called it a bubble that inevitably would burst and bring down the rest of the world's stock markets with it. That started in about 1990 and in a very short time dropped as low as 14,000. Today, by dint of the constant inputting of billions of yen into a kind of bottomless pit that has no effect on the economy, at the time of writing the Nikkei Average is between 12,000 and 20,000 points, half of what it was in 1988.

It is a bubble that all Japanese know has burst. It reflected itself in the collapse of the Pacific 'Tiger' economies — Thailand, Indonesia, Malaysia, South Korea, Singapore and Hong Kong. This was followed by Russia, Brazil and Mexico. They were propped up by the infusion of billions of dollars of aid from the International Monetary Fund, the World Bank, and from the central banks of the world. Every two or three years the same thing happens. There will come a time when the aid will not happen, and that very soon.

The US Government cannot maintain that bubble in the US, unrelated to the nation's true productivity. It is simply not feasible, and Maitreya is not the only one who has warned against it. Every senior economist in the world who has given an opinion has voiced it as a possibility, or even certainty in some cases, that there will be a world stock market crash. The only thing they do not know is when it will happen.

Maitreya first made that prediction in June 1988, and with every day that passes it becomes more and more likely to be fulfilled. The higher your stock market goes, when you clap hands and congratulate each other, the more likely the collapse will take place. To hear someone say, as I am saying, that the best thing that could happen is a stock market crash must make you wonder if I live on air or I am absolutely crazy. I am not crazy and I do not live on air.

Maitreya calls them the gambling casinos of the world. They have no function vis-à-vis the true trading system of the world. Ninety-seven per cent of all transactions on the world's stock markets are currency speculations. To the Masters, speculation is the major disease of humanity, which is driving us not only crazy with greed, but also to the edge of self-destruction. The best thing that could happen is the collapse of the gambling casinos which are simply agencies for greedy minds and idle hands, as the Masters put it. They have no true function. Only their end will bring humanity face to face with the reality. The governments are not in charge of their economies because they are not in charge of their currencies. The value of any currency, or the mode of action for or against a particular currency, is in the hands of a group of about 200 men and women in every country.

The financiers, speculators at certain great institutions, use your money that you have put aside for your retirement, for example. All the big insurance companies and banks gamble like everyone else on the stock markets. The world has changed from being semi-religious to being totally religious, but the religion has changed. The new religion is money. Money is the great altar at which everyone worships today. Everyone is taken up by greed, by the possibility of making quick money. The internet is fostering it. You have the NASDAQ Index, which goes up and down like a bigger yo-yo than the Dow Index.

Every avenue which could promote the well-being of humanity is being used as a way of making a few people rich at the expense of everyone else. That is the nature of market forces. It is based on the big, self-evident lie that we are all trading on a level playing field. That is the theory. If you have free market forces then by the law of supply and demand the economies of the world would be regulated. Nothing could be further from the truth because we are not all at the same level. You cannot compare the trading strength of America, Britain, France, Germany or Japan with Kenya, Tanzania, Zambia or Nigeria.

We in the West live our well-dressed, well-motorcarred lives at the expense of the health and well-being of the people of the developing world. It is gross and indecent. Maitreya calls it a blasphemy. "For how long," He asks, "can you support this degradation?" [Message 81] It is a degradation of the human spirit. It is the new slavery. We do not give it the name but such it is. Slavery has not died out. Slavery goes with every transaction on the stock markets. The time has come to end that disgraceful association, and it will happen by its own collapse.

Maitreya on television

When the stock market does collapse, as soon as it is obvious that it is on its final plunge, Maitreya will emerge. He will take up an invitation that He has received to appear on a major television network in the US, then in Japan. After that, all the networks will want to interview this extraordinary man.

He will not be called Maitreya. He will not be introduced as the Christ or World Teacher, but simply as a man among men, one of extraordinary potency, wisdom, obvious love and concern for the people of the world — not just one group but all people

25

wherever they are, whoever they are, at whatever level. They will listen to Him. His voice will be heard. He will reflect the need of the majority of the human race for justice and freedom, for the right to live decent lives which most of us in the West take for granted, knowing where their next meal is coming from, with work and the joy of bringing up their children without seeing them dying in front of their eyes.

When enough people are thus responding to His message, they will demand that the networks of the world allow Him to speak and develop His ideas more fully to the vast majority. Then the television networks will be linked together by satellite. This will be the most extraordinary event of all our lives, the most extraordinary event in history, like none other before it in its scope.

The Day of Declaration will be announced by the media. People will tune in at the given time, and see Maiteya's face, by now well known. As it says in the Christian Bible: "Every eye shall see Him" — on the linked television networks. They are in place for this event so that for the first time in history the World Teacher can address every individual directly, needing no churches or priests to act as intermediaries.

Maitreya is omniscient, onmipresent. He will come into *telepathic rapport* with every individual and each will hear Him, inwardly, in his or her own language. This will be a repetition, only now on a worldwide scale, of the true happening of Pentecost 2,000 years ago.

He will present a short history of the world, our journey from the extraordinary level from which we have come to the degradation to which we have fallen. He will urge us to change, inspire us with a view of the future, a future like none that has ever been presented to the world — the most wonderful, beautiful and extraordinarily brilliant civilization that this Earth has ever seen.

That is the future for humanity in the Aquarian Age which is now beginning. A world in which we will have energy for all our needs directly from the sun, which with a developed aspect of genetic engineering will provide us with the ability to create new organs. Instead of going to hospital, waiting for a transplant which might or might not take, and dying in the meantime if there is no organ available, you will simply go into a clinic and after a few hours come out with a new heart — your own heart remade, your own kidneys or liver remade. In this way people will live potently and with vitality much longer than they do today. With the sharing of the world's resources, all things become possible. Sharing creates trust. When there is trust among the nations there will be peace among the nations.

On the Day of Declaration, Maitreya will outline all of this. He will introduce the idea of His disciples, the Masters, to the world. The first to look for are the three Who were together in Palestine among the others 2,000 years ago: the Master Jesus, the one Who was Saint Peter, now the Master Morya, and the one Who was John the Beloved, now the Master Koot Hoomi. These three you should remember. These three Masters will work closely with Maitreya in the days ahead, and will be among the first to be introduced openly to the world, not on the Day of Declaration but soon after.

While He is conveying His thoughts to humanity, Maitreya's energy, the Christ Principle, will flow out in tremendous potency. He has said: "It will be as if I embrace the whole world. People will feel it even physically." This will evoke an intuitive, heartfelt response to His message. On the outer physical plane there will be hundreds of thousands of spontaneous, miracle healings throughout the planet. In these ways you will know that that One is the Christ, if that is Whom you await, the Imam Mahdi if you are Muslim, Krishna if you are Hindu, the Messiah if you are Jewish, Maitreya Buddha if you are a Buddhist; the World Teacher for all those who await Him under no name but simply have called Him into the world to help humanity face the future, restore and regenerate itself and enter the New Age in fitting fashion for the gods which essentially we are.

References

1 Overshadowing, in the spiritual sense, is the method by which a greater consciousness works through one of a somewhat less developed level, thus bringing down this consciousness to humanity.

2 For further information on the historical Jesus and His relationship to Maitreya, see *Maitreya's Mission Volume One*, and *Share International* magazine.

3 Published in *Messages from Maitreya the Christ*, Share International Fdn.

The Coming of Maitreya

"When He came before through His disciple, Jesus, men were unready to respond to His teaching. Today, through centuries of suffering, education and experience, are men prepared to understand and *act upon* His precepts. As Preceptor does He come; as Teacher, not saviour, does He fulfil His mission.

"Soon, the One for Whom the world waits will emerge and present Himself for all to see. Soon, men will engage in a dialogue with their Higher Selves and make their choice to live or die. Thus is being enacted the great drama of this time...

"Maitreya will use as signal the collapsing stock markets, the gambling halls of greed; then will He enter, openly, the arena of the world and state His case for justice and freedom, sharing and common sense." (From 'The end of chaos' by the Master —, *Share International,* May 2000)

Is Maitreya coming because we are heading towards a major crisis or because we are evolving as you say, to be able to join together? (April 1998)

Both. It is not one or the other. There are many in the world who are set on destruction. They do not set out to destroy, but they hold on to the old ways of living that inevitably will cause destruction. If we were to go on exactly as we are now, in which one-third of the world usurps and wastes three-quarters of the world's food and 83 per cent of all other resources, and one-fifth of the world's population lives in conditions of *official* absolute poverty, we would cause a crisis which would lead to a nuclear war.

29

Humanity is divided into two groups: those who compete, and those who co-operate. Those who compete are winning at the moment. They have built a market-forces economy based on unfair competition. The market-forces economy comes out of America, which is the richest and most powerful nation in the world, and so it is fine for America. Whoever is biggest and strongest is inevitably going to come off best. But can you imagine Zaire, Uganda or Tanzania advocating a market-forces economy? Of course not, because they are going to lose out every time. If it were a level playing field, there might be something to be said for it, but in fact market forces move in the opposite direction from evolution.

Evolution is moving towards greater unity, fusion, blending, the creation of the one humanity — not the sameness of life but the unification of all diversity. The greatest unity with the greatest diversity is the evolutionary aim. Market forces work in the opposite direction, by creating more and more divisions. Maitreya calls market forces "the forces of evil", because of their in-built inequality. They have created division in the world which has now reached crisis proportions. He can no longer stand aside and watch what He calls "the massacre of the innocents". So He has come into the world with the knowledge that there is a large body of people who are longing, and able, to co-operate, whose view of life is one of co-operation, justice and freedom for everyone. He is here to inspire and confirm those who see co-operation as the way forward, and awaken those who are holding on to the old competitive modes.

Maitreya comes in the nick of time to prevent humanity from destroying itself. If we do not co-operate, we will destroy our life, but Maitreya says that He knows already that we are ready for sharing. We will share the world's resources, if only because we have no alternative.

What about the people in the world who believe it is in their interest to prolong a warlike stance and find it difficult to accept what seems an impossible invitation to create peace? (September 1998)

When Jesus spoke 2,000 years ago He was not even recognized. Certainly there were plenty who would have followed Him if they had had any idea Who He was, but the minds of people of that time were totally dominated by the only ones who could read and write, namely the priests. The priests were filled with a special expectation of the Messiah as a warrior-king out of the House of David who would free the Jewish people from the Romans. Jesus came as a man of peace. He spoke His words of love, justice and right relationship. He propagated the nature of the human soul, and demonstrated the Love of God in perfection. He was not recognized as such because this was so against the expectations of the priests and, through the priests, of the populace, that Jesus had a tiny following indeed.

The teaching of the churches gives people the idea that He had a huge following and was very popular. Not at all. He had three specially close disciples, 12 of an inner group, 75 of an outer group, and 500 interested people. That was all the followers Jesus had at that time. It was very easy for the priests to direct the would-be followers to put Jesus down and have Him crucified because He did not fulfil their expectations.

Times have changed. Education on a world scale has completely transformed humanity. But no one should look for someone that everyone is going to believe in. Maitreya Himself has said: "Many will follow Me and see Me as their guide. Many will know Me not." [Message 10] He knows that the vast majority of people are hungry for change. Millions are hungry for food, and they are certainly not going to reject the possibility of change when they make up the bulk of the people of the developing world, which is nearly three-quarters of the world's population.

The people who might not, in the first instance, be overly delighted to share the resources of the West with the developing world are those who now control major corporations and financial institutions. But when the stock markets of the world collapse, these are the very people who will be helpless, who will no longer have the power to stand against the will of the people. The will of the people everywhere will be organized, educated, stimulated, galvanized and directed by Maitreya, and this will create a world public opinion against which no nation can stand for long.

How can I know that the Christ you talk about is the real one?
(September 1997)

There is no way I can prove to you that the person I am talking about is the Christ or the World Teacher. You have to satisfy yourself, from your own intuition, your own experience on the Day of Declaration and afterwards, through His teaching. The tree is known by its fruit, and either the fruit of Maitreya — His love, wisdom, insight, intelligence, advice, the effect of His energy on you, His blessings which are poured out to the world — convinces you or it does not.

If your mind is stuck in a fundamentalist religious mode, you will probably find it difficult to take seriously what I say, and on the Day of Declaration you could write any positive reaction out of your experience. But if you say: "That man sounds to me like someone of the stature of a Christ or Buddha," it does not matter if you believe in the name. That is immaterial. What matters is you and your relationship to the world. Is He asking humanity to do what you want for the world? Do you want justice, a rational economic system that allows people to live in peace, so that no one is starving to death in a world of plenty? If you want that, you are on His side, because that is what He wants. It does not matter who you believe He is, or whether you follow Jesus rather than Maitreya. Many Christians will follow Jesus because they know the name; they don't know the name Maitreya. But Jesus follows Maitreya!

Awareness is the key to all life. Where you are aware, life is in you. Where you are not aware, that life is still beyond you and that pertains to Maitreya as to everything else.

Will Maitreya save us like Jesus is said to have done?
(September 1998)

Maitreya comes to teach. Humanity has to save itself through correct response to the teachings. He does not come to save humanity. No one can save you — not Maitreya, not the Buddha, not any one who has ever been on earth. Only you can save yourself in the esoteric sense of fulfilling the nature of your Being and demonstrating that Being on planet Earth in its perfection. That is what saves you. It is called "Self-realization".

All the Masters are Self-realized, perfected, saved. If I were to say to you: "Believe in Jesus and you will be saved" (that is what every Christian tells you, especially the fundamentalists), or "Believe in the Buddha" or "Believe in Krishna" and you will go to heaven, it is a nonsense. Belief has nothing to do with it. Belief is to do with religion. Maitreya says religions have a function. They are like a ladder that helps you to get onto the roof, but once you are there you can throw away the ladder or give it to someone else.

It is to do with awareness, a growing, conscious awareness. That is the path of evolution; belief is not. You can be a convinced atheist, Christian, Buddhist or Muslim for 15, 20, 30 years and then suddenly 'see the light' and become something else — a Rosicrucian, Theosophist, or some other 'ism'. But life is not to do with 'isms' or ideology. It is to do with Action and

33

Reaction, which are opposite and equal. If we learn the meaning of that great Law, we learn what it is to be harmless. Harmlessness is at the root of Being, which keeps us 'safe'. If we are harmless we do not make the karma which drives people to war, to fear, and all the rest of it. Maitreya comes to show us that in the simplest terms.

It is said that when the disciple is ready the Master appears, so why do you rely on the appearance of one Teacher, Maitreya, to do things for us? (June 1998)

I have always emphasized that Maitreya has not come "to do things for us". He comes to teach. We have to save ourselves through correct response to the teaching. He Himself has said: "I am the architect, only, of the Plan; you are the willing builders of the temple of truth." [Message 65] The temple of truth is the new civilization, and we have to build it. Every brick, every stone, Maitreya has said, must be put in place by man himself. He comes to show the way, to advise, teach, inspire, release the energy to galvanize us, but we, willingly, gladly, must accept the changes. Otherwise they will not take place.

The phrase "When the disciple is ready the Master appears" should be understood on an individual basis. If an *individual* disciple is ready to serve humanity in a rather potent way, and has sufficient mental polarization and response to his own soul to enable a Master to contact and work with him, the Master may appear. But the sense in which I have been speaking is the readiness of humanity *as a whole* for the World Teacher. Maitreya is not an *individual* Master Who takes 'pupils'. He comes for all humanity. The Masters are His disciples.

*Your Master describes the Christ as "the Eldest of the great family of brothers". (**Share International**, October 1997) In what sense is the term "Eldest" used? There are Masters in the*

Hierarchy who are older in terms of time. Maitreya, I believe, was the first among Earth humanity to take initiation. Is it in this sense He is termed the Eldest of the great family of brothers, including all other Masters? (October 2000)

He is the Eldest because He is the most evolved (now that the Buddha is on Shamballa).

*(1) Is Maitreya aware, at all times, of everyone's thoughts? (2) Does He become aware when we're thinking of Him? For example, when we pick up our copies of **Share International** and read about Him, is a fragment of His attention drawn to that? (3) Could He pick up any musical instrument and play the most complicated piece? (4) Could He paint a masterpiece? Or (5) write a greater play than Shakespeare? (6) Could He sing like Elvis?* (September 2000)

(1) Yes. (2) Yes. (3) Yes. (4) Yes. (5) Yes. (6) No!

You say that Maitreya has incarnated in a physical body and is living in the UK. But why? Can't He do a lot more for all souls and the Earth from a spiritual level? (January/February 1999)

No, quite the contrary. Working on the physical plane, Maitreya and His group of Masters can do infinitely more for humanity than hitherto.

The Mayan Calendar, which began in the year 3113 BC, ends in the year AD 2012. The Mayans speak of the evolutionary rise/shift in human consciousness occurring at that time. (1) Is this related to the coming of Maitreya? (2) Is 2012 the year when He will speak to all humanity or will it be sooner (or later) than that? (3) If 2012 is not the year He will speak to all humanity, is this year significantly related in some other way? (November 1998)

(1) Yes. (2) No, it will be much sooner. (3) No, it is only an approximate time.

What are the ideas of the Vatican with regard to Maitreya living in London? (January/February 1998)

I know that at least one of my books — the first book, *The Reappearance of the Christ and the Masters of Wisdom* — was physically put into the hands of the Pope years ago. The Pope thumbed through it, and I understand that he read it later and does not believe a word of it. The Pope himself recently published a book in which he says that those who talk about the presence now in the world of a new Buddha should know that he is not "our Christ".

However, the Master Jesus has been living in Rome for the last seven years, and there are two members of the Curia (the group around the Pope) who are direct disciples of the Master Jesus. For years they have been trying subtly to reorient the Pope to the idea of the presence of the Master Jesus in Rome and of Maitreya in London, without, I think, any success. The Pope is probably too old and too rigid in his understanding of scripture to change. However, it will not have escaped your notice that over the years the Pope, in the economic field, has been extremely positive and progressive, going around the world advocating sharing and a more just society. This is the impression on his mind of the Master Jesus. Jesus does not overshadow him in the way Maitreya overshadowed Jesus, but He impresses his mind, and in so far as the Pope is open to that impression, which he seems to be, he goes out of his way to call for redistribution of resources. He is doing very good work in that respect.

Is there any sign that the Master Jesus is influencing the Pope? (April 2000)

When the Pope has made the sudden discovery, as recently reported, that Heaven and Hell reside in the human consciousness and are nothing to do with specific places — as people for 2,000 years have been taught by the Christian churches — it is a sign that the Pope benefits from the impression of the Master Jesus behind him.

Maitreya in London

If Maitreya is living in Brick Lane (London), there must be lots of people trying to find Him there. Does He actively avoid being found? (September 1999)

He is not living in Brick Lane. He did live in the Brick Lane area between 1977 when He came into London and January 1986. He had various contacts with the BBC; their vans came to the house in which He was living and He became very exposed. People saw Him going off in big limousines, in Western clothes which He does not normally wear. The BBC vans arrived carrying men with cameras, so He moved from the Brick Lane area. He has been in many other areas. Now He is in the northeast of London. He lives in a temple but He does not eat or sleep, He does not even have a bed, so He can live anywhere. He works with the Swamis of the various temples, trains and teaches them, then sends them around the world to spread His teaching. He is neither Hindu nor Muslim, nor Christian. He sees no difference between any of the religions.

The question was, is He avoiding being seen? If you read *Share International* on a regular basis and look up the Letters to the Editor you would think He did nothing else but present Himself to the groups around the world with whom I am associated. You would think He had endless time; sometimes people talk about, for example, the Master Jesus spending three days with them. I know a woman in Japan with whom the Master Jesus spent a month in her house and she did not know it was the Master Jesus.

What is the nationality of Maitreya? (July/August 1997)

Maitreya has, now, British citizenship but, essentially, He has no specific nationality. He has lived in the Himalayas for thousands of years but is not Tibetan or Nepalese. He lives in a self-created body, therefore of no national parentage.

How did Maitreya obtain His nationality? (November 1998)

After living for 10 years in London He applied for British nationality and was successful.

(1) Will Maitreya have a strong connection with Pakistan in the future as far as having an ashram there is concerned? (2) Are any of his current associates from Pakistan? (May 2000)

(1) No. (2) Yes.

How tall is Maitreya? (November 1998)

Six feet, three inches.

Does Maitreya have a navel? (October 2000)

No. He was not 'born'. His body is self-made.

Is Maitreya mortal or immortal? (December 1999)

As men or women, we are all mortal. As the soul or Self we are all immortal. Maitreya is a mortal man Who, through an evolutionary expansion of consciousness, has evolved to a degree of Self realization which makes Him one of the Great Immortals.

Maitreya is a very short name meaning "friendliness" in Sanskrit. Is it that Maitreya has no family name, as, for example, Mr Benjamin Creme has the Creme family name? (June 1998)

Yes. Maitreya has no family. His body is self-created. Maitreya actually means "The Happy One" — the one who brings happiness to the world.

Maitreya, the Fifth Buddha

You sometimes describe Maitreya as the fifth Buddha. I don't understand what that means. (1) If He is the fifth Buddha, are there four other Buddhas? Who are They? and (2) how is this related to the five Buddhas of Activity mentioned in your book **Maitreya's Mission Volume Two** *(pp. 79-80)?* (March 1997)

(1) Gautama was the fourth. Mithra was the third. Memnon was the second. (2) Not at all.

According to Buddhist teachings, Maitreya is a boddhisatva residing right now in the Tushita heaven. How can he be in the Tushita heaven and on Earth at the same time? If this Maitreya is the real Maitreya, has he come from Nirvana or from Tushita? Or will he go to Nirvana once he has accomplished his mission on Earth? (June 1998)

Nirvana and Tushita heavens are states of consciousness, not physical abodes. Maitreya is — in consciousness — a full Buddha Who has created a physical body to live among us in the world.

You have stated that Gesar of Ling is another name for Maitreya; Gesar was an historical figure, I believe, and you

39

have said that Masters have not lived openly in the world since Atlantean times, therefore he could not have been Maitreya himself. (1) Do you mean he was a disciple of Maitreya's, then? Tibetan Buddhism does not expect the "return" of Maitreya Buddha, for there has not been such a one in Buddhist history; the reference to Maitreya comes from a statement by Gautama Buddha — it's in the scriptures — that at some future date there would arise another "Buddha" ("enlightened one"), "like myself" (said Gautama, according to scripture), and his name would be Maitreya ... a new Buddha, not a return of one of the prior (four are cited) ones. All Buddhists should be familiar with this scripture. Gautama must have been a disciple; the previous ones to which he referred (or others referred) must have also been disciples; the prediction points to another such, Maitreya by name, yet Maitreya, here, is a Master. Therefore your reply is rather puzzling. (2) How could he have been Ling Gesar? (April 1999)

(1) Yes. (2) By overshadowing. Maitreya is the fifth Buddha and has 'appeared' many times through overshadowing different disciples. It is in that sense that He 'returns'.

When did Maitreya begin His evolution as a normal man? (May 1998)

About 8 million years ago, in early Atlantean times.

Who was the Christ going back past the 2,600-year period that Maitreya has held this office? (July/August 1997)

The office is that of World Teacher (not of the Christ) and was held previously by the Buddha, the Embodiment of Wisdom. Maitreya is the Embodiment of Love, the Christ Principle.

Is the World Teacher a collection of 'people' rather than one apparent person? (May 1999)

No. The World Teacher is an office held at this period (and for the next 2,500 years) by Maitreya, Who embodies the Christ Principle. He is the Lord of Love.

According to Jewish tradition, Enoch, who had maintained the line of righteousness, was taken up into Heaven. He was the first fully Self-realized person, and became, upon his transfiguration, the great being Metatron, also called the Teacher of Teachers. Noting the similarity between the consonants (vowels are not written in Hebrew) in Metatron (MTTR) and Maitreya (MTR), as well as in the office — namely Teacher of Teachers, is Metatron Maitreya? (January/February 1998)

Yes.

The female aspect of God in the Jewish tradition is the Shekinah; in the Hindu tradition it is Shakti. They also share two consonants. Is this coincidence? (January/February 1998)

No. They come from the same Sanskrit origin, SYKTI.

Maitreya's Television Interview

"Preparations for Maitreya's emergence are well under way. Naught can halt this blessed event; the timing, only, remains to be decided. This timing is more complex and difficult than men can know, based as it is on knowledge of the Law and on calculations beyond man's ability to comprehend. Notwithstanding these difficulties, it can be stated that the moment of the Great Lord's first appearance — which will allow Him to speak to millions though not by name — is near indeed. Despite the anonymity which the Law requires, there is little doubt that vast numbers will hearken to His words and align themselves with His cause. His message will touch and open the hearts of many who, knowingly or not, but wait for His appearance. Thus will He focus their aspiration and galvanize them into action for the common good." (From 'Humanity's response to Maitreya' by the Master —, *Share International*, December 1999)

When Maitreya comes on major television, why will He not use His own name? (November 1999)

For a number of reasons. One is that many people would not know Who Maitreya is. He wishes to be introduced to the world as a man among men, but one Who has ideas which, so far, most people have not thought about for the reconstruction of the world. In that way He does not create a division between Christians, Buddhists, Muslims and Hindus. If He were introduced as the Christ, Christians would be divided. Some would say "Hallelujah! The Christ is here!" Others would say: "He is not the Christ. He is a fake; he is the antichrist." Or, if they liked His ideas, they might accept Him, whoever He was. If they did not like His ideas, they would automatically reject Him. Many fundamentalist Christians do not like His ideas, even without seeing Him. They are convinced already that He must be the antichrist. They do not like the idea of sharing, and do not seem to like justice. Because He has not come down on a cloud into Jerusalem as they expect, they have a prejudice from the start. If He called Himself the Christ, there would be a huge division among Christians as to Who He was. If He called Himself Maitreya, the Buddhists would be divided. (I know dozens of people who call themselves Maitreya. They are no more Maitreya than you or I.)

If He comes out as a man among men, people without prejudice can approach what He is saying and respond to it without being influenced by the idea that He is the Christ, Maitreya Buddha, the Imam Mahdi, or the Messiah. These names get in the way of their spontaneous response to the ideas. We have to think the ideas are good ideas. We have to want sharing, justice and peace. If He is advocating a way towards sharing, justice and peace, we would be inclined to say: "Good thinking. I would like to talk more with that man. I would like to ask him a few questions."

You have said Maitreya will appear very soon on American television, but how can you be sure the media in the UK (and elsewhere) will take it up and make it known to the people? (January/February 1998)

I cannot be sure. They may or they may not. When the news of this interview goes out over the wires, the world's media would be foolish if they did not follow it up. At the least they should make it known that an interview with an unusual man has taken place.

43

The BBC knows this story, as do all the world's media. The BBC knows it rather better than most because they interviewed Maitreya in January, February and March of 1986, and even agreed to put on a press conference at which He could appear and present His credentials to the world. The fact that they reneged on this promise has meant that He has had to go through a long, slow process of doing it the hard way, without the backing of major media.

At last a major network in America has invited Him. The BBC has missed the boat in this respect. But I do not think that the BBC will be able to ignore it, at least after the American, Japanese, and probably the Dutch, German, French and other American networks have taken it seriously.

Is it possible to say why the television interview with Maitreya did not materialize by the end of 1997, as was hoped? Did it have anything to do with the US stock market not crashing yet? (March 1998)

If the collapse of the Pacific nations' stock markets had been repeated in the US and Europe (instead of the severe 'wobble' which did occur), Maitreya would have emerged as expected to bring His influence and advice to bear on the situation. Now that the huge infusion of funds, $57 billion, from the US and the IMF have stabilized (for the moment!) the situation in South Korea (the US Government's chief concern) and elsewhere, Maitreya has decided to wait — but not for too long.

The G8 nations and TV networks are based on commercialization. Would they allow Maitreya to appear on TV? (May 1998)

He has already been invited, so yes, presumably they would let Him appear on television.

The world is ready for change, and there are millions of people in the world who know this, though they may have no voice at the moment. Maitreya will become the voice of the people who see the need to change. He will galvanize world public opinion, and a properly galvanized, educated world public opinion is a force against which no nation on earth can stand.

Consider what has just happened in Indonesia. National public opinion forced the end of a dictatorship which had endured for 32 years. The Soviet Union was broken up into a federation of autonomous states as a result of public opinion. Capitalist West Germany and communist East Germany are reunited as one country as a result of public opinion. The transformation in South Africa — the new constitution, the end of apartheid — is the result of public opinion. The end of the Cold War is the result of public opinion. All of these events were predicted by Maitreya in our magazine, *Share International*. Maitreya largely brought them about by working through certain individuals like Mr Gorbachev and Mr Mandela. But the actual events were a result of the action of public opinion; otherwise they could not have taken place. In the same way, organized, galvanized, educated world public opinion will transform the world under the advocacy of Maitreya, Who will be a spokesman for all the people without a voice.

Sai Baba has been working in public for many years. Why does Maitreya need the invitation of media before His public work? (July/August 1997)

These two great Beings embody the same energy, the energy of Love, but have completely different roles to play. Sai Baba is in the second of three incarnational experiences on Earth: as Sai Baba of Shirdi, now as Sathya Sai, and early next [21st] century as Prema Baba. Maitreya comes as World Teacher for the

Aquarian Age (2,500 years). In a very definite sense, He represents humanity, and so needs our invitation (through our media representatives) to come openly before us, to teach us how to transform our lives in such a way as to respond correctly to the Aquarian energies and build the new civilization.

Recognition of Maitreya

"Very soon, the world will see the Teacher. The question arises: will people recognize Him? For the vast majority, recognition will not be difficult: seldom, indeed, does a man of His stature — demonstrating, radiating for all to see, the Love, the Wisdom, the Purpose and the Grace of God — come openly into our lives. Millions will respond and rally to His side, eager to implement the plans which, He will advise, are essential for the regeneration of life on Earth...

"Not all men, however, will recognize Maitreya as the One awaited by all the nations. Steeped deeply in the world's scriptures, however fragmented, and however discoloured by time, many will turn away, at first, from this latest manifestation of God's continuing Plan for the world. They will find it hard to reconcile Maitreya's simple and practical approach with their mystical expectations and dogmas. Do not be surprised, therefore, by their angry and anxious rejection. Thus it was in Jesus' time. Thus, also, when the Buddha began His work. Thus, too, did Krishna know dissent and condemnation. Thus has it always been when the New has presented itself to the Old.

"Be not afraid, therefore, when the 'men of cloth' raise their voices against the Great Lord, naming Him anti-Christ and arch-deceiver, for they know little of the laws which underlie their faiths and act and speak from ignorance and fear. They, too, are tested in this fashion." (From 'The recognition of Maitreya' by the Master —, *Share International,* April 1997)

47

On the Day of Declaration, when Maitreya speaks to the whole world telepathically while He is seen on satellite TV, will the majority of people be able to understand the meaning of what He is saying? (January/February 1998)

He will talk about the history of humanity, the high source from which we come, the evolutionary process, the Law of Cause and Effect, the Law of Rebirth, the need for harmlessness, the needs of the world, outlining our major problems — the ecological imbalance (this will become the number one priority), the fate of the starving millions, which is His major concern — and their solution through sharing and the creation, therefore, of justice and peace. He will speak simply, heart-to-heart.

If you read the messages from Maitreya that are published *(Messages from Maitreya the Christ*, Share International Fdn.), I think you will understand every single word, and so it will be on the Day of Declaration. He will speak in the simplest terms, not about esotericism. He might mention briefly, in simple terms, the Path of Initiation as the final phase of life on this planet. He will talk about a readjustment of our view of the nature of life, its meaning and purpose, why we are here, in terms which everyone can understand.

If He can speak to every individual in their own language He must experience every individual. For Him there is no separation, so that, inevitably, what He will say to each person will be brought down by their brain in their own language in words that they can understand. The more exalted the mind, probably, the more exalted will be the experience.

Is the Day of Declaration dependent on people accepting the principle of sharing? (April 1998)

No. The Day of Declaration is dependent on Maitreya being invited to speak to the entire world, which means that the media as a whole have to respond and make available a world link-up by satellite. This will be the result of previous interviews in America, Japan, the UK — all over the world.

The Masters do not go by dates. They have no sense of time. To Them past, present and future are co-existing. They see an event taking place, so Maitreya can make a prediction. There has never been such a body of forecasts, and of such uncanny accuracy, in the history of the world as that given by Maitreya between 1988 and 1991 (and published, as given, in *Share International*). This is because He sees, from a knowledge of the Law of Cause and Effect, that a particular event is inevitable, and He sees it actually taking place already. When it will precipitate on the physical plane, from the higher planes where it is already happening, is another matter.

What the Masters find difficult is to put the awareness which They have of the event into a time-frame for us. Whenever They give a time, They have to make an adjustment in Their consciousness to relate to our sense of time, which does not really exist. We have a completely false idea of time. We see a succession of events one after another; it is not like that. It is all one Now: the past and present are still active but not everything is going to precipitate. Every thoughtform we have will precipitate some time if it is powerful enough, held by enough people. If it is not potent, then it will not.

Is it really necessary that Maitreya manifests Himself in a great event like Declaration Day? (January/February 1999)

That is His plan so He obviously thinks it is necessary. I believe that nothing less than such an event would bring Him — quickly and effectively — into the hearts and minds of a sufficient proportion of humanity.

Why does He need television if He is omnipresent and omniscient? (September 1997)

He doesn't — we need it. It is a control. Maitreya could overshadow the whole of humanity at any time, whether on television or not. He will be on television for you to know that when you see His face the voice which you are hearing in your head is not your imagination, you are not going mad and giving yourself a short history of the world, the future of humanity and all the insights which He will give you on that day. You will be prepared in advance by the media, and will know when to switch on to listen to a talk the like of which you have never heard in all your life.

Will the telepathic link between Maitreya and humanity on Declaration Day be for that one time only? (December 1998)

Yes. Savour it!

You say that on the Day of Declaration Maitreya will overshadow the whole of humanity simultaneously. Does that mean He will overshadow all those both in and out of incarnation? (October 1997)

It will not take place for those who are out of incarnation. They will experience it on an emotional level if they are on the astral planes (as most people temporarily out of incarnation are); on the mental level if they are on the mental planes (as fewer are); and it will be a spiritual reality if they are on the spiritual planes (as even fewer are). If you were on the spiritual planes you would already know about it — it has already taken place — because on the spiritual planes there is no time. It has simply not yet precipitated on to the physical plane. For those in incarnation it will be a mental overshadowing. Each of us will hear His words in our own language. Our brains will automatically transform His thoughts and ideas, which are sent out into the mind-belt, into our own individual language, whatever it may be.

Will the Buddha play a supportive role on the Day of Declaration? (November 1998)

Yes. The Buddha has been playing a supportive role since Maitreya's decision to appear, which was made in 1945. The Buddha is no longer in the Hierarchy but is related to it. He is on a higher level than Hierarchy, namely Shamballa, the Centre where the Will of God is known. He is on the Council of the Lord of the World and acts as the Divine Intermediary between Shamballa and Hierarchy. Every year at the Wesak Festival He comes very close to the Earth and brings energy from Shamballa, which is distributed out to the world for the next year.

Every year since Maitreya's statement that He would return to the world, the Buddha has stood behind Him. There is also a closer association in that Maitreya now has the use of what are called "the Buddha's garments". The Buddha is the embodiment of the wisdom aspect of divinity on the planet, and His "garment" is that divine Wisdom. Maitreya can use the Wisdom of the Buddha, together with His own Love, to know the necessary teaching in approaching the people of the West and the East. He can see the world through the Buddha's eyes just as He sees it through His own eyes.

Maitreya and the Buddha are two of the earliest humanity to take initiation, back in early Atlantean days, and have been together ever since. Maitreya is still in the Hierarchy. The Buddha is now on Shamballa, and helps Maitreya in every way possible. There are other great Beings Who overshadow Maitreya, and add Their extraordinary cosmic energy to His energy. There never has been an Avatar as equipped as Maitreya now is, because no Avatar has ever had such a task as Maitreya has today.

51

Obviously many groups of people (ie fundamentalists of many religions) will not be immediately accepting of Maitreya and His message. Is there any one particular group of people (on the other hand) who will be the most receptive of Maitreya's coming? (July/August 1997)

Those whose altruism is well developed (ie aspirants, disciples and initiates) could be expected to respond quickly to Maitreya's ideas. As far as national or racial groups are concerned, the Master Djwhal Kuhl (through Alice Bailey) has indicated that the African peoples (I assume He means southern African peoples) will be among the first to recognize and follow His lead.

Do you think there are any negative forces — governmental, non-governmental, single organizations — seeking to prevent Maitreya from carrying out His work and to prevent humanity's advance? (May 1998)

Yes, I very much do. Indeed there are very powerful negative forces in the world which are generally called "the forces of evil". There are also powerful groups and individuals who see the advent of Maitreya as an end to their power and prosperity. They are in many countries, particularly in the Western world. They now control enormous financial and economic empires which they are determined to secure for as long as possible. They will not succeed for much longer.

Because of the extraordinary resistance to Maitreya's presence by certain forces in the world, will it be necessary for Him to destroy physically not only institutions but people, in order to come to the fore? (September 1998)

Absolutely, categorically, no. Maitreya is the Master of all the Masters. To the Masters, human free will is divine. It is

52

absolutely sacrosanct, and is never infringed under any provocation, and never will be. If Maitreya were to do what you are suggesting, it would be such an infringement of the Law that He would no longer be Maitreya.

I know people around Him now who have been invited by the BBC to come on television and talk about Him, and they have refused. All Maitreya has said is: "Somebody has to do it." He could use some influence: "Oh come on, be a sport. I'll give you a hand. I'll be behind you." Some of these are Swamis, men very established in their own department, and they do nothing. All Maitreya says is: "Somebody has to do it." Nothing which Maitreya will do will ever give humanity an example of violence, under any provocation. That is 100 per cent categorically so.

On many occasions you have mentioned the very important role that the mass-media will have in promoting Maitreya's ideas. I respectfully would ask whether you think that the private owners of these communication channels would accept such a sharing of their properties, or maybe we are facing the idea of socialization of the media. (September 1998)
Maitreya certainly expects public opinion to create the demand for His media appearances.

Is it possible for the "negative-new-world-order forces" to destroy the effect of Declaration Day in a technical way because the world knows they have UFO technology, etc? (July/August 1997)
No. There is no Earth government which has, and is able to use, UFO technology.

'Rehearsal' for the Day of Declaration

"When a nation loses a major representative, the people, as a whole, suffer trauma and shock. Thus it is today in the United Kingdom. The death of Princess Diana, the 'People's Princess', has wrung the hearts of millions, and an unprecedented display of 'People's Power' has conditioned the extent and the nature of her mourning.

"That the people loved her is manifest and not in doubt. That she, in turn, loved them and sought to serve them has evoked the aspiration of millions and shown their readiness for the message of Maitreya — the Lord of Love. It was the love, the concern and caring, of Diana which won the people's hearts.

"Nations, of course, are complex entities, and many and various are the strands which together form their nature. Britain now, however, is one whose soul is somewhat manifesting, and it is, indeed, the soul's love, of Britain, that the world is witnessing today. Nor is it by chance that Maitreya, the Embodiment of Love, resides in Britain's capital.

"When Maitreya appears openly before the world, He will likewise stimulate the love nature of the people of all the nations, thus creating a vortex of love whose radiance will transform the lives of men. In this way, through man himself, the Great Lord will work to complete His mission: restoring Divinity to Its true place in the hearts of men..." (From 'A nation

mourns' by the Master —, *Share International,*
October 1997)

As most readers will be aware, Diana, Princess of Wales, at the
age of 36, was tragically killed in a motor accident in the early
hours of Sunday 31 August 1997. It left a nation and much of
the world in shock. So familiar was she in her varied concerns
for the poor, the underprivileged, the sick, and the innocent
victims of barbarous landmines, that her death has evoked an
extraordinary wave of sympathy and grief.

On Saturday 6 September a funeral service was held in
Westminster Abbey, London, where not only the 'good and the
great' but hundreds of representatives of the many and varied
charities of which the Princess was Patron, were present.

Tributes from world leaders and representatives of groups of
recipients of Princess Diana's concern and care over the years,
and testimonies to her loving contact with individual members
of the public, have flooded in and awakened the nation to the
real extent of her influence and love. She was in every sense of
the words the "People's Princess".

In an unexpected twist of fate, we mourned also the death of
Mother Teresa, at the age of 87, who was, for Princess Diana, a
role model.

Information received from my Master throws fascinating
light on the extraordinary events surrounding Princess Diana's
funeral, as the following questions and answers demonstrate.

*On the day of Princess Diana's funeral there was an
extraordinary, heartfelt response by millions of people in the UK
— the like of which has never been seen before. Is it possible
that Maitreya gave a blessing to the nation?* (October 1997)

The unprecedented response was from the hearts of the people, their love for Diana who gave so much love to the needy and neglected. Maitreya potentized that love by a tremendous outflow of His energy — the Christ Principle, to which the people spontaneously responded without quite knowing why. It was, as it were, a rehearsal of what will happen worldwide on the Day of Declaration.

The soul ray of Britain is the 2nd Ray of Love/Wisdom. It is to its manifestation this past week, since Diana's death, that my Master refers in His article in this issue.

[For information on the rays of nations, see *Maitreya's Mission Volume One* and *Volume Two*]

Is it possible that Princess Diana had ever met Maitreya or knew about Him? (October 1997)

She had certainly heard about Maitreya and was becoming interested in knowing the full story. This would have thrown new light on the experience — a vision — which Maitreya had given her in 1989. This reoriented her life to dedicated service to the underprivileged and sick. From then on Maitreya magnetized her own love energy which was such a potent force in her subsequent charitable work. Among the thousands of testimonials after her death, many referred directly to her extraordinary healing presence and power. Even if gravely ill or dying, people felt immeasurably uplifted by her touch and words.

What explanation do you have for claims that some mourners saw Diana's face while they were signing one of the many books of condolences? (October 1997)

It is true. Maitreya put the image of Diana in the minds of hundreds of people during the week following her death.

Was Princess Diana's death predestined, meant to be? Perhaps as a kind of sacrifice, a symbol? (October 1997)

No. It was the result of a tragic accident caused by the photo-hounds who made her life a misery; technically, manslaughter.

Can you say whether the driver of the car in which Princess Diana died was drunk or not? If not, who was responsible for the accident? (October 1997)

My information is that the driver was perfectly sober and in full command of the car (up to the last moment) but was distracted by the encroachment of the paparazzi around, and in front of, the car. The paparazzi were thus directly responsible for her death and that of her companions.

Please, can you say if the car carrying Princess Diana and Dodi Al Fayed to their deaths was really travelling at 121 miles per hour as has been asserted? (October 1997)

My information is that it was travelling at 60 miles per hour when the accident occurred.

Why did the Masters not protect Princess Diana, as they protect others? (October 1997)

The Law of Karma governs the degree to which any individual can be protected. Several times in her life the intervention of the Masters had saved Princess Diana from harm. Unfortunately, at this time of major threat, the Law did not allow a degree of intervention which would have kept her safe. The impact of the crash resulted in such terrible inner injury that her body would have been no longer viable or useful to her.

I am puzzled about your statement that the death of the Princess of Wales was a complete accident. I thought from my esoteric reading that there was no such thing (spiritually) as an accident. In other words, 'higher powers' would be aware of events leading to a particular outcome and that there is always a reason for everything? (November 1997)

From the higher point of view there are no accidents but on the physical plane there are. An accident is an explosion of energy. If we build up an emotional energy, a tension, which has to explode, we will have an accident. We create it; it works out when the tension reaches a certain critical point.

Miracles

"The present phase of miracles, now worldwide, will continue and accompany this process until no one can deny its significance at this time..." (From 'The Blueprint of the future' by the Master —, *Share International,* October 1999)

What is the real meaning of the miracles appearing worldwide? (July 2000)

Over many years Maitreya and His group of Masters have saturated the world with miracles. In the 10th message from Maitreya given in 1977 at one of my public meetings in London, He said: "Those who search for signs will find them, but my method of manifestation is more simple."

All religious groups look for signs. It is through the signs that they know the teacher is in the world or is coming into the world. You only have to keep awake and you will see that signs

58

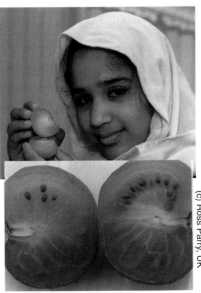

Clockwise from upper left: (1) In many countries, statues and icons of Jesus and the Madonna are seen to weep tears, blood and oil, and even move. This Madonna statue in Mura, Spain began to cry tears of blood in 1998. (2) Photograph of sunset taken from aeroplane reveals image of Kannon, the Buddhist Goddess of Compassion, when the film is developed. (3) "There is only one God...Mohammed is the messenger." This Muslim holy message appeared in Arabic script in a sliced tomato in Huddersfield, Yorkshire, UK, in June 1997, one of many such miracles. (4) Hundreds of crosses of light appear in windows worldwide beginning in 1988 in El Monte, California, USA. Many healings, both physical and emotional, are associated with the crosses.

are everywhere. In every country in the world, in every religious setting, there are signs of one kind or another.

Throughout the Christian world there are signs in the form of the appearances of the Madonna Who was the mother of Jesus 2,000 years ago. She is now a very advanced Master. She is not in incarnation, but creates all the Marion mysteries: healing wells, statues which cry real tears and blood, statues of stone which walk across the garden, which open their eyes or hands and close them again. *Share International* and other magazines such as *Time* have devoted entire issues to the existence of these miracles.

In a small church in Knoxville, Tennessee, five crosses of light appeared in the sanctuary windows. When the sun went down, 40-foot-high crosses could be seen from inside the church. This miracle was created by the Masters and is being duplicated all over the world. There are crosses of light in California and some southern cities in America. They are in Europe, China, and Malaysia. There is a doctor in the Philippines who had patients recovering in half the normal time. He was dumbfounded. He then found there were 12 crosses of light appearing in the windows of the room where he treated patients.

The first cross of light appeared in 1988 in a suburb of Los Angeles. Thousands of people came from all over the United States to see that extraordinary miracle. There were reports of people being healed by the cross. In that town there were eventually 30 crosses of light. The character of the town even changed. Previously it was a rough, crime-ridden town, but after the crosses appeared it improved remarkably.

Perhaps the greatest miracle of modern times, or maybe of any time, was the milk miracle. It took place over four days in September 1995. It occurred throughout the Hindu world, not only in India but wherever Hindu *puja* was performed. Statues

59

AP/Wide World Photos

Above: Over four days in September 1995, sacred Hindu statues around the world 'drink' milk offerings. Millions witness the milk dematerialize in this extraordinary global phenomenon.

AP/Wide World Photos

AP (Photo: Eyal Warshavsky)

Clockwise from upper left: (1) Birth of a white buffalo calf in Wisconsin, USA, in September 1994, fulfils Native American prophecy heralding return to spiritual values. (2) In December 1996, thousands flock to see 35-foot rainbow-coloured image of the Madonna on a finance building window in Clearwater, Florida, USA. Many are healed. After damage by vandals, image reappears. (3) Since first reported in October 1996, thousands of pilgrims of different faiths, including Christians, Muslims and Jews, have witnessed an icon of Jesus weeping and blinking in Bethlehem's Church of the Nativity.

of gods made of stone, wood, copper, brass, steel, bronze, and silver began to lap up the milk which was offered to them. There were small statues and huge statues. Milk was given in large quantities and small quantities. In every case it disappeared out of the spoon, cup or saucer in which it was offered. In Delhi everything stopped, even Parliament. Milk shops ran out of milk; other shops closed. Carrying their jugs of milk, hundreds of thousands of people lined up in the streets to visit the temples. Many had never been to the temples before. In England we saw it on television. Visiting a temple, a British reporter offered the milk and said: "Maybe I can get it to do it," and it did. This event was created by Maitreya and a group of Masters around Him Who specialize in that kind of miracle. They simply transformed the physical milk into its etheric physical counterpart. The milk was made to disappear — that was the miracle.

There is a huge 30-foot-high brilliant colour-image of the Madonna in Clearwater, Florida. It is on the outside of a finance building. That building is now dedicated as a temple to the Madonna. People come from all over the United States to worship there. They bring flowers and other offerings. At one time vandals destroyed a part of the image, but over the span of a few days it miraculously restored itself.

All of these miracles are there to strengthen the hope and faith of religious people, to reassure them that there is a God and that God is concerned with human well-being.

Maitreya mysteriously appeared 'out of the blue' to 6,000 people at a prayer meeting on Saturday, 11 June 1988 in Nairobi, Kenya. He spoke in Swahili for 15 minutes, then disappeared, leaving dozens miraculously cured of their ailments. Photographs of the event were carried by media around the world.

Encounters with Maitreya and the Masters

*(1) When people have encounters with Maitreya or the Masters, as reported in the Letters to the Editor of **Share International**, are they the only ones who see Them? (2) Does Maitreya materialize a body for them or does He overshadow an existing person? (3) Does everybody have Maitreya/Jesus experiences but most people just can't remember them? I can't imagine They only appear to an elite few. (4) What is the function of these experiences? (5) Why is it always Maitreya and/or the Master Jesus that get mentioned and never any of the other Masters (apart from the Master in Tokyo)?* (November 1998)

(1) Not usually, but sometimes. (2) He materializes a 'familiar'. Occasionally He bases the 'familiar' on an existing person. (3) No — but a very large percentage do have experiences in one way or another. (4) To awaken people to His presence; or to corroborate the intuition or belief of those who work to make His presence known; or to uplift and help the depressed and sick. (5) They are taking on this special role.

*How is it that Maitreya can get involved in the everyday lives of very ordinary people? I'm thinking of the 'Letters' page of **Share International**.* (March 1997)

He appears to people in the groups with which I work, all over the world. These are people, for the most part, who have been working for years in making known the fact of His presence, so they are in a special category. Occasionally they are people who — although they do not know it now — are going to get involved in the near future.

Why are some people and not others seeing the Masters and Maitreya and recognizing Them? (1) Are They making

Job Mutungi, editor of the *Kenya Times*, witnessed Maitreya's miraculous appearance in Nairobi: "The tall figure of a bare-footed, white-robed and bearded man appeared from nowhere and stood in the middle of the crowd...Everyone was murmuring something. People were flat on the ground, weeping uncontrollably in praise and worship, in total submission to the occasion...In clear Swahili, which had no trace of accent, the strange man announced that the people of Kenya were blessed..."

Kenya Times

Themselves known to lots of people, but only some are aware enough to see Them? (2) For instance, could I have or have I seen a Master or Maitreya and I was just so absorbed in my own world that I didn't notice? (3) Or is it that karmically, or for some other reason, I don't have a need to see Them? (May 1998)

(1) Yes. (2) Yes. (3) No.

When Maitreya or the other Masters appear, as they do to people who write in to **Share International***, it does not seem like these encounters are beneficial to people. Why do they create such apparently ridiculous encounters?* (May 1998)

A: There is no way we can judge what benefit these encounters have for the people involved. I know many people who have seen Maitreya or one of the Masters in this way, and they seem always to have benefited tremendously. They feel uplifted. If they were depressed or unhappy, they feel full of joy; they feel relieved. These encounters have extraordinary value for the people who experience them. As a group, the Masters come from that centre in the planet where the love of God is expressed, and the vast majority of these encounters demonstrate this love aspect. In many of these encounters people are saved from certain destruction — in car accidents, falling down a cliff, in all sorts of terrible situations — by the Masters Who intervene.

I have read many of the letters in **Share International** *with great fascination — they are so varied, strange, personal and often seem to have great significance for the person involved. Some experiences seem simple enough; others seem more meaningful. Could it be that sometimes Maitreya or the Master Jesus is trying to point to a glamour or prejudice held by the person?* (May 1999)

Yes. Very often, even if obliquely, They do point up a major fault or glamour, usually by imitation or humour. For example, They might well ask relatively 'stingy' people for money.

I have found that there are certain times when my thoughts of Maitreya are periodically heightened more than others. It is at these times that I will look about wherever I am and ask myself: "I wonder if Maitreya is here" or: "I wonder if such and such is Maitreya ..." etc. Is it plausible that at these times of heightened awareness or thoughts of Him that He is, in fact, very near? (May 1999)

It is, of course, possible but not very plausible. Hundreds, perhaps thousands, of people go around with the expectant desire to see Maitreya. I believe that is the case here.

If you met Maitreya would you recognize Him? If you had one question for Him what would it be? and thirdly, what would be His answer? And would you accept it? (December 1999)

I don't think I would have a question for Him. He has given so many answers I would not have any question to ask. Would I accept it? If I could think of a question and He gave an answer I would most probably accept it. I would recognize Him. I have recognized Him. I have also seen Him when I did not recognize Him — as a woman, and also as a well-dressed beggar asking for a couple of dollars for gas [petrol], even though He had no car. I did not recognize Him then but I recognized Him later — when the penny dropped, as we say. I also did not recognize Him (and the Master Jesus) when They appeared long ago as polite and cheerful policemen and changed a tyre of my car for me when I found it punctured.

Maitreya and the Master Jesus appear in all sorts of guises, ages etc. Are all of these persons imaginary, or are any of them based on real live people? (March 1998)

The vast majority are purely imaginary creations but from time to time They base a character on a real person whom They imitate more or less exactly. I know of several such among the scores of contacts and experiences sent to *Share International*. A clear case is when, as has happened several times, Maitreya appears looking exactly, or almost exactly, like me. Sometimes, the contactee may see Maitreya and the real person on different occasions. In this case, the contactee will experience them — as it were, the same person — differently. That is the key.

If the Masters cannot yet take female bodies, how is it that Maitreya can and does appear to some people as a woman? (July/August 2000)

The fact that Masters do not take (incarnate in) female bodies does not mean that They cannot. It is to do with the present relationship (which is dynamic) between Spirit and Matter. In any case, when Maitreya or other Masters appear as a woman it is not an incarnation but the use of a *mayavirupa* or 'familiar', a thoughtform.

I was fascinated by a recent "Letter to the editor", but was perplexed to read that Maitreya had a cigarette in His hand. With all the anti-smoking drives going on around the world in the interest of better health, this could be seen as a rather extraordinary endorsement of cigarette smoking by the World Teacher. Is there some significance that I may have missed? Could you please explain this? (April 1997)

He often 'lights up' in His meetings with people, at least according to the letters. The point is this: He is not presenting

Himself as the World Teacher in these encounters but as an ordinary person, one of us. The person involved has to recognize Him despite these various disguises; and they would not expect Him to smoke. Also, occasional letters report Him to be drinking beer — which I am sure He does not actually do as the World Teacher. These different guises are usually 'projections' He creates rather than the Teacher Himself. Also, when He smokes during such an encounter, it is usually before a person who is strongly, even fanatically, against smoking. He is teaching them tolerance.

In one guise or another, to how many people does Maitreya appear, on average, in one day (24 hours)? (September 1999)
Twenty-six.

I am concerned about all the various guises that Maitreya uses. Sometimes He is dark and at other times He is fair. Sometimes He is Asian, sometimes American. Sometimes as male, female, young, old, etc. He seems to appear as a real body of illusion. Perhaps we have all seen Maitreya already, but did not realize it was Him. (1) Will it always be like this — even after Declaration Day? or (2) will He take a definable and consistent form such as in the Nairobi picture? (December 1997)
(1) No. (2) Yes.

*When Maitreya makes appearances: (1) Does Maitreya operate His London **Mayavirupa** simultaneously with His other appearances? (2) Does Maitreya ever dematerialize His London **Mayavirupa**, or put it to sleep? (3) When Jesus appears in various male and female bodies (Letters to the Editor) what kind of bodies are these? (4) What state is Jesus's Rome body in during His other appearances?* (May 1997)

(1) Yes. (2) Dematerialize it, yes. Put it to sleep, no. (3) Materialized thoughtforms. (4) Its normal state.

You say that Maitreya is appearing in various parts of the world. What would you say when Jesus Christ states in Matthew 24: "Take care that no one deceives you, because many will come in my name saying: 'I am the Christ' and many will be deceived, even the elect, but do not believe them"? (October 1997)

The elect, of course, are the fundamentalist Christians who believe they know exactly how the Christ will return (that is, on a cloud at the end of the world). You would be surprised how many 'christs' I have met. You cannot do the work I have been doing for 20-odd years and not meet a succession of people who believe themselves to be the Christ. Dozens of evangelistic Christian preachers on television in America believe that they have the "word of God" in their pocket, that everything they say, quoting word-for-word from the Bible, is literally true. The Bible is not meant to be taken literally but is couched, rather, in symbolic language. I believe the Bible to be a work of profound prophecy and truth when understood from its inner meaning; if taken literally, it becomes something else.

The would-be Maitreyas, the would-be Christs, are in every country. That prophecy is being borne out in the world today. You should note very clearly that I have not said where Maitreya exactly is but only that He is in the Asian community of London. For years I could have pin-pointed the very place where He is, and if I had done so the world's media would have been there straight away and this story would have been proved true and fulfilled years ago — no later than 1982, when He was ready to come forward. The media listened then to the information, and in large measure believed it but did not act.

Maitreya's Appearances to Religious Groups

Since 1988, Maitreya has been making a series of appearances round the world to large groups of mostly fundamentalists of all religions and the frequencies of His appearances have been increasing. They are published in the *Share International* Questions and Answers pages every month, and a summarized list of His appearances is printed at the end of this book as an appendix. He appears to the groups out of the blue in a form which they will recognize and speaks to them in their own language for 15-20 minutes. He does not say Who He is.

Most importantly, Maitreya creates (usually in advance of His appearances) healing waters in the areas where He will appear. He charges the water sources with the energy from the constellation Aquarius. The healing waters contain positive hydrogen atoms and their pH is altered. Eventually, He will create 777 such water sources throughout the world. They will vastly improve the health of humanity. So far, four such water sources have been discovered. They are in Tlacote, Mexico; Nardana, India; Nordenau, Germany and Nairobi, Kenya. Maitreya controls the timing and the manner in which a water source will be 'discovered'.

[For more information on the healing waters, see *Maitreya's Mission Volume Three.*]

Preparing for Maitreya's Emergence

"Many there are who accept and believe that the Christ is in the world, who await impatiently His emergence into the open, yet who do no more than wait and wish, leaving the work of preparation to others. Sad it is that thus they waste the opportunity to serve uniquely at this unique time, a time like none before and none to follow.

"My earnest wish for these is this: that they seize this opportunity to be of service to the Christ, and to their brothers and sisters who know not yet that He is among us. Tell them what you believe: that the Great Lord is here; that Maitreya knocks loudly upon the gate. Very little time remains to do this and prepare them for this precious experience. Seize the time and *act*." (From 'The requirements of the future' by the Master —, *Share International,* April 2000)

If the emergence of Maitreya is inevitable, why should we not simply wait for it to happen? (October 1999)

The opportunity to work for the transformation of the world, for the saving of humanity, the lower kingdoms, the Plan of Evolution, is a gift of grace, an opportunity never before offered to so many. I know it is easier to believe than to act on the belief, but if you believe it at any level, make it known at that level. This will be the only opportunity you will have to do that. When Maitreya comes forward, millions of people will gather round Him, the world will be transformed really rather quickly — but you have the chance to know beforehand, and to create the climate of hope and expectation which is required.

How do we convince ourselves of Maitreya's presence?
(September 1997)

You should not need much to "convince" yourself; just look at the changes in the world, at the signs of His presence — all of those extraordinary miracles which have been taking place for years throughout the world. These, and the political changes, are the signs of the presence of the Christ.

I attended one of your lectures in London which was presented as "A message of hope" but I felt emotional, guilty and responsible for the suffering in the developing world. I felt confused that it is also a message of hope. (December 1999)

Feeling guilty — that is as it should be. If all people felt guilty, we would do something about it. In the main, people are so complacent that they do nothing at all. They know people are starving but they say: "I'm all right, Jack." Maitreya calls complacency "the source of all evil", because it expresses precisely the separation which is our main illusion. We think we are separate, we maintain that separation and therefore we have a divided world, a world in which millions are suffering. Even those who are creating the divisions are suffering.

We have crime, drug abuse, all sorts of terrible conditions in the developed world because we create two worlds. By separating ourselves from the developing world, making them build up enormous debts which they cannot repay, they get poorer and poorer, paying not only the debt but the interest on the debt. If we gave them loans without interest it would be different. We pretend we are giving them aid but it is not aid, it is usury. We are making millions from the interest on the loans to the developing world. Our own government and others are beginning to realize this and call for cancellation of the debt. We cannot do it quickly enough. We have also to cancel the process

69

of greater debt by giving interest-free loans. We make more money from our loans than they receive in loans.

If you feel upset and emotional about it, it does not mean that you cannot have hope. First of all, the sense of responsibility should strengthen you, and give you the urge to act. It is action which will bring about the changes. Maitreya says: "Nothing so moves Me to grief as this shame. The crime of separation must be driven from this world. I affirm that as My purpose." And: "For how long can you support this degradation?" "How can you watch these people die before your eyes and call yourselves men?" [Messages 93, 12 and 11]

How do our positive and negative attitudes affect Maitreya?
(April 1997)

Very much. In 1945 Maitreya announced His coming and it was hoped it would be around 1950. It was hoped that the pain and suffering of the war (1939-45) would have chastened humanity and brought about a change in our direction. But not all the nations had suffered and they quickly went back to the old greedy, competitive ways of the past. The date was therefore put back until, in 1977, Maitreya said He was coming whether we were ready or not.

If we had wanted, at any time since 1945, we could have transformed the world and Maitreya would have been revealed immediately. He has been ready to come forward, if invited, since the end of May 1982. So, if you believe that Maitreya is here, make it known, shout it from the housetops. If you tell others that you believe He is here, it encourages them to do the same; it lifts their spirits, their hope, and Maitreya can enter our lives without infringing our free will.

His coming has to take place under law. It has to be prepared for in advance. Making this story known is part of the preparation for His coming. You can ally yourself with that and in so doing help to create a climate of hope and expectancy. It is probably the most important thing you could do at this time.

For what purpose does the group that organized Mr Creme's lecture come together here? Is this a religious group? (May 1998)

The group has come together today for the purpose of mounting this lecture and enabling me to share my information with you. It is not a religious group. It is a spiritually-oriented group concerned with the spiritual life. The religious path is only one path of the spiritual life. I have not asked the members of the group here for their affiliations, but I am sure there are people here from many different religions and from no religions.

Other information tells us that the world will be destroyed, but Mr Creme confirms a bright future. I quite agree with Mr Creme. Why are there so many predictions of doom? (May 1998)

These predictions of doom always emerge at the end of one era and the beginning of another. We are at the end of the era of Pisces and the beginning of the new era of Aquarius. These prophecies of doom and destruction emerge at this time from the various levels of the astral planes — the planes of illusion. They come through the various mediums, who find it very profitable to make known these prophecies of doom. They write books and make lots of money, but these mediums are really doing a great disservice to humanity. These predictions of doom and destruction are, for the most part, projected onto the astral planes by groups of beings which we generally call the forces of evil. Their aim is to frighten humanity, to keep humanity enthralled. These mediums are playing right into the hands of the forces of evil, and they compete with one another in predicting the next 'terrible catastrophe'.

71

These forces act against Maitreya and the Masters of our Spiritual Hierarchy and their efforts are directed to prevent the open manifestation of this spiritual group in the world. They will not succeed. The emergence of Maitreya into the physical world *has taken place* and 14 Masters are already in the world. They are joined by other Masters every year or two and that process will continue. If no one read the books or listened to the mediums and their prophecies of doom, everybody would be happier — except the forces of evil. The world is not going to be destroyed.

How can we give Maitreya and Sai Baba our true devotion? (May 1997)

Sai Baba and Maitreya do not need your devotion. You cannot give Them anything; They have everything in Their own Being. Could you give Maitreya your love? He is the Lord of Love; what can you give to the Lord of Love, beside Whom your love is minuscule? He wants you to give your love to the world, and He comes to inspire you to do it, to awaken in you the love which is inherent in the heart of every human being, but which is frustrated in its expression, largely by the unjust political, economic and social conditions with which we surround ourselves. When these conditions are changed, the love of humanity, inspired by Maitreya, will demonstrate in a way which today you probably could not imagine, and will transform the world.

Benjamin Creme as a Spokesperson

Why did Maitreya choose you (Benjamin Creme) as a spokesperson? (April 1998)

He was scraping the bottom of the barrel and found me! I was sitting around doing nothing serious. I am a painter, which is serious, but it also gives me the opportunity to say what I know. If I were working for the government, for example, I would probably be afraid to go out and talk, because they would just give me the sack. Literally hundreds of journalists know this story, and though some are totally cynical, many of them, who may not actually believe it, take it very seriously indeed. But they never do anything about it, they never mention it, because they are afraid of losing their jobs. Everyone is looking after their 'career'.

What are the qualities which have made you the spokesman for Maitreya? (June 1999)

The main quality, I suppose, is doggedness, steadfastness — by which I mean holding on, never giving up — and the ability to go on and on saying the same thing over and over again. For 25 years I have been doing this work of preparing the way for Maitreya to a public which is sceptical to a degree, to a media which is almost totally cynical, trying to put forward very complex, difficult ideas to people without the background of experience or reading to absorb them easily. The people who come to my meetings are self-chosen — they would never attend such meetings if they were not somewhat open to the ideas. Why are my meetings not full of journalists? Because every journalist thinks he or she knows everything about everything, and mostly they know little about anything. That is a factor in the dissemination of this profoundly important information. The other, probably most important, factor is that I can be contacted, telepathically and consciously, by my Master and by Maitreya if necessary.

Maitreya has 40 disciples. What is the position of Mr Creme?
(May 1998)

Maitreya has 62 disciples Who are Masters. He is the Master of all the Masters. The Hierarchy is made up of 60 Masters and three Great Lords: the Manu, the World Teacher or Bodhisattva — that is Maitreya — and the Lord of Civilization or Mahachohan. Many of these Masters have disciples. Maitreya is a seventh-degree initiate. A Master is a fifth- or sometimes sixth-degree initiate. The Masters have disciples who are fourth-, third-, second- or first-degree initiates, and even those who are not quite at the first initiation, aspirants to discipleship. For myself, all I will say is that I am a conscious, working disciple of one of the disciples of Maitreya. My Master lives in the Himalayas and is very well known in esoteric circles, but His name is not being released for the time being.

(1) How did you catch a signal from Maitreya in the beginning, and (2) how can we be sure the signal is a real message and inspiration? (November 1998)

(1) I did not by chance "catch a signal" from Maitreya and begin this work. I was contacted by my Master — one of Maitreya's Disciples — and later by Maitreya Himself, in 1959, and, after strenuous training, began my public work in 1974. (2) You have to decide for yourself whether my message has the ring of truth or not. Look around, look at the changes in the world — forecast by Maitreya and published ahead of the events in *Share International* magazine. Look at the thousands of miracles which are happening all over the world and which are suited to different cultural and religious groups. These are 'signs' promised by Maitreya as evidence of His presence. [Message 10]

Do you believe you are channelling Maitreya's vibrations; or do you believe you are getting telepathic messages? (October 1999)

Both. Most people would call any communication from any entity, whether it be an astral entity or a Master working on the higher planes, 'channelling'. I do not like the term so I do not use it.

I am not 'channelling' anything, but a channel has been created, first of all between my Master and myself, and then between Maitreya and myself. There has been a gradual process of overshadowing over the years, growing deeper and deeper, until He came into London in July 1977. Several times in August 1977 I was taken before Him and on one of these occasions He asked me if I would take publicly, at my open, public lectures — which were then weekly — communications of a kind which, for a couple of years, I had been receiving from Him in the privacy of my own group. So we have many messages from Maitreya dating from before 6 September 1977 when the first of the published messages was given. Perhaps one day we shall publish those messages.

I do not call that channelling. It is a telepathic rapport which is established through the overshadowing of my consciousness by some (minuscule) part of Maitreya's consciousness, and for which I have gradually been prepared. It is overshadowing at the soul level, which is only possible if it has been built up over a long period of time, to acclimatize the recipient to the level of vibration. With the overshadowing (whether or not a message is given) is released the vibration of the various energies of Maitreya.

Two things, more than anything else, convince people that what I am saying is true: the reality of the energies during the overshadowing at the beginning and end of my meetings, and the reality of the overshadowing itself, seen by many people who are, to a greater or lesser degree, clairvoyant; they actually see the overshadowing as it takes place, and have described it.

(1) What is meant by the word "channelling"? (2) Does it apply to Madame Blavatsky, Alice Bailey and Mr Creme? (March 1997)

(1) 'Channelling' means simply an active conduit or channel from one plane or level of consciousness to another. In its modern, general connotation it describes the reception of teaching, information, or instruction from the astral planes (usually the 5th astral, occasionally the 6th) through an astral sensitive or medium. The information and teaching thus received, it should be understood, will suffer from the distorting mechanism of the astral planes — the planes of illusion.

(2) Madame Blavatsky and Alice Bailey were not, nor am I, astrally sensitive at all. We are (as was also Helena Roerich of Agni Yoga) "mediators", conveying information received on the mental level from its source — the Buddhic level of the soul planes direct from one or other Master.

If a recording is made with a videotape camera or a tape recorder during the overshadowing of you by Maitreya and Sai Baba in your lectures and Transmission Meditations, (1) are the videotapes and cassette tapes being magnetized with any energy? (2) If yes, what kind of energy? (3) Will these energies be transferred to new videotapes and cassette tapes if copies are made? (October 2000)

(1) Yes. (2) Love energy from Sai Baba. Love and blend of other energies (Spirit of Peace, Shamballa Force, Will, Buddha, Avatar of Synthesis) from Maitreya. (3) Yes. But they should not be duplicated at higher speed than the original recording.

Transformation and New Approaches

"The counsel of Maitreya is for nothing less than the complete reconstruction of human life on Earth.

"A mighty programme of change will be proposed, leading, step by step, to a fundamental transformation of structures — political, economic and social — by which men work out their interchange and relationship.

"At the present time, men might hesitate before such far-reaching changes, but in response to the advocacy and inspiration of the Christ, and faced with the threat of economic chaos, many will see the need for a new approach and a new urgency in tackling the pressing problems of our world.

"These problems, if ignored, would continue to fester, and would erupt in tragic happenings around the world. Pain and suffering for millions would be the inevitable consequence of our present neglect. Thus will speak Maitreya. Thus will He show the need for change." (From 'Maitreya's counsel' by the Master —, *Share International,* September 1995)

After the Day of Declaration, will Maitreya be a political leader? (May 1998)

No. Maitreya is a spiritual teacher. Humanity is going through a great spiritual crisis because we do not know who we are. We do not know why we are here nor the purpose of life. We have replaced our reverence for life with commercialization, a market-forces economy and the worship of money. The economy is the new religion of the world, and it is this commercialization that is driving us to the very edge of destruction. Humanity's spiritual crisis is focused through the political and economic fields and must be resolved in these areas.

The Master Djwhal Khul has written through Alice Bailey that it is the greatest triumph for the forces of evil on this planet that the religious groups have been allowed to monopolize the concept of spirituality, thus implying that the religious path is the only path to divinity. It is not. To the Masters, the religious path is only one path among many paths to the same divinity. We will have to expand our awareness of what constitutes spirituality. Everything we do — political, economic, religious, social, cultural, scientific — should be, must be, spiritual. It must be based on the good of all the people.

We have put a ring around religion and said: "That is spiritual, and every other thing we do can be as corrupt and destructive as we like. As long as we go to church or temple one day a week, nothing bad will happen." We have to recognize that every aspect of life is spiritual because life has a spiritual basis. There is only the divine. The divine underlies everything we know, everything we see, and everything we do not see.

In the divine plan for our evolution, the next aspect planned for humanity is the creation of right human relationships. Politics and economics control these relationships, so they are central to our understanding of what right human relationship is. Governments should see themselves as serving the needs of the people: food, shelter, healthcare and education for all. That is the role of government. No one can make a blade of grass. It is made by divine providence. The food and resources of the world are given by divine providence for the whole of humanity, not just for the Japanese, Europeans and Americans. We measure the right to live, to eat, to create, to move, to be happy, by the amount of money that we happen to make, as if that were a measure of our worth.

The Masters are the most evolved people in the world, with the greatest heart and the wisdom of the ages. You cannot imagine anyone more worthy than a Master, and yet they have no money. They do not need money. Their life does not depend on money, nor does ours. There is nothing wrong with money. It is simply an energy we can distribute. It is a means of distribution. If we worship it, then we distort the entire nature of our lives. People say money is the root of all evil, but they should say the worship of money is the root of all evil.

Maitreya says complacency is the root of all evil. That complacency makes us able to watch people starving before our eyes and yet live as if nothing were happening. We are all right: it does not matter about anybody else. That is the root of all evil.

As Maitreya emerges into open public life, He will be talking about political and economic restructuring and transformation. Once that is established you will find that He has come to teach us, as He says, the Art of Self, or God, Realization — in other words, how to evolve, how to become a Master. The Masters are Self-realized. That is what makes you a Master. Then you are free to go on to higher planets. That is the goal of life.

If, 2,000 years ago, Love and Wisdom were ushered in by Jesus and Prince Gautama, what spiritual gifts will be issued in the Age of Aquarius? (May 1999)

Maitreya embodies the energies of Love and Wisdom and now the energy of Will. Behind Him stands the Spirit of Peace or Equilibrium, Whose energy is already changing the world; and also the Avatar of Synthesis, Whose fourfold energy — Love-Intelligence-Will and the Principle of Directed Purpose — will increasingly transform and unify humanity. The energy of Aquarius is itself the energy of synthesis and will unite and blend us into one human group.

How fast do you think the changes will be? (November 1997)

There is a complete transformation coming which has to take place at the grassroots level; and it has to satisfy and be real for everyone, otherwise it would not last. The changes have to be logical. They have to be fast but slow enough for people to accommodate to them, so that there will be the minimum disruption, at any given time, of the existing social order.

However, the changes will be so far-reaching that if you were coming from Mars in 25 years' time, you would see a completely transformed world, a world in which the people have come of age, have made their voices heard. Who pulled down the Berlin Wall? It was the people, not the politicians!

When I read books on Sai Baba, I understand that Sai Baba is encouraging the building of hospitals and schools and wells. Is this a model case for the reconstruction activities after the Day of Declaration? (October 1999)

Yes. You will find that with all the great teachers of the world, the truly great teachers, the main thrust of their teaching is always to do with service — service to the planet, to people, the elimination of disease and suffering, all that which concerns the human condition. It is not about personal advancement, techniques of evolution and so on. It is about service, and, likewise, with Maitreya, you will find He is teaching about service.

Commercialization

"Commercialization, that burgeoning but stealthy and often hidden menace, controls now the lives and destiny of countless millions, and reduces to a cypher the God-given individuality of man. People are now statistics without purpose or needs, pawns on the chess-board of market forces and company profits.

"The arid desert which we call the modern world leaves men bereft of that which makes them human: happy, creatively fulfilled, quick to respond to each other's needs, and free. Deadly competition corrodes the human spirit and now sits in judgement on the 'battle' of life. Life, the Great Adventure, has been corrupted and replaced by an agonizing and unfair struggle for mere survival." (From 'The end of the "barbarian age"' by the Master —, *Share International,* April 1999)

Maitreya says that commercialization is more dangerous than an atomic bomb. Living in America, commercialization is around us. Everything is set up in this country to perpetuate commercialization. How can someone like myself who sees the evil in our economic structure keep from perpetuating this evil? Or is it that we must wait for the total collapse of the economic system? (July 2000)

It is neither totally one thing nor the other. Commercialization is not only all over America, it is now everywhere. America has exported commercialization, and all that it means, around the world. Globalization is a fact. It is seen in trade and in the distribution of resources. But it is also a concept, an idea in the mind. Commercialization creates the idea that if you have problems, they can best be solved by the most efficient business methods which have been evolved to produce the greatest profit. Through the market-oriented economy and what Maitreya calls the blind following of this market-oriented philosophy, as if it were some magic wand that solves the economic problems of the world, all problems are seen as solvable in terms of marketing.

If you have a product, you have to market it. You have to sell it through a market. You create a market, you buy a market, or you steal somebody else's market. The bigger and more powerful you are, the more powerfully you can manipulate the market. It is this advantage that America has over even the European nations or Japan, and so it is eminently successful in securing the lion's share of the markets of the world for its products. Its products obey the law of commercialization, which is the agent of market forces. That is, you maximize the business efficiency of any activity in order to bring about the greatest profit for yourself. That is the basic law governing all business activity in this country [USA].

I am sure that somewhere in some small town in the middle of America there is some businessman who works in an altogether different way: as a service for the community. And I am sure there are many such people in a small-town sense who do not try to maximize their profits, who try to keep the group of workers together, and pay them well and share the profits with them. It is service-oriented, but it is not terribly potent in the larger picture of the commercialized instincts and activities of American business.

This has now become global, with all that that means in investment and control over the way the economy of any individual country is based. The capital investment is applied in such a way as it is guaranteed that perhaps 90 per cent of the investment's benefits come back to the source, which is the business, usually in America. It might be Germany, France, Britain or Japan, but to a large extent it is America. American corporations have perfected the means.

The danger of commercialization, apart from the exploitation of the peoples of the Third World, is the commercialization of our concepts, our values, our ways of looking at the world. This is why Maitreya says it is more dangerous for the world than an atomic bomb. It just quietly, subtly, infuses all aspects of life. It takes over. The business economy and the need for profits simply become the norm in politics, healthcare, education, transport. It has no place in education or in healthcare or in the democratic political process. Yet it is allowed to infiltrate and then control each of these essentially service activities of humanity. That is its danger. It is so subtle. We do not see it happening.

Suddenly, the language changes. You are in a hospital system and they start talking about the market. "Well, of course, we would love to give everybody this drug, but with the market as it is today the money just is not there." So people die because they cannot get the treatment. They cannot get the treatment because it is too expensive, and so it becomes privatized. This is privatization of every aspect of our lives.

Water is privatized, can you imagine? They take the fundamental resource for all life on the planet and they privatize it. Our water in England belongs partly to France because they bought the shares. The Americans, too, have a big investment in British water, British gas and British electricity.

This is global commercialization. In one way it can be projected as a benefit for humanity because it is international. It is giving humanity the sense that everything is international, that we all belong to everybody else, but, of course, we do not. We all belong to the big corporations. They do not care in whom they invest so long as the rewards are sufficient to pay the huge, bloated salaries of the executives. These corporations have to make outrageous profits because the bonuses to their executives must be justified by the profits made.

It is utterly ruthless, and right human relationships, which is what service is about, goes out of the window. That is the danger and few seem to see it — except Maitreya. More and more people are beginning to question the value of this commercialization of the world. But few see the true urgency of it, the true, poisonous effect.

Since we are all competing, the only thing we can do is to lower the cost of our product. That is the number one thing, so that the edge in this competitive market is that the product, which is not much better or much worse than the French, Dutch, British or Japanese, must be priced that little bit less. So we have to produce it at the lowest possible cost. Everyone else is doing likewise. Everyone is trying to reduce their costs, produce a product which is acceptable on the outside, at least as good as everybody else's, but just that little bit better value for money.

Every effort is made to do that but the cost is jobs. The personnel are cut down to the absolute minimum. When the companies expand there are always job losses. The way to maximize your profits is to unite. They look for the major competition, their rivals, and buy them out, take them over. That means the price of their shares goes up in the Dow Index and then more people pour their capital into that company which makes it stronger. It is able to take over another and another and another. Then they can take on the giants across the world.

The stock exchange is used to register the financial standing of any particular corporation — which is only on paper. So long as it is written up on the stock exchange, people will invest in it if it is going up, because it is a good buy. If it is going down, they will sell. They are gambling. That is why shares go up and down. People are not doing anything. They are just lending their money for a time to that company at such and such per cent. They are sitting back. They are living off their winnings. It is money for nothing.

The whole thing is built on this lie that you get something for nothing. You do not. The cost to the world is colossal, the cost in jobs and heartache when families suddenly have no one who can support them because the breadwinner is out of work. Hundreds of thousands are laid off because when you take over a new corporation it enables you to use the same managerial staff. The top levels remain the same. To make the whole thing pay more, they cut down the staff. So the same big executives who earn the huge sums are retained, and the people who actually produce the goods on the work floor are put out in their thousands.

So unemployment rises throughout the developed world. That is the key reason for unemployment. It is put forward as recession. It is not recession, it is competition for markets. Since all the major developed countries make almost precisely the same goods, it is just a battle of competition. It is like the jungle.

Americans (this question is from America) are brought up on competition. For many, it is the 'be all' and 'end all' of human existence. You have to compete to live. It should no longer be true. That was true of early animal man but 18½ million years later we could live together in harmony, without conflict and competition, simply by reordering the distribution of resources and co-operating rather than competing.

This is why Maitreya puts commercialization so high on the evil list, 'more dangerous than an atomic bomb', because it is more insidious. It is now everywhere in the world. Even the Russians have accepted it, and they do not have the infrastructure to make it work, even badly. They create millionaires every week, and put more and more people on the poverty line. This is new for Russia. They always had degrees of poverty, but never the desperation that there is today. At the same time they have a huge Mafia who control the wealth. It is like Chicago of the 1920s all over again. They are going through their Chicago period. They have the gangs, the hoodlums, and all that goes with that — the breakdown of law and the breakdown of society, in the end.

It is becoming a kind of nightmare for many people here. When children go into a schoolyard and shoot half a dozen of their colleagues and a few teachers, people wonder why. What is happening in the world that children are doing this? They are doing it because they are part of the same scene. When all of these energies are misdirected, when they are directed to competition and retribution, the child who is offended by a teacher or ostracized by his friends takes his dad's gun into school and shoots as many as he can. That is what the American people have settled for. If you settle for it, you get it. You should not ever settle for it. You have to organize a complete transformation, a completely different view of life.

That is what Maitreya is about. It is a completely different view of life from that maintained in the developed world, perhaps in America more than anywhere else because America is so big and with such a varied population, with different levels of education, different social and vastly different economic levels. It is a huge melting pot, in which anything could happen. And, of course, if anything could happen, it does. There is no rule. There is no law. It is a Wild West story.

"Must we wait for the total collapse of the economic system?" You do not need to accept the present system. You have to see what is happening. You have to be aware. If you are aware, you do not take the whole thing at its face value. You do not say: "You know, we are getting this pretty cheap. That is great. Prices are coming down on this. Great." You have to realize the price comes down because someone in Africa has been paid even less for the products which created it. You have to be aware, and not identify with the system. You cannot change it individually but you can change your attitude towards it and recognize what is actually taking place. Because if Maitreya is right, it is at the end of its life. You can give it that push which will end it.

The Energy of Destruction

Could you talk about what will happen to the energy that came out of the East/West conflict and went into commercialization? Where will it go? How will it be transmuted?

The energy of destruction, which focused itself in the two world wars (which were actually one war), and in all the confrontations between the nations since, is now focused in the market-oriented mode of dealing with the economic needs of the world, and the commercialization which is the direct result. Commercialization is so destructive because the energy is already destructive. It is simply the energy, as Maitreya put it, which sent the aeroplanes into the sky and the tanks into the battlefield. That battle has been cut off but the energy does not just go away. It has circled the world over, and it has found a 'new womb'. That 'womb' is commercialization, the agent of market forces. The question is, what will happen to it now? When market forces are seen as the destructive agencies that they are — because they benefit the few at the expense of the many — and when commercialization is recognized as the destructive mode by which that destructiveness works out, then the energy of it will be resolved. It will be reconstructed. The law governing action and reaction, which is the law underlying the work of the Spirit of Peace or Equilibrium, the Cosmic Avatar Who overshadows Maitreya, will re-create, out of that destructiveness, its opposite, and in the exact proportion. That is being done now. The energy of Equilibrium is the most

87

powerful energy in the world today and is already at work transforming the prevalent violence, hatred and competition into their opposites. Greed will become sharing, competition will become co-operation. That is the transmutation which will, hopefully soon, happen to commercialization.

Stock Market Crash

"...the 'gambling casinos', the world's stock markets, continue their dizzy climb to a still higher platform from which to fall headlong into chaos.

"The marvel is that many wise heads shake and warn, but in the excitement of greed few hear the warning voices. Thus the stage is being set for the collapse of the present economic disorder. Thus men stoke the fires of their own undoing.

"Into this turmoil will step Maitreya. Men will turn to Him for answers to their dilemma.... Maitreya will show the answers are simple but until then difficult for all but a relatively few to accept: that sharing is the natural, if untried, way for men to live together. That thus will begin the end of men's major problems." (From 'The voice of the future' by the Master —, *Share International,* March 2000)

You said that Maitreya had predicted a world stock market crash. We've had the Asian financial crisis. My impression is that that is 'not bad enough', we need a worse crash than that. The responsibility of saying that will affect every person — our jobs, our homes, our lives — and that will cause tremendous economic and social upheaval. Do you realize the responsibility of the scenario that you are postulating? (May 1998)

In 1988 Maitreya gave a series of forecasts which were passed by one of His closest associates to two journalists with instructions to pass them to me for publication in *Share International.* We published the forecasts one after the other as we received them, and sent them as news releases to all the media and government agencies throughout the world. They were kept informed month by month for about three-and-a-half years of Maitreya's forecasts. In this way He was making quite clear to intelligent observers that there lived in London a man of extraordinary knowledge, prescience, clairvoyant ability perhaps, but certainly with insight not only into the happenings of the world but into future happenings. One after another the events He predicted have taken place.

One of the forecasts was that there would be a world stock market crash which would begin in Japan. The Japanese market immediately began to collapse and is now, as far as the Japanese are concerned, collapsed. The Japanese economy is on its knees, and the banks and other institutions are becoming bankrupt one by one. That is not my responsibility, but something which is happening in the world. Maitreya made it known that He would come out openly precisely to help cope with the effects of such a crash. If the crash had happened in the Autumn of 1997, as it might have done, He would have come out immediately to offer His insight and advice to the governments of the world — not to get round the crash but to deal with the results of it.

World markets have steadied themselves, especially in the West, but every crash of a major type occurs when the index is at its highest. The Western stock exchanges are at their highest ever, and it is precisely when something reaches a point of maximum tension that the reverse swing takes place; there is a breaking of the spring and a collapse occurs. That is what Maitreya expects in the Western markets, and He is prepared to come out as soon as that appears to be continuing and is not merely a phase — *before the chaos starts.*

How will the financial melt-down of developed markets result in a more fair distribution of wealth to underdeveloped countries? (May 1998)

90

When the world's stock markets crash, the priorities of all governments will change. The first priority will be the provision of adequate food for all the people; second, the provision of adequate housing; and third, the provision of adequate healthcare and education for all the people as a universal right.

That does not sound terribly revolutionary: enough food, shelter, healthcare and education, which many people take for granted. But there is no country in the world in which all of these pertain as a universal right. When they do, life on this planet will be transformed.

When humanity asks Maitreya: "We accept the principle of sharing. We wish to share. How do we set about it?", this will be the answer.

There is a group of initiates, disciples of the Masters, who are men and women of great achievement in their own lives, in fields such as finance, economics, public administration. They have worked out a series of interrelated blueprints, plans, that will solve the redistribution problems that are at the heart of the economic problem today. Each nation will be asked to make an inventory of what it produces so that the world's 'cake' is known: what we need, what we create, what we need to import. Each nation will be asked to make over in trust into a common pool that which it has in excess of its needs, and out of that common pool the needs of all will be met. A sophisticated system of barter will replace the present system.

Central to the entire transformation of humanity is the acceptance of the principle of sharing. On that depends justice, and on justice depends peace for the world. Strangely enough, that most important step of sharing is the easiest to accomplish. With the acceptance of the principle of sharing all the other problems will be more easily solved.

I think the people in the developed countries should change their minds to bring justice into the world. Does Maitreya think all the people in the industrialized nations can change? (May 1998)

Maitreya ended one of His messages, Number 11, by saying: "My heart tells me your answer, your choice [the choice between sharing or death] and is glad." So He knows already humanity is ready to change. It is obvious the people of the developing world will be the first to gather around Maitreya and respond to His message. There are also many people in the developed world who see that we cannot go on in the present circumstances, and see the necessity for change, although they may feel powerless at the moment. When there is a stock exchange crash throughout the world, the whole world will change. The priorities of the governments will change.

They have never had Maitreya, the Master of all the Masters, among them. Every time He appears on television, His energy of love will pour out into the world. That itself will transform the people who are watching. There will also be His analysis of the situation. Maitreya's mind is razor-sharp and can cut through to the heart of every problem and illuminate it for us.

The Masters have experienced everything on this planet, so They know the problems. They have been like us. Every pain, suffering, illusion, everything that we experience, They too have experienced. Maitreya can speak from heart to heart with every individual. There has never been a teacher so well equipped to deal with the problems we face today.

He is confident that the developed nations will change and lead the way. Humanity has to suffer to change. The suffering is already happening throughout the world. The developed world is crippled by crime, drug abuse, competition, disease, unemployment, bankruptcy. It is not all easy sailing in the developed world. That is why Maitreya is waiting until the stock exchange crash is total, East and West. Humanity needs this to come to its senses, to come into reality. Then we will turn to Maitreya for guidance.

In order to mitigate the effects of the collapse, Maitreya wants to come forward openly just at the moment it is obvious that the Western bastions of power, the stock exchanges of Europe and America, are crumbling. The collapse can take place in chaos and lead to pain, suffering and confusion, or it can take place in a more ordered way and reconstruction of the world can begin immediately. This latter course is what He will seek to advocate.

*In **Share International** (June 2000) your Master recently indicated that He and other Masters see the merging of stock exchanges as folly: "As the stock markets teeter uncontrollably under the twin onslaught of greed and fear, the 'men of money' now seek to bolster their power by combining the major markets into one. In our view, this will but hasten the total collapse of these 'gambling casinos' of the world" — why?* (September 2000)

Until now, the world's markets moved up or down in relation to local as well as international pressures. There was seldom total 'across-the-board' movement which can be massive in effect. With the merging of stock exchanges this 'buffer' against total collapse is being abandoned. It is meant to have a strengthening effect, of course, and in times of stability and growth this would make sense. However, in the present highly volatile, unstable situation it does make for a dangerous vulnerability to market pressures on a much wider scale.

Is the movement towards a single European currency a small step to "Seal the door where evil dwells", ie with one financial market in Europe instead of the current nine or so, the currency speculators have a reduced field of play, or will this European 'State currency' cause a further divide between the G8 countries and Third World (and other such) nations? (October 2000)

It will cause a further division.

When the world stock market crashes (1) How can we protect ourselves from the chaos of a stock market crash? (2) Will there be a shortage of everyday necessities like food, medicines, water, gas, electricity and jobs, etc? (3) Will there be pensions in the future? (4) What will be the consequences of joining the Euro currency? (July/August 1998)

(1) Everyone will be affected to a greater or lesser degree. The best protection is not to invest in the stock market. (2) Not if properly organized and people do not hoard. Obviously, jobs in some sectors will suffer, as now. (3) Yes. (4) I do not think Britain will join.

(1) Some time ago, going more or less on your advice to sell stocks and shares, I did so, and have lost a lot of money since. The value of the markets went up, not down. (2) What is your advice now? And, (3) could you clarify this please: when you say the markets will crash, do you mean only some will and others will continue? Or do you mean all will crash but only temporarily? If you mean that the whole system will fail and permanently — what is to be gained by that? Instead of millions of poor desperate people in some countries then we would all be desperate and resourceless. (4) What good will that do? (September 2000)

(1) With respect, if you sold stocks and shares and the value of these went up instead of down (the reality of gambling anywhere) you did not lose money but simply lost the opportunity to make more with no personal effort. (2) The same. (3) I believe,

according to Maitreya's forecast, first made in 1988, that we are witnessing the process of a world stock market crash which began, as predicted, in Japan, which will be total, and will pave the way for the establishment of a new, fair and just economic order. (4) Only such a situation will bring humanity into reality and make possible the needed changes worldwide.

The questioner writes as if a stock market crash were being forced on humanity against our will. Such a crash is inevitable in the present system through the Law of Cause and Effect.

Going more or less on what you said about the Euro in **Share International** *I sold my Euros. Now I've lost quite a bit of money. Do you still think the Euro will not become common currency in Europe replacing all the individual national currencies? Should Britain adopt the Euro?* (October 2000)

The Euro has lost 20 per cent of its value since it was introduced so there is little wrong with my advice. I still think that Britain should not adopt the Euro.

You said that "if Japan withdraws its investment in US Government Bonds, 25 per cent of your (US) national debt is shaken at its foundation. You have to find the rest or collapse. You will collapse." My question is, why wouldn't other buyers snap up these bonds? Certainly the US is one of the most stable of all the countries to invest in. Wouldn't there be plenty of buyers from other countries who would rush in and snap up these bargains? (May 1998)

The US economy looks stable — even booming — at the moment — despite the trillions of dollars of national debt. However, this is not a true picture; the US will be caught up in the world economic crash as predicted by Maitreya. No country today is an island.

Sharing

"From time to time, I have spoken of the need to inculcate the spirit of sharing whereby the world's resources can be more equitably distributed. This would lead to a reduction of tension and of incalculable human suffering. It would also bring about a revitalization of the life and of the economies of the already developed nations. The life-blood of the planet must circulate. The stagnant economies of the richer nations can only be galvanized into motion through the recognition that the poorer nations, too, have a right to live and to enjoy a reasonable standard of life. Only sharing can make this so...

"Soon, the world will know for certain that men must share or perish. Maitreya will lose no time in bringing home to all, this truth." (From 'The future beckons' by the Master —, *Share International,* March 1983)

I don't see how the rich and powerful will automatically give up their riches and power and share with other people. (October 1997)

I have not said it will be automatic. There is only one way humanity will share, and that is when it is brought face to face with reality, when the pain hurts enough. Then we will take the necessary steps but until humanity sees the need it will not share. The need will be shown by the collapse of the world's stock markets which Maitreya calls the "gambling casinos" of the world. They have no part to play in the New Age structures which, eventually, we will build.

Share International seems to be against free trade: why? (June 2000)

Share International is not against truly free trade. The problem today is that there is *no* free trade. Huge barriers exist in many rich nations to cheaper imports from developing countries. Self-protectionism is rife everywhere. Only the principle of sharing can produce really free trade based on an *agreed value* for the world's produce.

If we assume that everything is as it should be, then people in Africa have to learn from poverty and people in the West from wealth. Why then should there be any changes?
(January/February 1999)

How can we assume that "everything is as it should be" when half the world lives in poverty and the other half lives in relative luxury? When, as Maitreya puts it: "the rich parade their wealth before the poor"? "When millions starve and die in squalour"? Such an idea — that "everything is as it should be" — seems to me to be the most blatant rationalization of greed, complacency and self-deception I've heard in a long time.

Please discuss "helping" others by giving assistance in cash or kind. On the one hand, one wishes to help the less fortunate, but, on the other hand, for example, it has been demonstrated that "food aid" can and does undermine people's ability to feed themselves. In addition, it would appear that various kinds of "aid" can and do undermine people's ability to feed themselves. In addition, it would appear that various kinds of "aid" can undermine the lessons a soul has set out to learn, or the challenges it has set out to meet. Another example of ill-placed "aid" would be giving cash or booze to an alcoholic. Some "aid" may also simply trivialize the individual's own efforts.

Clearly one needs considerable wisdom to guide one's assistance to others. To the extent that we lack that, and given that there are situations wherein giving, as a form of sharing, may turn out harmful rather than beneficial, please give us some guidelines on giving so as to truly aid, and not harm, the recipients. (November 2000)

With respect, to my mind the above reservations about giving aid are but rationalizations of a resistance to giving at all. As Maitreya says, "Sharing is divine. When you share you recognize God in your brother." It is up to 'the brother' how he uses what has been shared.

It seems that, for Maitreya, by sharing resources we can find a way to solve many of our earthly problems. But at this "sharing stage" an important question arises in my mind: I would like to know Maitreya's way of thinking about the private property of people. In my specific case, my family and I have put in many years of dedicated effort and hard work to have an honest and clean means of subsistence, through which now we can have a better life. I'm completely sure that many other working persons will be in this same position. For sure, I would like to give a hand to a person that needs help, but I cannot consider it fair to share the result of years of my personal work with other people, just because this is supposedly the only way to fix this world. (September 1998)

Maitreya is not talking about individual private property but about the unacceptable differences in living standards in the developed and developing worlds, the tensions of which threaten world stability and peace. These can only be resolved by the universal acceptance of sharing world resources.

*How will a general freewill be maintained when the methods proposed by **Share International** seem to entail a centralized* *world bureaucracy? Will the rights of those individuals or groups who choose not to share be respected?* (September 2000)

Nothing will be imposed on humanity; our freewill is sacrosanct and will never be infringed by Hierarchy. In practice, all changes will require the freely-given assent of the majority — otherwise they would not work or last.

Today, the rights of millions of the world's poor are denied and trodden on by the powerful nations without an outcry about freewill from their citizens.

*About a decade ago the Brandt Commission came into existence; it provided compelling reasons for the case for a new economic system; it tried to redress the imbalance of power in the North and South and promoted better access to resources for all. It seemed very accurate and well-founded; (1) what happened to those ideas? (2) Has anyone come up with anything better so far? (3) Does **Share International** know of any efforts to implement some of the Brandt Commission's proposals?* (January/February 2000)

(1) The Brandt Commission was inspired by Maitreya in 1977. The proposals were, unfortunately, rejected by the major powers, especially the USA, Britain and the other European nations, and Japan. They are still relevant and will be reintroduced and recommended by Maitreya. (2) No. (3) No.

You are right to criticize the imbalance between the First and Third Worlds. Yet, because of wars, corrupt regimes, bad weather, etc, help is frustrated or impossible. How should we deal with this when we want to help? (January/February 1999)

The NGO aid agencies are still of vital importance in helping to *relieve* suffering in the Third World and thus require constant donations from those who are concerned to help; but the real

99

transformation — precisely because of the hindrances mentioned above — must come from a *global* attack on poverty and starvation by the united efforts of the rich Western countries. It is this which Maitreya will seek to inspire. The governments will act when the people *demand it.*

Politicians

Do you have the opportunity to speak to politicians and scientists — who are the people in a position to make the great leap forward? (November 1997)

It does not depend only on the politicians and scientists, but on the countless millions of ordinary men and women who have no voice. Maitreya will become their voice. He will create through them a world public opinion calling for justice, sharing and right relationship in every nation. That world public opinion — focused, educated and organized by Maitreya — will create a force against which no government in the world can stand.

Politicians, many of whom I think will respond to Maitreya, are as varied as everyone else. The present politicians, with some exceptions, are of the past, upholding the status quo. Standing in the wings is a group of younger men and women who have been trained by the Masters since 1975. They will be elected, through the democratic process, to positions of power and influence to implement the new structures, the change in direction, which the Masters will advise. Through them the Masters can work without infringing human free will, because they are men and women in the world. By their obvious altruism, common sense and grasp of the problems, they will be elected to positions in many countries (perhaps most countries) which until now have been held, in the main, by the diehards of the past.

How can we share our food with the starving people? First of all, should we start to choose politicians who have the same opinions? (September 1999)

Absolutely, yes. If a politician knows that he will only get your vote if he is positive about the process of sharing and wants to advocate it then he will do so because he is interested in your vote. But if you say: "Well, you do what you like," he does what he likes. If you say: "I will only vote for you if you are for the principle of sharing with the other countries of the world," then you will see he will speak up for sharing. Any politician will say: "Well, there are no votes in sharing." Nobody will advocate sharing because there are no votes in it. But if he knows that the only way he will get your votes is if he advocates sharing, then he will speak up about it. He wants your votes.

Ethnic Conflicts

"We, your Elder Brothers, are never advocates of war but neither do We advocate a lame acceptance of genocide and human degradation; the world, today, is too fraught with dangers for such appeasement.

"From now on, the nations must plan ahead for such contingencies, and let be known their will to act. The sentimental call for peace at any price is not Our way; the Path of Love must also be the Path of Justice and Sanity.

"The question arises: how to proceed to end a tragic episode in recent European history? Nothing less than the complete abandonment of this cruel endeavour of separation by the Serbian leadership should be acceptable under the rule of law. Otherwise this evil adventure will inspire others to emulate its ambition and prove a constant threat. The return of the refugees and their rehabilitation is a major priority; the reconstruction of their torched and pillaged villages a daunting task. The Serbian people should be held responsible for the reparations required and thus, in some measure, assuage their guilt. Huge loans will be needed by the Yugoslav Federation to enable them to meet these obligations and to rebuild their own war-shattered homeland. They must be made to see the unacceptability of their nationalistic ambitions and the need to abandon a leadership which leads them so astray." (From 'A hard lesson' by the Master —, *Share International,* July/August 1999)

*I would appreciate hearing your Master's views on the NATO/Yugoslav conflict. In the April 1999 issue of **Share International**, He states: "[Man's] present, triumphant ability to kill from places continents apart sets the seal on his progress to self-destruction. War has been made clinical and impersonal; no longer need the warrior witness the look of terror on his victim's face."*

This might be construed by some as a condemnation of the NATO bombing. Yet my recollection is that He was critical of world leaders a few years ago for waiting so long to stop the genocide in Bosnia. Any clarification would be much appreciated. (May 1999)

The article for the April 1999 issue was written early in March before the NATO bombing began. In His article, my Master was making a general statement about the impersonal nature of modern war in terms of intercontinental nuclear missiles which can destroy millions of lives in seconds. In relation to 'local' wars, as for example today in Kosovo and previously in Bosnia, His statements in the April article should not be seen as a condemnation of the NATO bombing.

The Masters see it as most important that the nations police the world to ensure the upholding of international peace. As my Master says in His article in June 1993: "Nothing less will guarantee a future free from the threat of fratricidal war. War, today, must be made illegal and the instigators answerable to Law. The nations must be prepared to enforce the law and to accept the price of action. Until true and lasting peace is assured such policing of the world remains the sole recourse."

What is the Hierarchical advice on how to solve ethnic and religious conflict such as in Kosovo, Bosnia, or inter-tribal conflict such as in Rwanda? (January/February 2000)

The partners to the conflict must meet, discuss, and with wise compromise (on both sides) come to solutions which resolve the conflict.

Am I missing something? I keep hearing refugees referred to as 'valid' and 'merely economic refugees'. It is argued that governments have the responsibility to protect or defend, but xenophobia is on the increase; protectionism is, too. Surely if people are prepared to face terrible dangers, even death, precisely because they are economic refugees, then the world should take them and their situation seriously? How would Hierarchy advise dealing with this and related issues? (June 2000)

Open the doors!

Recently, 58 illegal Chinese immigrants were found dead in a container-truck entering the UK. Governments and the people of various Western countries are clearly afraid to open the doors and allow an influx of foreigners who might threaten the livelihood of others. The factors causing people to be so desperate as to risk such terrible deaths still remain. Surely opening the doors is not the only solution? (October 2000)

Of course 'opening the doors' is not the only solution. I was asked the Hierarchical viewpoint on a difficult problem. The answer lies in the principle of sharing. If the world's produce were more equitably distributed there would be no incentive to risk life as happens today. 'Open the doors' means 'share the resources'.

The tourist industry in a number of Western countries is demanding that local government or city councils find a solution to the problem of the homeless and beggars. Their presence, it is said, is having an adverse effect on the tourist trade and on local trade. Is this a problem that the implementation of sharing would solve? How? Talking about sharing with reference to such problems is sometimes dismissed as utopian or unrealistic. (June 2000)

A more just economic system is the solution for this growing social problem. The implementation of sharing is the obvious and only answer.

What is the best way to solve the race problem? (July/August 1997)

Everyone should realize that, in their long incarnational experiences, most people have been members of every race, colour and religious tradition. Also, in humanity's age-long wandering and intermarriage, there is no such thing as a pure race. When people really see and accept these facts, and when the principle of sharing is implemented, fear of the stranger, the foreigner, will go, and race hatred with it.

(1) Is the Truth and Reconciliation Commission in South Africa an experiment in right human relations inspired by the Hierarchy? (2) Is it really justice to ask the families of victims of the apartheid regime to forgive injustices and crimes committed against them? (3) Is there a better approach to such matters? (January/February 2000)

(1) Yes. (2) Yes. Otherwise, if animosity persists, there will never be social peace and well-being in South Africa. (3) No. It is the recommendation of Maitreya to Mr Mandela.

There are some who say that the confusion and chaos in the modern world are due to a conspiracy of the Jews. What is your opinion about this? (November 1997)

105

This is an ancient calumny used again and again by authoritarian governments to draw the attention of their people from their own shortcomings, mistakes and misdeeds. Because of their tendency to separation, the Jews, throughout the centuries, have provided an easy scapegoat and suffered endless pogroms as a result.

Legal Systems

Could you say something about how the Masters view the role of the International Court of Justice in the Hague, the Netherlands? (1) Do the Masters think that demagogues like Milosevic should be made to stand trial? (2) What sort of laws should come into effect to ensure that the Court does not spend its time convicting small fry while the big fish escape with apparent impunity? (3) Does not this tendency undermine its validity? (January/February 2000)

(1) Yes. (2) The laws are adequate. It is a question of political will to enforce them. (3) Of course, yes.

With the energy change, will we see a change in our legal system? Or will the time come when we will not even need a legal system? (September 1999)

In the first place, we do need a legal system. There are 6 billion people in the world and we have to have an international legal system, the rule of law, without which you get anarchy, chaos, war and all the rest.

The legal systems of today are corrupt, as all our systems to some degree are corrupt, and inevitably they will change. Greater equilibrium will be the result. Today, there is one law for the very rich and another for the very poor. This is so obvious in our day-to-day reading of newspapers and watching of television that something must be done to change that structure. There is an inbuilt caste system, by whatever name you call it, in every country, whereby the law acts unequally for those with influence and power and money and those who have none of these. The influence of Maitreya and the Masters will bring about a sense of fair play, of justice. As justice grows on the economic and political level, it will inevitably infiltrate every aspect of society, including the legal system, and those large, fat, well-paid judges, some of whom are blameless but some of whom are corrupt, unfair and unjust in their justice, will have to make way for better exponents of the art.

How common is vote-rigging in the democracies of the world? (May 1998)

In the older democracies it is now relatively rare. Unfortunately, in many of the newer and still emerging 'democracies' this is far from being the case; vote-rigging is rampant.

The USA in a Quandary

Looking at the recent American Presidential election (November 2000), I am wondering how rampant vote-rigging is in the US. I suppose in the US it takes a more subtle form of discrimination — such as in the way they count votes or the way the voters of certain communities are treated, etc. I would appreciate it if your Master could shed some light on this. (January/February 2001)

Vote-rigging is not 'rampant' in the US (unless it is necessary to ensure a Republican victory, as was the case in Florida!) Many tricks and trumped-up procedures were used in Florida to deny the vote to many black citizens and others who traditionally vote Democrat. And the counting machines used in parts of Florida (installed in 1960) have shown themselves to be inadequate and out-of-date. It is up to *all* Americans to vote and to *ensure beforehand* that the system is fair.

The recent US presidential election, fraught with controversy and legal challenges, resulted in victory for the conservative Republican Party candidate, George W.Bush, with some military leaders now in seats of power. These leaders represent ideas very contrary to Maitreya's priorities, so many of us are concerned about this turn of events. Can you comment on the significance of this? Is this a major set-back for Maitreya's mission, or is there possibly an unseen reason for this change, which may indeed be part of the Plan? (January/February 2001)

It is certainly not part of the Plan; Mr Gore actually 'won' the election. Nor do I think that it is a set-back for Maitreya's mission. The American people (the small percentage who voted) actually voted for Mr Gore and continuation of the policies of the Clinton administration. If Mr Bush and his advisers plan an increase of US military strength (which is likely) it will undoubtedly upset the present balance of power. This, I believe, would bring Maitreya more quickly into the open, whatever the state of the (already shaky) stock markets.

Could the Master say which US presidential candidate the majority of Florida voters intended to vote for when they cast their vote? Did Bush win the election fraudulently? (January/February 2001)

Yes, very much so. Some Republicans think of their party as having a 'Divine right' to rule and that any and every trick is valid to ensure a Republican victory. The Florida vote, if it had been allowed to proceed, would have shown Mr Gore to have won by thousands of votes.

I feel the majority group of the justices of the US Supreme Court acted politically, essentially deciding on George W.Bush as the President. Would you say this is a part of the process of bringing out the corrupt legal system of the US to the surface in such a way that everyone could see? Can you say how corrupt the US Supreme Court justices are? (January/February 2001)

The US Supreme Court undoubtedly did act politically and thereby showed how easily the legal system of the US can be corrupted. The implication in the question is that this was perhaps part of a plan of Hierarchy or an esoteric process. This was not the case. It was simply corrupt.

I am most concerned about George W.Bush's totally backward attitude toward foreign policy. He says America should not become involved in the affairs of other parts of the world unless they interfere with American interests. I fear the effect the Bush administration would have on world affairs. How will Bush's election affect the US response to Maitreya's public emergence, when it occurs? (January/February 2001)

I do not think that the response to Maitreya's emergence will be very much affected. The loser won and the winner lost the election but the result was close and only a small percentage of people actually voted. However, I believe that the Bush 'victory' does increase the tension in world affairs, particularly if the new administration proceeds with the $60 billion anti-missile defence system. That would frighten and anger both Russia and China who are reluctant to engage in another arms race. For that reason alone I think the Bush success will have the effect of making the emergence of Maitreya sooner rather than later.

National Identities

Maitreya has said that the identity of a person and a nation is sacred. At the same time the melting of the ethnic groups in the USA is considered an experiment of Hierarchy, while on the other side the (cultural) development of the ethnic groups in the UK is considered another experiment for maintaining their own group identity and integrity. How can it be that in one case the identity of an ethnic group is gradually lost and in the other case is maintained? (July/August 1997)

That is the very nature of the experiment which also involves the various — now autonomous — states of the former Soviet Union. It is not the case that whole nations are absorbed into the "melting pot" in the USA, but only *representatives* of the various nations — mainly from Europe. The original nations retain their own identity while something altogether new is gradually emerging through racial admixture in the USA.

You said that each nation has its own ray-structure and according to this, I suppose, its own role to play in the Plan of Earth evolution. (1) If that is so I am interested to know the ray-structure of Croatia. (2) Until today Maitreya hasn't made any appearance in Croatia. What is your opinion about the reason and will He make one soon? (3) Do nations also have "points of evolution"? If so please give a few examples? (June 1999)

(1) Soul 6; Personality 4. (2) I do not have an opinion. I do not know. (3) No, but certain nations are more evolved (older as nations) and express more of their soul energy than others. At present these are Great Britain, France and Japan.

[For the rays of nations, see *Maitreya's Mission Volume One* and *Volume Two*]

Could you give us the ray structure of Serbia? (July/August 1999)

The rays of Serbia are 6th-ray soul and 3rd-ray personality.

Maitreya has said that the countries of Europe would retain their individuality as this comprises different soul and personality rays for each country which manifests in our unique individuality. (1) Does He see the launching of the new currency as affecting this individuality in any way? (2) If not, should the United Kingdom be joining in now? or (3) Are we right in holding back from monetary union with the rest of Europe? (January/February 1999)

(1) Yes. Monetary union is a misconceived idea despite its obvious practical advantages. (2) No. (3) Yes.

Is there a kind of alliance forming between Prince Charles and Tony Blair which will perhaps act as a focus for the emerging soul of Britain? (December 1997)

No. However, it could become so in time. The soul aspect of every nation is demonstrated through the initiates and disciples of that nation. The personality, the lower aspect, which should eventually reflect the soul aspect but for most nations still does not, is demonstrated by the mass of people.

The soul quality, as far as Britain is concerned, is the love aspect of the 2nd ray, though the 1st ray of power has dominated the personality life of this country for centuries. It has created parliament — we (the UK) have the 'mother of parliaments'; it has created the militaristic history of Britain, the colonizing force which went all round the world and captured most of it. We were repeating what this nation did as Romans. This nation is largely a reincarnation of the Romans. Not everyone in Britain was a Roman, but most of today's population were. The Romans

111

opened up the world and their armies conquered it, just as Britain conquered the later known world. They built roads; we built railroads: that is how the world became as small and interconnected as it is today.

During the Second World War we came through a period in which we had great leaders, necessary for the wartime trials and traumas. In Britain we had Churchill, who was a third-degree initiate (three-fifths of the way to being a Master). At that time also there was, in America, Franklin D.Roosevelt, who was 2.7; in China, Mao Tse Tung, who was 3.2; and in Yugoslavia, Tito, who was 2.5. Even Hitler was a second-degree initiate: to be as effective and powerful as Hitler was you have to be an initiate of some level because you have power if you are initiate. The forces of evil, as we call them, the forces of materiality as the Masters call them, could thus work through Hitler, as they did. Hitler was a medium with a deeply evil personality.

The Axis powers, in the war from 1939-1945, embodied the energy that Christians are still waiting to be manifested, namely the Antichrist. Christians are afraid that Maitreya might be (and many call Him) the Antichrist. Many of them really believe me when I say that Maitreya is in the world but they are afraid because their interpretation of scripture says that the Christ can only come at the end of the world, on a cloud, into Jerusalem, to take them up into "the rapture". So Maitreya must be the Antichrist, they believe. The "rapture" is a symbolic statement for the expansion of consciousness, the awakening of the Christ Principle, the demonstration of the nature of God in everyday life by the reconstruction of our political, economic and social structures, necessary to demonstrate our innate divinity. Our innate divinity is our humanity and we cannot demonstrate our humanity because of the corrupt and evil political and especially economic structures with which we surround ourselves today; structures which by their very nature divide and separate people.

That is the nature of market forces. They benefit the few at the expense of the many.

However developed Prince Charles and/or Tony Blair might be, being among the leaders of the nation they can give expression to some degree to the love nature of the soul aspect of the country. This is one reason why we have a Labour Government after 18 years of corrupt, reactionary rule which divided Britain and turned it into two countries, one rich, the other poverty-stricken. An end of that separation is awaited by the people, and I am sure the aspiration of Tony Blair is for that, and the aspiration of Prince Charles is to get closer to the people, to serve them.

China

What is the destiny of China? (December 1998)

No government of the present time will remain. All the countries in the world are at various stages of development, but when the Principle of Sharing is accepted, which is inevitable, and seen as the *sine qua non* for a progressive society, it is obvious that the present government will no longer be in control. Maitreya has stated that China will emerge as the most powerful — economically but not militarily — nation in Asia. My Master has stated about China that at the moment there are many different experiments of a political/economic nature going on. Some of them, He says, are very unusual and particular to China but also are throwing a light on the possibilities for other nations; experiments which He says other nations could look at and benefit from. The Chinese Government has been set for years on opening up the country to markets while at the same time keeping the people under sufficient control so as not to make the mistake which the Russians made in opening up the whole thing and expecting in two weeks to transform the system. That is the calamity of Russia, if I may say so. Russia's 6th-ray revolutionary zeal has swept her up into making vast changes without evolution. Such evolution takes time.

In the past, China has been communist. Now it is opening up more to capitalism. (May 1998)

It is indeed, but it will emerge as a mixed capitalist-communist state. China is going through a great transitional phase and many interesting experiments are taking place there. There are new aspects which have not really been tried on that scale before. The Chinese, with a 3rd-ray personality, are extremely adaptable. If China had not been adaptable there would be no China today. China has lasted for 4,000 years by adapting to circumstances.

It has more than 1,000 million souls, the biggest population in the world. Its neighbour, India, is next with about 900 million people, but it is not organized in the same way. The Chinese have, still, the disciplining, organizing power of the communist regime, when everything was organized from the top (which is what brought down the Russian experiment).

However, the Chinese are much more adaptable and less ideological than the Russians, and are managing it in a completely different way. They are, with a 1st-ray soul, somewhat ruthless in their application of the necessary disciplines, but if your population is over 1,000 million you have to take steps to limit it and you have to organize very carefully the economy of the country. If you are starting from a very poor level but emulating the capitalist West, you have to take very little steps. That is what they have done, and now are emerging with a series of experiments of a blend of communism and capitalism.

Maitreya has said: "A cart needs two wheels. A cart with one wheel will not go." One wheel is capitalism and the other socialism or communism. Of course it is not capitalism or communism in the classic sense but a blend, bringing in the best aspects of both. The Chinese have an enormous capacity for hard work. Many have two jobs, and seem to need little sleep. They see the country as one totality, the New China. That gives an enormous spirit to the work.

*Since Hong Kong is scheduled to be returned to China by the British on 1 July 1997, and Maitreya has predicted (**Share International** September 1989) that Hong Kong would never become part of China, does that mean that Maitreya will prevent the handing-over of Hong Kong by emerging before 1 July?* (June 1997)

No, I am afraid not. I very much doubt that Maitreya would "prevent" such an agreed return in any case, and I expect the formal handing-over of the island to take place as planned. Does that mean that Maitreya's prediction will prove to be wrong? Again, I think not. I feel sure that His meaning is that the *way of life* of Hong Kong will continue more or less as at present despite the formality of the island's return to China. As the Chinese leadership has recently reiterated, they see the situation as "One nation, two systems." The Chinese very much need Hong Kong — as it is — as a window on the world and as a powerful source of foreign (hard) currency.

The Falun Gong movement, which claims 70 million adherents in China alone, has been condemned as being an "evil cult" by the Chinese Government, and many of its followers have been rounded up and jailed. Why is the government reacting so viciously against a movement that says it is based upon a

115

philosophy of Truthfulness, Compassion and Forbearance? (April 2000)

Because of the very size and popularity of the movement which detracts people's attention from the practical aims of the Chinese Government. The government's reactions are complex but basically it sees this movement as a threat to its purely materialistic long-term plans for China.

Falun Gong and its teachings of deep breathing, strenuous exercises and a philosophy drawn from mystic Buddhist teachings, is beginning to catch on in the West. (1) Is it a dangerous cult, or (2) does it offer genuine physical, mental and spiritual benefits? (April 2000)

(1) No. (2) Yes.

Crime and Violence

The crime rate has really dropped in New York and Los Angeles.
Have the Masters come forth there? (July/August 2000)

I am sure there are a lot of factors to do with this, but in 1975
the vanguard of the Masters came into the world: five Masters,
one into New York, one into London (I don't mean Maitreya),
one into Geneva, one into Darjeeling, and one into Tokyo. These
are the five major spiritual centres in the world. I don't mean
that they are beautiful spiritual cities, but they are the major
outlets for spiritual force in the world. Then two other Masters
followed, one in Moscow, and one in Rome. The one in Rome is
the Master Jesus. These were followed by more, until now there
are 14 Masters in the world. Their presence in the world does
not make the crime rate drop, but several things are happening.

Maitreya is the embodiment of the energy which we call
Love, the Christ Principle, and He pours that Love into the
world all the time, daily, in an unending flow. This has a subtle
but very definite effect on the way people think and act. It works
in two ways. In the Bible it is called the "Sword of Cleavage".
He comes as the Sword of Cleavage, not to unite people but to
"set brother against brother and father against son". This is a
symbolic way of talking about that energy of Love which is
completely impersonal. It stimulates everything, the good and
the bad, the selfish and the altruistic, all at the same time. So it
takes enormous knowledge and skill-in-action by Maitreya to
make sure that more people absorb it who can use it
altruistically than do those who would use it selfishly. It is a
juggling act. It stimulates everybody, so that the selfish become
more selfish, and the altruistic become more and more altruistic.

In this way the choice which humanity has to make becomes very clear. We have the bad, the selfish, the narrow, the exclusive, that which makes for separation and division, the destructive aspects of humanity. They are stimulated, but not to a degree which prevents those who can work in a more constructive way, more altruistically, more inclusively, from doing so. Humanity can thus see very clearly what actions will lead to catastrophe, to total destruction, if we continue in the insane way in which we are acting now, where everyone is out to make as much money as they can in the shortest possible time.

Everyone wants suddenly to be a millionaire, or if they are a millionaire, then a multimillionaire, a billionaire. Everyone is caught up in a kind of hysteria of greed, and it goes through every nation. All are suffering from that same syndrome; and with market forces speeding it on, with commercialization making it almost impossible to live in any other way, we have come to a point where the world is teetering on the edge. We either change direction totally, or we destroy all life on the planet. That is what Maitreya will say. We have not much time to make up our minds. Maitreya says: "My heart tells me your answer, your choice, and is glad." [Message 11] "The end is known from the beginning", and He knows that He has not come in vain.

But we have to know what we want. We have to see very clearly, with a sharp edge: that way leads to chaos and self destruction and that way leads to — what? The most marvellous civilization this earth has ever seen. That is how the Sword of Cleavage works; that is the Energy of Love. We are beginning to see the effects of it.

There is also another tremendous energy, the energy of a great Avatar Who overshadows Maitreya in a very similar way to how Maitreya overshadowed Jesus in Palestine. This Avatar works with the Law of Action and Reaction, which, as you know, are opposite and equal. The effect of this energy is to change the present violence, destructiveness and disharmony into its opposite, so that we will enter an era of tranquillity, of mental and emotional poise, in the exact proportion to the existing chaos and disharmony. That is now the most powerful energy in the world, and it is that which is affecting the crime rate.

There are other factors working in the opposite direction, because all is stimulated, the 'muck' is rising to the surface where it can be eliminated. It is like your unconscious. While your unconscious is unconscious, all the unconscious motivations, of which you are unaware, are doing their harm without your being aware of why you are doing certain things. When they come to the surface, you can make your choices, and get rid of them. That is what is happening.

Children and Violence

You say division causes crime; the have-nots taking from those who have. What, then, causes the crimes of unprovoked violence among our teenage children and young adults, who take lives and create havoc, seemingly for the fun of it? (March 1997)

Everyone, without exception, is responding to the new, powerful cosmic energies which are pouring into the world. This has a profound effect on everybody. If you have a slight mental or emotional unbalance, it does not take very much to upset that balance and cause this crazy outburst of violence with seemingly no cause. That is one of the reasons for this growth of unprovoked violence around the world. People are responding to powerful energies which they cannot control, cannot sustain, and to which they cannot adapt. Their unbalanced mental/emotional bodies are over-excited and they 'flip'. Everyone goes out of balance at some time: every mother 'flips' in relation to her children, and the children simply pass on the violence they themselves receive.

Everyone should realize the extraordinary importance and responsibility of having children and looking after them. Violence promotes violence — it is inevitable. Everything is passed on: from parent to child, child to child, and so on, down the ages. There is a long history of violence which is simply called 'teaching them manners', or 'teaching them how to behave', or, above all, 'teaching them right from wrong'. We teach them wrong by doing wrong. We teach people violence by being violent to them. Many say: "Well, I'm not really violent, I don't really beat them up. I just give them the odd slap." The odd slap, to a child, is an affront. It is receiving from their loved parent a kind of violence which is unexpected and unprovoked from a child's viewpoint. From the mother's or father's viewpoint, they were naughty and deserved everything they got. That kind of relationship is coming from what we would consider a violent background.

Another cause is that weapons of violence are so readily available in this country [USA]. The gun is everywhere, but in America it is a big symbol of personal freedom that goes back to the early days of the founding of this huge and great country. But a fantasy is lived today through the gun. You have a problem of the association of gun-owning, rifle-owning, weapons-owning groups against the rest of society. Until you ban the gun and make it illegal on a wide scale, you will find that young children, teenagers and young adults will go for the gun when they 'flip'. The more readily available guns are, the more likely it is that these violent outbursts will happen.

People have asked me many questions about why young people are so difficult: why do they not go to school, why do they want to kill each other, why have they become uncontrollable, why do they not live the lives their parents want? (May 2000)

Great new spiritual energies in great potencies are pouring into the world on a daily basis. This is transforming human consciousness including the consciousness of young people. Young people are sensitive. They feel themselves to be souls in incarnation, and yet everything they experience in their family, in school, and in the streets seems to be totally materialistic. It is against the very nature of the soul. The soul is oneness, wholeness, seeing humanity as one. But the child goes to school to compete with other children, to be the best, the very opposite of the nature of the soul. Schools are not there to prepare children for life. They are there to prepare children for business. Business has taken over all life. That is why children don't want to go to school. It is called commercialization.

Education and healthcare are run as if they were businesses. They are not businesses, but services absolutely essential to evolving human beings. Commercialization is the greatest danger to our life today. It dominates the thinking of all institutions, all governments, all nations. Maitreya calls commercialization more dangerous to humanity than an atomic bomb. Commercialization is creating in the young people a situation in which they are at conflict within themselves. They know at some level that they are a soul, but the life around them is the very opposite and so they are in conflict. They are at war with themselves, and as the extension of themselves, the society of which they are a part. It is important to recognize this process and not simply blame young people for not doing as they are told, or what you would like them to do. This is happening all over the developed world. Wherever commercialization reigns supreme, the young respond in this way. The parents, like the

121

young people, also need a spiritual basis to their life. By spiritual I don't necessarily mean religious. The religious path is only one of many paths to divinity. But all spiritual paths lead to that divinity. Competition is unspiritual.

Environment and Pollution

"More and more, the planet's precarious state of imbalance, created by man's misuse, sounds a warning note which men ignore at their peril. The very breath by which men live is threatened, the air, polluted and poisoned, wreaks havoc on the lives of many millions.

"Into this crisis has come Maitreya. He knows the dangers better than any man. What can He do to help men save themselves from further suffering, and to restore the planet to full and vibrant health?

"The Karmic Law controls the nature and the scope of the aid that He may give. Advice and guidance will be man's for the asking but men must be prepared to change the present modes of living to ensure the planet's future and the future of their children. The resources of the Earth are finite but with good husbandry and sharing, adequate for the needs of all.

"Men must, therefore, redefine these needs, and enter into a new and truer understanding of the meaning and the purpose of their lives. This will come when a measure, even, of sharing has replaced the present destructive competition, and led man away from the precipice edge. The choice is man's: to share and flourish, or to continue in deadly competition and together die.

"That men will choose the way of Life is not in doubt — the hearts of men, when tested, are found ever to be sound." (From 'The choice is man's' by the Master —, *Share International,* November 1999)

Will the new civilization restore the environment? (September 1999)

If the environment is not restored, in a very short time there will be no new civilization. There will be no planet. We have probably another 20 to 30 years in which to restore this planet to health. Again the key to this change is the acceptance of the principle of sharing. We also have to create a sustainable economy, one which uses only resources which are renewable and correctly husbanded for future generations. The present economy enjoyed by the developed world is completely non-sustainable. If we continue as we are doing now, there will be no forests; pollution of the rivers, the seas, the air, the land will be so tremendous that disease will decimate humanity.

Pollution, according to the Masters, is already the number one killer in the world. It so diminishes the activity of the immune system that people succumb to many diseases such as pneumonia, influenza, AIDS, HIV and so on. The very air we breathe, the water, the soil, is totally polluted and we are destroying the very planet which we need for our continued existence and that of our children.

One of the major things which will happen after the Day of Declaration is the turning of the attention of humanity really strongly to the cleaning up of the environment and making this earth viable again. Every human being, of whatever age, will be involved in this process. As soon as the needs of the starving millions are met, as soon as the process of sharing is under way, then the attention of all must turn to the support of our eco-systems, otherwise there will be no planet.

Maitreya Himself has said that the saving of the environment must become the first priority of *all* people, young and old. Since we have to do this to survive, I have no doubt that — with Maitreya and His group of Masters and initiates working openly as advisers — we shall do it.

124

Our inner feelings and thoughts — what we actually put out — how do they influence the world? (December 1998)

We are not separate from the world. Our sense of being separate is an illusion. Through the action of the Law of Karma — the Law of Cause and Effect — every thought, action and feeling sets into motion causes, the effects stemming from which make our lives — for good or ill. When our thoughts and feelings are positive, creative and harmless, the effects are likewise positive and harmless. When our thoughts and actions are destructive, however, they create negative reactions or karma. When very large numbers of people are caught up in such negative feelings in, for example, war; when hatred and bigotry are powerfully affecting large numbers, the impact on life generally is very destructive. In this way we influence even the devic elementals whose actions control the weather patterns and natural forces like floods, hurricanes, earthquakes, and so on.

Can you say what is really behind the present extraordinary weather conditions? Are they really the results of global warming or are there other factors at work? (December 2000)

There are several factors simultaneously at work: global warming caused by our misuse of resources; the effect on the *deva* (or angelic) evolution responsible for nature's action, by the destructive thoughtforms of humanity. As we are out of equilibrium so we cause disequilibrium in the *Deva* evolution; the deforestation of large areas which exacerbates the tendency to flooding; above all, global warming caused by the fact that the revolution of the planet has been slowed (see *Maitreya's Mission Volume Two*, Chapter 6) and the planet brought slightly nearer the sun. These effects are temporary but inevitable at the present time.

125

It seems that the world's weather patterns and seismic and volcanic activity are more unstable than in recent decades: could you explain this please? Will natural disasters (floods, earthquakes and so on) get worse? It sometimes looks rather 'biblical' when we see the scenes of floods and earthquakes on our television screens. (January/February 2000)

These 'natural' disasters (often man-made or -induced) will eventually cease when the elementals are restored to equilibrium as we regain our equilibrium by greater 'right relationship' inspired by Maitreya. New and higher energies are doing their beneficent work but this takes time to 'work through' to the physical plane.

*In **Maitreya's Mission Volume Three**, on page 106, is written that Maitreya's associate sent a letter to American President Bill Clinton. In the last paragraph, referring to Yugoslavia, Maitreya's associate pointed out that the forces which have been triggered and unleashed upon humanity, imposing murderous sufferings, "will now reverberate in terms of major earthquakes and disastrous floodings and aerodynamic failures. Let your generals and scientists now watch and analyse these happenings." It is interesting to note that within one week in September 1997 six US military aircraft have crashed; some have even come apart in mid-air. (1) Are these aeroplane failures, and also floods and earthquakes, because the US procrastinated in getting involved in the war in Yugoslavia? (2) Is Bill Clinton or anyone else in the US Government starting to "analyse the happenings" of these plane crashes?* (January/February 1998)

(1) Yes, not only the US but the United Nations in general and the European nations in particular. (2) No.

Why is there no mention of natural shifts or disasters (warming, plate-shifts, El Niño, eruptions)? Surely, if Maitreya was the Christ, Benjamin Creme would have included some passages in his first two books? Yet there is none. (January/February 1999)

Natural and man-made disasters abound but the prophecies of cataclysms on a world scale are exaggerated. They come, through mediums, from the 5th astral plane — deliberately placed there by the 'forces of evil', the Lords of Materiality, to frighten humanity and so help, if possible, to bring about these catastrophies by creation of a mass thoughtform of expectation. They should, therefore, be ignored and given no energy.

About the environmental disaster that has happened in Spain, how can such a disaster happen? It was the last place in Europe where there are (maybe for a short time now) beautiful and rare animals? What does it mean? Is it man's fault or a punishment? I appreciate humanity very much but animals also deserve respect and love. (July/August 1998)

It was entirely man-made, like an oil-spillage disaster. There is no 'punishment', only the working of the law of Cause and Effect.

What triggered the Turkish earthquake? Was it karmic factors, the result of the Indian and Pakistani nuclear tests, a release of energies built up from the war and bombardment in Yugoslavia, or was it simply a natural and overdue movement of the tectonic plates? (October 1999)

Karmic factors to do with civil tensions in Turkey.

It has been reported that the dogs howled in unison throughout the city three times, the last time being 24 hours before the

127

Turkish earthquake. Was this because they heard or felt pre-quake vibrations or was it intuition? (October 1999)

They heard the (to us) ultrasonic vibrations leading to the earthquake.

We have been taught that earthquakes naturally follow nuclear tests. When can we expect to see this happen in India? Any other comments you care to make about the repercussions of the testing would be appreciated. (September 1998)

Not all nuclear tests result in earthquakes but many do, often many thousands of miles away from the test site. The recent Indian tests were the direct cause of the Bolivian earthquake which immediately followed them.

Was the recent earthquake in Afghanistan due to Pakistan's underground nuclear testing? (September 1998)

No. It was a continuation of the earthquake which caused much destruction in the same area earlier this year.

(1) What was the cause of the recent earthquake in Taiwan? (2) Is there any link between this and the recent Turkish earthquake? (November 1999)

(1) Natural earth movements of tectonic plates. (2) No.

Big earthquakes have occurred all around Japan since the Kobe earthquake in January 1995. Are these warnings of something? (September 1997)

No. They are the result of natural movements of the earth's tectonic plates. Japan, unfortunately, is in an earthquake zone.

(1) Was the recent (April 1999) eruption of Mount Usu in Northern island (Hokkaido) of Japan caused by natural volcanic activity? (2) How about the more recent (August 2000) eruption of Mount Mihara in Miyakejima island located off the coast of Tokyo? The residents of the island have been forced to evacuate and have not been able to return to the island yet after four months.

(1) No. Maitreya used Mount Usu to 'siphon off' energy which was growing in intensity in the Tokyo area and would have been very destructive. This is similar to the occasion (in May 1980) when Maitreya used Mount St Helens in Washington to redirect pent-up energies which would otherwise have devastated much of California. (2) The eruption of Mount Mihara, on the contrary, was a natural, deep eruption.

The Planet's Environment and the Space Brothers

Has there been interference in world affairs by extra-terrestrials? (October 1998)

All Hierarchies of all the planets in this system are in touch with each other, and everything that takes place in an extraterrestrial sense takes place under Law. All the planets of our system are inhabited, but if you were to go to Mars or Venus you would see nobody because they are in physical bodies of etheric matter, finer, subtler, than gas. If you were to go there and had etheric vision they would be as real to you as they are to each other, but if you do not have etheric vision — and the bulk of humanity does not as yet have etheric vision, though some people here and there have the beginning of it — to all intents and purposes these planets would seem to be uninhabited.

There is ample evidence in the craft which we call UFOs to show that there has been a surveillance of this planet for many years (at least since 1945, but in fact since the beginning of time). This means that this planet is kept intact. There is a huge star out in space which is exerting a magnetic 'pull' on our planet, hence the growing incidence of earthquakes over the last 180 years.

What we call the "Space Brothers", the people who use the vehicles we call UFOs, who come mainly from Mars and Venus but also from Jupiter, Mercury and a few other planets, have put around our planet a ring of light which keeps it on its axis. It is very slightly off its axis, but this ring allows it, within karmic limits, to be held so that the poles do not flip, which is predicted by many 'prophets of doom' to take place. It will not take place. Nothing can shift that ring of light which is put in place by our Space Brothers. Without their help this planet would probably be in chaos.

One of the major activities of the Space Brothers is to neutralize the pollution with which we are destroying our planet — caused in the main by nuclear radiation which is pouring out from the nuclear powerhouses all over the world. Every underground nuclear explosion also puts into the air dust which is totally contaminated by nuclear radiation with a half-life of thousands and thousands of years. Within karmic limits they mop up as much radiation and pollution as possible. They also go down into the oceans and neutralize waste which we have dumped there and which otherwise would kill off marine life and further poison the planet.

The planet is already polluted to a degree which is now dangerous. Pollution is the greatest killer of all diseases of humanity, and much of it is of nuclear radiation. The advice of Maitreya and the Masters will be to close down immediately all nuclear-fission power stations in the world. They could be replaced tomorrow with a safe, fusion process of nuclear power as an interim measure before the coming Technology of Light.

One of the main factors in maintaining our eco-system is our Space Brothers: we owe them an enormous debt. There are various tales in magazines and newspapers of people being taken up, experimented on, and things being inserted under their skin and so on. All of this is totally untrue. There is not a single instance of such happenings. All of these stories are the result either of the fevered astral imagination of people who *want* to feel these things and do so in an astral sense, which they then describe to others and so build up a climate; or work of certain negative forces in the world whose aim is to keep from the public the reality of the extra-terrestrial connection of this planet.

All the planets at Hierarchic level are interconnected and are all in communication. This solar system acts as a *unit* — it is not one planet and a whole lot of dead planets. They are all teeming with life at different stages. We are at a midway stage; Venus is unbelievably evolved compared with this planet, as is Jupiter, Mercury, Saturn and various other planets. They have *no need* to carry out experiments on us; they *know*. They are so advanced that they can make the UFO craft, which are made from etheric matter. They create the crop circles as a means of letting us know, obliquely, that they are here — that the Space Brothers are real. Only *they* could simultaneously, in fields all over the south of England, in a few seconds, create unbelievably complex and beautiful crop circles. The technique is programmed into the vehicle; they only have to hover and in a few seconds the work is done.

How are crop circles actually formed? (December 1997)

The occupants of the UFOs visualize the shape they want to create. With their focused mind they decide the shape in any given circle — sometimes with extra additions, like 'second thoughts'.

131

They then bring their machines down to near the surface of the field. Using their technology, operated by their minds, the patterns are created. It is a combination of advanced technology and thought; the machinery responds to their thought. The whole process takes place in seconds, even for the most complex pattern.

In a conversation between Sai Baba and His biographer, Dr Hislop, Sai Baba said UFOs are in the imagination only. Could you please comment. (July/August 1999)

Firstly, I do not believe that statement for one moment. I think that that is what Dr Hislop believed and, like many other people, he has given an answer from Sai Baba which would seem to support his own contention — whereas it does nothing of the kind.

I believe that Sai Baba knows, probably better than anyone on the planet, the reality of the UFO phenomenon, but it is not His task to make it known. If it were, everyone who believes in Sai Baba as an Avatar, who sees Him as, at the very least, an expression of divinity on the physical plane if not the Creator of the Universe, would take His word for it, and it would have an authority which He Himself does not want to give it: it would infringe the free will of those who ask. Likewise, if you were to ask Sai Baba: "Is Maitreya a real person, and is He living in London?" He might say that that is all imagination, too. But He works with Maitreya daily and knows perfectly well that He is a reality and living in the world; but it is not Sai Baba's place to say so.

Sai Baba has many millions of devotees; His word, therefore, has enormous authority, and if He said of UFOs: "Yes; they exist; they are friendly; they come from the other planets of our solar system," — which I contend they do — every one of these devotees, and many who are not devotees, would believe Him. There is nothing wrong with believing, but that would be an imposed authority. The Space Brothers, who use the UFOs, perform their task of salvage, which is their real work on this planet, in a way which does not infringe our free will. They leave tangential proof of their presence. They create the crop circles, for example, in corn, which is seasonal and after a time is cut down. Governmental officials bribe farmers to cut the corn as soon as the circles appear. This is happening all over the world: there is a huge international conspiracy against the revelation of the true nature of the UFO phenomenon. Sai Baba knows with absolute certainty that that is true. It is not His task to say it, so He does not say it.

UFO Spacecraft

You have said that many of the Space Brothers who visit our planet are highly evolved beings — Masters within the Hierarchy of their planets, or in the case of Venus they are more like Gods. They could travel anywhere by thought. Why do they need, or use, space ships? (December 1997)

Because the technology of the space ships allows them to help us in very many different ways. Many of the large ships (they can be up to four miles long) are mother ships, laboratories and so on.

Was the spacecraft that crashed near Roswell, New Mexico, in 1947 a genuine "alien" craft with aliens as crew? (September 1997)

The occupants of the spacecraft were coming from Mars. The crash was not an accident but a deliberate act of sacrifice on the part of each individual in the spaceship. Normally those spaceships cannot crash — they are made of etheric matter, so

133

they have no weight, they cannot be destroyed. The occupants deliberately brought down the vibrational rate of the matter into the dense physical and crashed the spaceship, so that we would have the evidence of the spaceship and five spacemen who could be studied and seen to be certainly similar to humans on this planet, if not identical.

The American authorities have known this for years but of course the evidence — the vehicle and its occupants, because they were really etheric — disintegrated quickly back into the etheric. However, autopsies were carried out on the bodies and there is a film of this, so we have major evidence that this whole UFO question is real.

Probably it will take Maitreya to confirm to the people the reality of those visitors from outer space.

During space exploration in 1957, Russian scientists sent a dog (Laika) up into space. What happened to it? (April 2000)
The Space Brothers rescued it.

In the province of Cordoba, Argentina, there are people who claim to have physical contact with Space Brothers. They also assure us that the experience with them is not traumatic and that they are harmless. They can speak with them and when asked who they are, they answer: "We are ourselves". (1) Are these experiences real? (2) What do they mean when they claim "we are ourselves"? (April 2000)
(1) Yes. (2) They are avoiding being specific about who they are.

In another town of the same province, Villa Carlos Paz, Argentina, distinguished for its beautiful green hills, there are stories of "landing platforms" for visits from the "Space

Brothers". This also happens in the Pampa provinces. There they wait on top of hills to sight UFOs and bring torches to draw figures of light in the air for the visitors — and the Space Brothers make the same patterns with their UFOs. Are these experiences real? (April 2000)

Yes.

Were the Space Brothers (1) the ones who drew the lines at Nazca, Peru, and (2) the ones who engraved the statues at the Eastern (Pascua) Island? (April 2000)

(1) Yes. (2) No.

Beings on Other Planets

How do beings evolve who are not in dense-physical bodies (for example, on Mars)? Is there something similar to our death or do they evolve always in the same state? (April 1997)

They know death and reincarnation as we do. However the intervals in "life" are much longer than with us and the incarnation is always in etheric-physical bodies.

What kind of beings live on planet Pluto which is less evolved than planet Earth? (April 1997)

Beings you would not like to meet on a dark night!

During Neil Armstrong's televised first steps on the moon there was a loss of picture for a two-minute period. Radio hams in America claim that Armstrong and NASA had a conversation on a separate channel during which Armstrong reported three UFOs landing nearby. Did our Space Brothers have a ringside seat for man's first landing on the moon? (May 1997)

135

Yes.

Are there any 'artifacts' on the moon (except those left by NASA)? (May 1997)

No.

The planet Vulcan was discovered by the French astronomer Le Verrier but modern-day astronomers refuse to believe in its existence. Does this planet still exist and if so what function/purpose does it serve? (June 1998)

The first-ray planet Vulcan was known to the ancients and, of course, is very much still in existence. It is the most advanced of all the planets in our system, nearing the end of its sixth 'round' (Earth is in the middle of the fourth round). It is very near the sun, is small, and for these reasons its light is masked or blotted out by the sun. It is not possible to speculate about a planet's purpose except to provide an environment for its incoming Monads.

Might the comet approaching earth be a harbinger of good news for the planet Earth? (May 1997)

The Earth is not exactly the most important planet in this (or any other) system but in the long term the cosmic energies distributed throughout space by the comet will benefit this Earth. I suppose that is good news!

PART TWO

THE GREAT APPROACH

The Great Approach

The following article is an edited version of a talk given by Benjamin Creme at the Transmission Meditation Conference held near San Francisco, USA, in July 2000.

My Master has written a large number of articles for *Share International* on a wide variety of subjects. A recurring subject, as in Maitreya's Messages, is the Great Approach, the return of the Masters of Wisdom to the everyday world. There are many articles of which at least some part is devoted to the idea of the return of the Masters and what it will mean for humanity — the nature, to some degree, of Their work with disciples, and Their role as guides and teachers.

I could have chosen perhaps 20 or 30 such articles to read but that would take an enormously long time. So I have cut it down, but still there are many articles that are to a greater or lesser extent devoted to this subject. My aim is to read an article, or part of an article, and then comment on it, perhaps enlarge on it and explain some things that may not be apparent in the article itself. Because of the nature of the content of the articles, we will keep coming back, in the Master's words, to the same ideas, and perhaps a deeper realization will come to you apart from anything that I might say about this extraordinary event.

When you think about it, the return of the Masters to the everyday world, the Great Approach, is the most extraordinary event ever because it is taking place for the first time in 98,000 years. It is a climactic event not only for humanity but also for the Masters Themselves. Most of the Teachers have not lived openly in the world. They have been hidden away, sometimes totally alone, sometimes in a small group, meeting every 25 years or so and then going back to Their retreats. They have become used to this silent, focused, concentrated way of living. They have to give that up and come out into this noisy, everyday world where 6 billion people are fighting, quarreling, researching, creating, living and dying. All of that is taking place around Them in a situation which is entirely new, hearing sounds that They never hear.

Can you imagine sitting up in the Himalayas, the Andes or the Rockies, with wonderful weather most of the time and seeing nothing but sky and beautiful cloud formations, hearing only the wind, the sound of a deer passing quietly in a meadow below, and bird calls? There is constant telepathic communication but it is silent and They can switch off or tune in if They want to.

The Masters have to learn to live in the everyday world which for Them must be painful in the extreme. Can you imagine what it means for Them to come down Sunset Boulevard in Los Angeles late at night, and every passing car has rap and hard rock music on full blast? For years many of Them have been preparing Themselves, making sorties into the world, going down to the Bronx, Piccadilly Circus and Times Square. They have seen the horrors that we live by and among and for, getting to know us, and getting acclimatized to this cacophony. They have to take up this extraordinary task now.

For the Masters this must be something terrible, not a picnic at all. I think most people imagine that the return of the Masters is for Them rather easy. They do not need to look after planet Earth quite so intensively. They leave that to those who do not come out, but They have to look after Their health, Their breathing, Their inner ear. They have to subject Themselves to all the strains and impacts of our discordant and disoriented society, in many cases for the first time in hundreds of years. Some of the Masters have been making these sorties for a very long time, of course, and have contacted disciples and various dignitaries. In this way They have come to know what to expect. But for many of Them it is obviously going to be extremely challenging.

They have been preparing Themselves for over 500 years, at least mentally and psychologically, and also by learning to speak again. The Masters do not usually speak. They use telepathy as the normal mode of communication between Themselves, and also with those disciples who have that ability. They will have to formulate Their ideas into words, ideas that will help humanity reorganize itself and change its social, political and economic conditions.

They have obviously a hard task ahead, but I am sure if you were to ask one of Them He would say: "In some ways, it is not going to be easy, but we are all looking forward to it." I am sure They are looking forward to it in the way Masters, or people close to Them, look forward to challenges. It must be a tremendous challenge for Them, even though They know that They are equipped spiritually and mentally to carry out this momentous task of transforming the human way of life into something more resembling the Plan of God, the destined mode of living according to the Plan.

There is even more to it than that. If one gives talks or writes articles, one tends, for the sake of the audiences, to emphasize what the Masters will do for humanity, what a great gift, what a great experience it will be for humanity to have these perfected men at our service. This is how Maitreya has put it. Many people have the idea that the function of the Masters is to be at the service of the men and women in the world.

To be sure, that is part of Their work. It may not be why They are returning to the world, but in returning to the world They do indeed take up that work of service because They know nothing else to do. They are only concerned with service. They know the Plan of evolution — the source, extent and depth of that Plan — so They seek to serve the Plan. Their coming into the world is not done with trepidation but with a certain *élan*, a looking forward to a time of earnest endeavour. The fundamental purpose of the return of the Masters, however, is not to do with humanity at all. It is really to do with the evolution of the Spiritual Hierarchy as a Centre on planet Earth.

The human race is the Centre where the Intelligence of God manifests. The Hierarchy is the Centre where the Love of God is expressed. That stands between humanity and Shamballa, the Centre where the Will, and therefore the Purpose, of God is known. Everything the Masters do is determined by Their knowledge of the Plan, the Will, therefore, of God from Shamballa, and the needs of the Centre below Them, the human race, and the eventual linking of these three as yet separate Centres.

The long-term Plan of the Will of God, the Plan issuing from Shamballa, is that the Centre we call humanity gradually, stage by stage, becomes synthesized into, involved in and a part of the Centre we call the Spiritual Hierarchy. Eventually these two together become synthesized into the highest Centre, Shamballa, the Centre where the Will, Purpose and Plan of God is known and issues from.

So although the Masters come into the world gladly, readily and happily, looking forward to serving humanity in a way altogether closer, the fundamental reason is really to do with the evolution of Hierarchy as a Centre on this planet, and not with having a good time serving us. That is a side issue as far as this movement from the inner planes to the outer physical plane is concerned.

For over 500 years the Masters have known that sooner or later Their return would have to take place. Sooner or later They and humanity would be ready for this extraordinary event — the recapitulation on Their part of Their life experience as individuals, men and women in the world, who, by the same steps that we take, have evolved to a point of perfection which to Them may be relative but for us is perfection indeed. They have nothing more to learn on planet Earth. They have to re-enact this life experience in such a way as proves Their ability to function simultaneously on all planes, from the dense physical to the highest spiritual plane open to us on this planet, and so show Their readiness for what They call the Way of the Higher Evolution, about which we can know little or nothing. All Masters have completed this task of perfection, but now in group formation, They must show Their ability to function at will with total control on all the planes.

There is one path on that Higher Way of which we might get an idea, but for the most part this is beyond our conception.

The Path of Earth Service
I would think this is the only path of the seven that we might imagine something about.

The Path of Magnetic Work
There too we might just have a glimpse of what this could be about.

The Path of Training for Planetary Logoi
Is there anyone who understands what that is about? It is about training to ensoul a planetary scheme, as part of a great solar

system. You have to train for it. Obviously, you do not wake up one morning, even as a Master, and say: "I am ready. I think I could. Perhaps not a big planet, a rather small kind of beginning planet." And for a few million years you sit on it or near it, whatever you do, and ensoul it. You sit and imagine. You go into deep meditation and get in touch with the Solar Logos of that particular solar system and say: "Well, what do you want me to do?" And He outlines His plans for that solar system. He says: "Well, you can have that new little planet, and good luck, my boy." One should not joke about these things, I know, but they are so far away from human consciousness.

What is the training for Planetary Logoi? What books do you have to read? Do they exist? Not on this plane, I am sure. A Planetary Logos. That means you can visualize everything about that planet, its relationship to the sun and to the other planets, and how to maintain that relationship. What speed to go round at, dizzying or not. That is, I would say, a full-time job in itself.

Then you have to visualize all the kingdoms of that planet. First of all, you have to establish water. You cannot go far without water. Very nice if you have mountains, forests and streams of water down the mountains, and it looks good. It is nice for picnickers.

You have to create all the kingdoms, starting at the bottom. You create the mineral kingdom. You have to be good at judging jewels. Do you put a lot of diamonds in, sapphires, rubies? Or do you just put in gemstones, the cheap stuff? You have to make all these decisions by yourself. If you are a Planetary Logos, I do not think anyone is going to teach you in the training period how to choose between one jewel and another. I am talking on a large scale.

Later on when you have humanity, you have to decide which tribes are going to live in which areas where there is gold, silver, rubies or diamonds, so that they do not necessarily all get it at once and share it. You must have a time when they will fight over it, and then you get discord because out of that disharmony you will try to create harmony. You would not be a good Logos if you did not meet a few obstacles! You do not want it all easygoing, everyone with everything that they need spread out on their front lawn, and they just go out and take up a diamond if they need it.

You have to arrange your planetary scheme in such a way that the greatest difficulty is presented to the various kingdoms. For the mineral kingdom, you will have to provide a series of earthquakes and volcanic eruptions to mix it all up. So your planet will cool down in such a way that it will be absolutely impossible for later generations to use.

You have to learn how to do it right, but you are not going to get it right the first time. Whoever did anything of such a magnitude right the very first time they took it up? I am sure the training is good; but nevertheless there will be obstacles like volcanic eruptions and earthquakes on a magnitude that we cannot imagine.

And what do you do about dinosaurs? You have to decide whether or not you are going to have dinosaurs. What about later generations of little boys? They will want there to have been dinosaurs like they see in films. A planet without dinosaurs is not worth having, is it? They would want those little toys, Tyrannosaurus Rex and the flying Pterodactyl.

I would say that is probably the most difficult path that any Master could choose to approach. I just asked my Master if He agrees with that. He says: "Something like that!" He says much of the training is in pointing out the difficulties which exist in present solar systems — for example in our own! You cannot imagine what that training could be. I would say that the vast bulk of the training is to do with mathematics to keep your planet where it should be and not too close to the sun or the other planets. Learn to drive with consideration. While you are steering your planet round the solar system, you do it according to laws. When it says stop, you stop.

The Path to Sirius

That is an interesting path. That is a path which, if you have any sense, you will put your name down for pretty soon. By the time you are knocking on the door of the fourth initiation, put your name down quickly because I am sure a lot of very ambitious people want to go to Sirius. There will be a lot of competition for a place. Try at the third initiation. You might even need to do it then because humanity is advancing all the time. By the time you get to the third initiation, you might find that you were overtaken and there are no seats on the bus to Sirius. If you get to Sirius, you will find it is fantastic. It is absolutely perfect. If you are looking for perfection, then Sirius is the place to be.

We are a very lucky solar system, not a very advanced one. It is not bad, it is a little solar system at the edge of the galaxy, not very advanced in real terms. But we are living next door to one of the most advanced solar systems in the entire galaxy, one of the Seven Sacred Solar Systems. It must do us some good to have as our next-door neighbour such a Being, such an extraordinary entity, one of the Seven Sacred Solar Systems out of hundreds of thousands of solar systems. We get to sit beside Sirius.

That is why we have the Law of Cause and Effect, the Law of Karma, by which causes have effects, and the effects work out in relation to the causes in perfect symmetry. That law is directed to us from Sirius. It creates everything we know about Earth, everything in life, because it is the major law governing all life on this planet. The Law of Karma or Cause and Effect is generated out of the Being of Sirius. That is a law which only a great cosmic Being could create.

The Path to Sirius means that when you go there you make spectacular progress. If you are really ambitious in the spiritual sense and want to advance very quickly, then try and get to Sirius because it is so fast.

Let me give you an example. In Palestine 2,000 years ago Jesus was a fourth-degree initiate. He took the fourth initiation in that life, which is demonstrated by the Crucifixion, the Great Renunciation. His cousin, John the Baptist, was a third-degree initiate at that time. Now the Master Jesus is a sixth-degree initiate. John the Baptist became a Master relatively soon and went to Sirius. If He were in this solar system, He would be equivalent to Maitreya, a seventh-degree initiate with two levels of cosmic consciousness. In fact He is coming here in about 500 years' time as an avatar from Sirius. That is the kind of evolution you can make. If a Master of the fifth degree went to Sirius, He would be like a novice.

The Ray Path

We know about the rays but we do not know about the path called the Ray Path. The ability to handle these great electrical energies, the seven rays, and to distribute them scientifically at a cosmic level, that is extraordinary. The seven rays stem from seven stars in the Great Bear. They are focused through various constellations and planets, and through advanced Masters on the Ray Path Who manipulate these great energies in such a way as to create all that we have in our solar system. That is, in a nutshell, the work of the Master Who takes the Ray Path.

The Path the Logos Himself is on

What would that be? If you do not know what the Logos is like, you do not know what path He is on. I suppose you could only enter that path if you had Logoic consciousness. Someone like the Buddha or Maitreya, and the Chohans, sixth-degree initiates, would have the beginnings of Logoic consciousness. Maitreya is a Planetary Life so He would know the Plans of the Logos. That path fits you for that kind of consciousness, whatever it is.

The Path of Absolute Sonship

That is the path which leads you to be a Cosmic Christ. The Absolute Son is the One Who can embody the Christ Principle, the God-the-Son Principle at a Cosmic level. On our planet that is, potentially, the Lord Maitreya, and He, therefore, is on the Path of Absolute Sonship. He is a Christ, and that path will take Him eventually to be the Cosmic Christ. You continue and become a greater manifestation of that which you already are, in His case the Christ, the Son, and eventually the Cosmic Christ.

Maitreya will live on this planet for the next 2,500 years and then go on to higher work in the system. At the end of this planetary scheme, at the end of all the work that our planetary Logos has planned, when all is achieved and perfected, Maitreya will return as the Cosmic Christ. It is that idea, which is mentioned by Madame Blavatsky, that allows some semi-informed Theosophists, followers of Blavatsky, to believe that it is not possible for Maitreya to come into the world until that time. (They are semi-informed because it is not wrong; it is only part of the truth.) That is such an unconscionable time ahead, millions of years, that that time is put off in their minds. They think that there is no way Maitreya could be in the world because they rule out altogether His plan to come Himself at the beginning of the Age of Aquarius at the head of His group, the Masters of Wisdom. As one of the three Great Lords, the Lords of Compassion, Maitreya comes to lead His group back into the world and to take humanity on a journey of perfectionment parallel to that of the Masters. The Masters help humanity to become the disciples that eventually everyone will become. Those who are already disciples go higher. Some will become

Masters, some fourth-, some third-, some second-degree initiates.

An extraordinary event is in the offing in this age. In about the first half of the age, the Christ Principle will be awakened in the hearts of so many people, literally millions, that humanity will undergo *en masse* the first initiation, the 'birth of the Christ in the cave of the heart'. That birth, which is symbolized by the birth of Jesus in Bethlehem, the House of Bread, will be an actual physical experience in full consciousness on the physical plane for millions of human beings who are now approaching the first initiation. Some several million people stand on the threshold of that great climactic experience, not only for the individual but for humanity, the world disciple. As far as humanity is concerned, that is really what the return of the Christ is about.

Since I have been working publicly, there have been many groups who have claimed that the Christ will not come into the world. They believe that the birth of the Christ is the manifestation of the Christ Principle or Consciousness, and that that alone is needed and will make the great change in consciousness in humanity. That is not untrue. The true reappearance of the Christ is the birth of the Christ Principle in the heart of humanity (the heart at the right-hand side of the chest). But, of course, that occurs eventually *because* the Christ is actually among us as a physical man.

This is extremely important. The reappearance of the Christ in relation to humanity is fundamentally about the birth of the Christ Principle in the hearts of all humanity. That awakens the love aspect, and therefore sharing and justice, right relationship in a word, is guaranteed in this coming age. Right relationship does not happen by itself. Humanity has to make it happen. The awakening by Maitreya of the Christ Principle in the hearts of all humanity is the method by which His major work, which is on the astral plane, is carried out. This will galvanize the heart response of humanity and awaken them not only to the need for brotherhood but also to the actual expression of brotherhood, and therefore sharing, justice, peace and freedom for all people everywhere. This will show the reality of the identity of all individuals as potential Sons of God, having equal rights to the love and protection of God, and the gifts of God, which are the food, raw materials, technology, and all that we take for granted in the developed world but which are so lacking in the developing world. When the Christ Principle is awakened sufficiently in the hearts of all humanity, a tremendous transformation will begin to take place.

Let me read a few parts of my Master's far more eloquent comments on this subject to get a deeper grasp of the enormous event that is taking place. This article is called 'The day of destiny'.

The Day of Destiny

"There is growing evidence, in the changes now taking place at an accelerating pace, that some force (or forces) guides the destiny of the world. Few can believe that the historic transformations, the upsurge of aspiration for freedom and participation now witnessed on a massive scale, result from mere coincidence and have no inner cause. Few would deny that the speed alone of these momentous changes suggests otherwise, points to the growing awareness by millions that their day of destiny has come, and that power, from now, rests with the people, and must be wielded for their good. A new sensitivity to energies is manifesting today, and it is to new and powerful energies, scientifically blended and directed, that we must look for the origin of the outer events. Energetic stimulus precedes change, always and everywhere.

"Whence do these energies come, and who directs them? Students of the Wisdom Teaching will know that behind all outer events stands the Spiritual Hierarchy of Masters under the leadership of the Christ. It is They, in Their Wisdom, Who guide the destinies of the world and wield the energies and forces which bring about all change. Theirs is the task to oversee the present climactic world situation and to ensure that out of chaos harmony and equilibrium prevail.

"Much has been written about the Masters and Their work; much more, as yet, awaits elucidation. Not all that is written and taught has the hallmark of Truth, but, nevertheless, vast numbers today know of Their existence, acknowledge Their divinity, and look to Them for guidance and succour. They seek Their inspiration and value Their counsel.

"The time is fast approaching when the Masters Themselves will make Their appearance, and, scattering the clouds of superstition and doubt, will reveal Themselves as normal and human, albeit divine and perfect, men. The world awaits the appearance of the Christ, and, soon, the expectations of countless individuals will be fulfilled. His mission has already begun; the changes which proceed apace bear witness to His presence. The signs are there for all to see, not only for the discerning, but for those who must hear a thunderclap to sense a storm.

"Soon, the final preparations for His emergence will be in place, awaiting the outer events which must precede His declaration. Dignitaries around the world await His Call, ready to reveal their experience of His blessing. Many who already know Him stand poised to speak. From all nations and peoples will come the representatives of each, eager to add their voice to the hosannas of esteem.

"Maitreya's task has but begun yet already the nations shake off the stranglehold of the past. What then can be imagined when in full vision He stands before the world, His teaching and counsel uplifting the hearts and minds of all?" (*Share International*, January 1990)

The New Revelation

"Whenever man stands at a crossroads, as he does today, he becomes the recipient of close attention and aid from that group of Elder Brothers, the Spiritual Hierarchy, Who, from ancient times, have stood guard over his welfare and progress.

"Thus is it now as we await the formulations of the new age structures. To assist and guide man in his deliberations, the Masters are taking up Their posts in the cities of the world. Unknown, as yet, to all but a few, They represent the highest man can achieve on this planet: a perfect expression of the Love nature of God, consciousness and control on all planes and a knowledge, tested and tried by long experience, of the Plan of Evolution and the process of its implementation.

"Never before in man's long history have the possibilities for rapid advance been so great. Never before, in such numbers, have the Masters dwelt among men. This alone is remarkable; it presupposes

great changes, already occurring and still to come."
(*Share International*, March 1988)

Can you imagine when the Masters are actually working openly, known for what They are and advising the leaders of the world, the major statesmen, professors, educators, the great financiers and administrators? You can imagine what effect the Masters' advice will have on these men and women, trained in their own particular professions, with all the expertise at their finger tips, though sometimes an expertise that has led the world to the very edge of a precipice. That expertise will be turned to good, to the needs of all humanity, and will show an insight, a technological clarity and ability which will quickly, if we wish it, transform the world.

The only thing that will hold it up is ourselves. We determine the speed of transformation. If we want it quickly, it will be quickly. If we want to slow it down, we will slow it down. The Masters will not push us. They will simply present us with the information and guidance and leave it to world public opinion to decide which way to go and at what pace. In this way, the free will of humanity will never be infringed. That is the plan. That is the way the Masters have always worked, but now They will be doing it openly.

So openly that people will begin to turn to Them for the answer to every problem (just as people turn to me to ask my Master for the answer to every problem, whether it is personal or to do with their group. Whether they should take a new job or not? Should they leave this house? Are they where they are meant to be? What do I think of this book? Is it authentic, should they buy it? People think up these questions knowing in their heart that they are not questions for Masters. Masters do not have time or interest to answer such questions. Nor, to be honest, do I).

'The new revelation', continued:

"Chief among these changes is the readiness of men for new revelation. The thirst for knowledge has brought man to the door of knowledge unlimited. Beyond that door, man senses, lies a treasure trove of mysteries to be solved, worlds of meaning to be conquered, vistas of beauty to be experienced and known. Man begins to question the purpose of his existence and to search for means whereby that purpose can be fulfilled.

"Thus it is at the dawn of the new age. As always at such a time, man approaches life with a deeper reverence, sensing its spiritual basis, and raises his eyes and heart to those realms from which all revelation comes, thus invoking the revelation for which he longs.

"'God works,' the adage goes, 'in mysterious ways.' Yet always is that mystery open to interpretation and understanding. Age after age, the mysteries have been revealed; new insights have opened the door to greater knowledge and a new light has entered the minds of men.

"Today, a great new light is awakening humanity to its purpose and destiny. That shining brilliance will reveal to men the Purpose underlying the Will of God, and will galvanize mankind into the creation of those relationships and forms which will serve to demonstrate that Purpose in all its beauty and power.

"Such a time as this has seldom been. Man is on the threshold of a new understanding of himself and of those forces which lie behind all appearances. Soon he will know, beyond all gainsaying, that God is, and that man is God."

The Plan is not some vague, cosmic idea in the mind of a great cosmic entity, but something that has exact relevance to our lives. It has to do with right human relationships, and therefore with politics, economics, religion, science and education, and whether the poor get enough to eat, whether there are too many poor and too many rich, and whether the gap between them is too great.

All of this is part of the Plan of God. God's Plan is not a set of rules that you have to obey, but ideas which in themselves have an inner beauty, an inner relevance because they are at the very heart of the spiritual basis of our lives. When we aim at right relationship, we automatically create structures — political, economic, and social — which allow that to take place. It does not take place in the abstract; it has to work out in this dense, physical world. Therefore we need connections between ourselves. These connections might be of ideas, plans and hopes, but they are connections because relationships make connections. We are not separate. This is the reality of the human condition whether we realize it or not. If we are not separate then we are all connected.

These connections take place in all the different departments of life, in the way we live our lives. Whether we live in the town or the country, we live in a way which relates us to other people. That might be a lot of people or very few, but in a planetary sense we are related to every other person on the planet. At the moment there are about 6 billion people in incarnation with whom we are knowingly or unknowingly in relationship. (Eventually it will be less, between 3.5 and 4 billion as the ideal number for planet Earth.)

You cannot be consciously in relationship with every individual in the world for every moment of the day, not even with radio, television and the internet. Because of the different ray-structures which nations have, they find it easier, or less easy, to live together in harmony and therefore in peace. Close relationships are necessary to ensure that it is harmony and peace rather than the opposite which prevail.

Right human relationships come about when we recognize that we are one. It is the fundamental need for all humanity to see that the human race is one group — different colours, different backgrounds and histories, but one single group coming from the same source, all souls in incarnation. As souls we are divine and perfect, and on an evolutionary journey towards demonstrating that perfection.

Since we are souls in incarnation, everything that we do, ultimately, is the result of being a soul. If it is in line with the Plan of God for the evolution of humanity, then everything we do as souls will be right for that individual and for his or her environment, which means everything and everyone else, both in terms of the planet and all creatures on the planet. At the moment, of course, this is not the case.

Humanity is sadly lacking in all the requisite modes of conduct: in relation to one other; to what we call God, to the purpose of our lives. Also in relation to the kingdoms below us like the animal kingdom, much of which we abuse and kill for no good reason and force to live horrible, unnatural lives; the vegetable kingdom which we destroy from our negligence; and the mineral kingdom, the very substance of the planet on which we live, which we pollute and destroy until in a relatively few years' time it will be almost impossible to live on planet Earth — unless we change direction.

The coming into the world of the Masters is a sign that They have something to give us, that we have something to learn, and that They have come in time to guide us away from the danger of self-destruction. We could destroy ourselves in war or by the despoliation of our planet which will no longer uphold human or sub-human life if we continue in our current ways.

The Plan

"Step by step and stage by stage, humanity is achieving a degree of Oneness. Each day that passes brings some new insight or event which underlines this process and shows conclusively that the Plan is working out.

"The Plan of which I speak embodies the Purposes of the One we call God and focuses His intention for all the kingdoms of Creation. No one can know, in its entirety, the manifold aspects of this Blueprint of Evolution, but the broad outlines, at least, have long been the concern and privileged service of the Spiritual Hierarchy under the leadership of the Christ. With the many aspects of this Plan They daily work, seeking to inspire, through humanity, its gradual fulfilment.

"The time has come for humanity to enter more deeply into a knowledge of the Plan and thus, in full consciousness, to evolve according to the Will of God. Where man's will and God's Will coincide, all proceeds normally and well. Where this congruence is absent man is afflicted by all manner of ills, each of his own engendering. Thus it truly can be said that man creates his own destiny; his halters and fears are his own, his suffering self-made.

"Today, the Plan unfolds at an unprecedented rate. Miracles of change are occurring on a global scale, confounding the hopes of those who would for ever enthral the peoples, and keep them submissive to a nefarious foe. New energies saturate the world, awakening man to new possibilities and relationships. New teachings and teachers present themselves to men, each in his own way illuminating a strand of the complex pattern of the Plan. Thus does the Plan proceed through mutation and change, bringing all gradually to the envisioned goal. Wherever men turn their eyes today they can witness this happening; a paroxysm of change engulfs the world.

"The task of the watching Brotherhood is to oversee these changes and contain them lawfully within the confines of the Plan. Thus do the Masters work, relating the Plan to the possibilities presented by men. Each step towards synthesis taken by men gives opportunity for further unfoldment under law. Thus do men, themselves, control the progress of the Plan." (*Share International*, April 1989)

"The task of the watching Brotherhood is to oversee these changes and contain them lawfully within the confines of the Plan." People may not really understand what this is about and how important it is. There are, at present, two great forces in the world. The conservative and reactionary forces are responding to, and are exponents of, the Piscean energy of the last 2,000 years which has created the divisions and separations which are so evident today. They are idealistic to a fault and deeply entrenched in their own individual interpretation of that idealistic vision. The more progressive forces are the forward lookers, responding to change, looking for new forms, new ways of thinking and relating. They tend to be younger people, but not necessarily so. There are many of the old who are young at heart and forward looking; many of the young are old men before they are out of short pants.

If the forces of progress followed, too forcefully, their desire for change, they would sweep away everything, both the good and bad, that exists at the present time. At the beginning of each new age this process takes place, because the old energies are waning, the structures are crystallizing, and inevitably they begin to break down. The conservatives want to hold these structures together, the bad parts as well as the good, and resist change for as long as they possibly can. Not all structures are bad simply because they are from the past. We have to hold on to the best of the past and build the new upon it.

Left to themselves, there are many progressive forces who would destroy everything in their wake, everything that is resisting their ideal. They can be as fanatically imbued with the ideal of change, and the form that that change should take, as the diehards who are holding on to the old structures willy-nilly, preventing any kind of reconstruction and regeneration. So Hierarchy have to oversee and balance this process.

Great divine ideas — brotherhood, equality, sharing, liberty and freedom — have galvanized people ever since they were enunciated clearly in the French Revolution, an event which was inspired by the Masters. These ideas, of course, had been enunciated somewhat before, for example in Greek times at the birth of a kind of democracy. But in a very powerful way they set alight in France the idea of individual human freedom. This was very much in the air, too, in America and was watched carefully. There were many contacts between the American Government and the French.

If the Masters had not intervened, as They had to do many times, there would have been an even greater blood-bath in France because of the revolution. As it was, there was an extraordinary blood-letting. Those marvellous ideals of fraternity, freedom, justice, sharing and equality went 'down the drain'. Down that drain, too, went the blood of thousands of people. It was as if all the pain and suffering of the under-classes had been let loose, and one goal was allowed to demonstrate in the killing of everyone who, they thought, had stood in their way and oppressed them. It was revenge writ large, and it profoundly influenced Europe and America.

The same thing happened in the Russian Revolution when Hierarchy had to step in to prevent a similar blood-bath. Many aristocrats, men of great wealth and power, were killed. Again, this was the rising of the people, allowing their pent-up hatred and sense of injustice to overflow into violence, sweeping away everything in the ideal of the new — the new brotherhood and justice. Of course, it did not work. There was no new brotherhood or justice any more than in the French Revolution. However, these revolutions left humanity with the thoughtforms of freedom, brotherhood, equality, sharing, and a better relationship between the peoples of any country.

Hierarchy intervened again in the American Civil War. That war was a ghastly affair in which brother fought brother, cousin fought cousin, people fought those living on the other side of the field. Hundreds of thousands of people died because they wore a certain colour uniform. The Civil War was devastating and still has a profound effect on the psyche of America. It is a sickness which has never gone away, and America from that point of view is still a deeply divided nation. The Hierarchy had to step in and keep the slaughter to a minimum.

In this way the Masters prevent too great an upsurge of hatred and violence and keep the Plan going forward on a reasonable basis.

'The Plan', continued:

> "Entering our life today are forces altogether new, heralding a civilization based on Brotherhood and Love. These forces likewise herald the re-entry of the Christ into the midst of men, accepting the challenge as Teacher for the new time. Working in full knowledge of the Plan, His task is to take humanity in the direction of its ordained destiny: the fulfilment of the Will of God for the perfection of all men.
>
> "Thus today does the Christ work to accomplish His task as the Great Mediator, the Representative and Knower of God."

I think people are rather unaware of the precise scientific relationship between how we live, the relation between each other and the nations, whether we have peace or war, and what that has to do with the Plan or Will of God. They do not see the connection. To begin with, most people do not know there is a Plan, and that it is the outcome of the Will, the Purpose of God. They do not see God, so how do they know about a purpose? They do not see the Custodians of the Plan, but from now on they will. From now on, the Custodians of the Plan, the Masters of Wisdom, and one of the Lords of Compassion will live openly in the world, accessible to all peoples for Their advice and training, and Their enlightened view not only of the Plan itself but also of what procedures will aid humanity in working out the Plan on the outer physical plane.

We are going through a spiritual crisis: we do not know who we are; we do not know our divinity; we do not know why we are here or our relationship to what we call God. We say: "If there are wars and children die from cancer, how can there be a God?" as if these wars were created by God. We do not say: "If there are wars, and children die from cancer, we are not acting out God's Will." That is a completely different thing to say. It is not God's Will. God makes perfect conditions and we destroy them.

When humanity realizes that there is a Plan, that evolution proceeds according to a Plan, that it is a scientific process, people will begin to wonder about their part in the Plan. Then the Masters can give us Their advice, and we can see the good sense of that advice. It should be obvious to intelligent humanity that living in peace and harmony is more useful to evolution than living with war or the threat of war, competing all the time, one half getting all the goods and the other half getting nothing. That does not seem sane or logical, not a good idea. I am sure God's Plan for the Earth is a very good idea. If it is based, in the beginning, on sharing and justice, and therefore something we can manage, that is practical, then I think it is a good idea. I think most people will see this.

Presented by Maitreya rather than the sermonizing advocates of Christian fundamentalism, I think people in their millions will turn to that kind of God, whether they call it God or not. People will turn to the *ideas* that are divine — brotherhood, justice, sharing, right relationship, peace, harmony, creativity — a world in which "no man lacks", as Maitreya has put it, "where no two days are alike". Can you imagine such a world where no two days are alike? The only people who have access to that kind of world are those who have enough money to live without being forced to work in the drudgery of a factory or office or field, where most days are the same. The lower down the scale you are the more all days are alike: hard, boring, drudgery, and the same drudgery day after day. That is the reality for countless millions of people.

Can you imagine, when Maitreya says "where no two days are alike", when every day is a revelation, every day a new experience? And not only every day but every moment; moment to moment throughout the day a new experience, when the world is changing so fast for the better that you can hardly keep up with it. When every radio and television news broadcast tells you what has been done that day for the world. Only good news. Can you imagine it? Of course, there will be the odd accident, but good news every day. The Good News Show. "Ladies and gentlemen, I have good news for you tonight."

In this way, humanity gets a graph of how it is evolving and changing, how the outer political and economic forms are changing, the conditions which are unifying, synthesizing humanity until we really see ourselves as brothers and sisters of one society. That is the aim. I can see it, of course, as not being an overnight event, but relatively very quick.

God's Representative

"Whenever man is bereft of hope, seeing no way forward, no way to solve his problems, he sets up an instinctive cry for succour, an appeal to God to help him in his anguish. Thus it was during the war-years earlier this [last] century that the travail through which humanity was passing invoked the Christ, called Him forth once more into the world. Never before, through all vicissitudes, has so much depended upon His coming, for never before has man controlled such forces of destruction." (*Share International*, July 1987)

For the first time in our history we can literally destroy all life, human and sub-human, over and over again. We have a destructive power now at our disposal that could end the human experiment on planet Earth. If it were used, and it is in the hands of some dangerous individuals — in particular in the Pentagon, the Russian equivalent of the Pentagon and various smaller countries — humanity would not stand a chance against these nuclear weapons, and the biochemical and biological weapons of even more sinister destruction. Nothing could save humanity. There is no antidote to any of that destruction that would be thrown into the air by ballistic missiles on every country. It would be a devastation beyond anything that the Pentagon or the Russian Pentagon imagines.

If people think: "The people are alive and well and living in Hiroshima and Nagasaki where the two atomic bombs were dropped," they do not know what they are saying. These were two little atomic bombs beside which the modern equivalents are gigantic monsters. These atomic bombs killed hundreds of thousands of people in a flash. The bombs created today would cause literally millions of deaths per bomb. And enough anthrax or other chemical agent, a biological monster, could destroy all that was not killed off in the first dropping of the hydrogen bombs.

You can see, therefore, how much depends on the ability of Maitreya to turn the tide, to change human thinking. The Masters say, my Master has said it several times, that the tide is turning, that humanity is passing the test for entering into the Hierarchy, taking the first initiation. It is doing so by gradually changing its view of things, by coming to its senses, by lessening, broadly speaking, its claim to power and domination.

There are still groups in the United States, Russia, various European countries and elsewhere, where economic or military domination are of paramount importance. The mass of humanity, however, from the Masters' point of view, are turning away from that. The tide really is turning, and not too soon, because had it been otherwise we would now be really sitting on the edge of a precipice.

The US Government is talking very publicly about spending $60 billion for an umbrella against such attack but all of the experiments have proven so far that the umbrella does not work. There is no 100 per cent guarantee against ballistic missiles. As for biological and chemical weapons, this is something completely devastating. They can be released in all sorts of ways, popped from a submarine and not by a huge international ballistic missile. A little rocket can drop into New York or Boston or any of the coastal towns and paralyse many millions of people, literally in minutes. It is too devastating even to talk about.

'God's Representative', continued:

> "Today, the nations are divided, as ever. Each claims to be the repository of the world's wisdom, offering men the choice between freedom and justice. How absurd it is that men should be proffered such a choice. Freedom and justice are divine and that divinity is indivisible. There can be no freedom without justice, no justice bereft of freedom. Shortly, men will be offered the opportunity to end for ever this travesty of truth and so heal the breach between the nations. It requires but the simple realization that all men are divine and have the same divine right to share in God's gifts and plans. Lacking such realization men would know no peace."

That is the simple secret. All men are brothers, all men are divine and have the same divine right to God's gifts and plans. The resources of the planet do not belong to America, Britain, France, Russia, Japan or anyone else, but to the whole world. Divine providence, according to the Plan of the Logos, provides what the planet needs for its sustenance.

Because there are people, they have to eat. That is the way we are constructed. We have to eat to live, to maintain the energy source that will keep the life in the form. We have to eat two or three times a day. However, not all people eat — many are starving to death. It is part of the divine Plan that the wherewithal is provided for all creatures to eat. There is enough food in the world right now so that no one anywhere need go hungry. The food is not distributed, it is not shared, because we do not see the need. We do not see that we are equal, that equality under God is a reality. It is not that we all need so many ounces of bread and so many ounces of sugar. But we all need what we need, whatever that happens to be. With Americans it seems to be big, big plates. With Japanese, little tiny plates. I think the British have it about right!

'God's Representative', continued:

> "When men see the Christ they will realize that they are not alone, that God's Representative has answered their call and returned to help them. He will remind them of their source in divinity and of their kinship, brothers all. He will place before them the choices for the future and exercise His right of counsel. He will outline the steps towards a better life for all, a life more in keeping with the spiritual nature of man. He will teach and lead and thus change the world through the actions of men.
>
> "At first, progress may be slow as men grow accustomed to the benefits of change but in due course the pace will quicken until all is caught up in a ferment of change. Naught can stop this process, for it finds its origin in the Mind of God. Naught can for long resist the magnet of God's Plan."

This is not something casual, unplanned, hoped for but unlikely. It is something that is absolutely certain to take place. The

Christ is in the world now, although not openly revealed, because it is part of a Plan. It is a Hierarchical Plan and the Hierarchy know the Plan of God. By God, I mean the planetary Logos. They know the Plan of the Logos, and that Their work is to put that Plan into action through humanity and the lower kingdoms. They seek to extend that Plan into all aspects of its nature. One of these is guiding humanity in such a way that we keep in right relationship to the Plan. They are not taskmasters. You can put your foot over the line a little bit from time to time, but eventually you are encouraged to get into line and follow the laid-out path because that is the safe path. It is the path that makes for right relationship, harmony, justice, and the expression of love and intelligence in the world.

It is really about loving intelligence, intelligent love — self-interest, if you want to give it another term. It is human self-interest that will drive us to accept the advice of Maitreya and put it into effect. Nothing can resist this for long because it finds its origin in the mind of our planetary Logos.

'God's Representative', continued:

> "Without doubt, the greatest hindrance to the Plan's successful working is the present insecurity of men. They see around them a hostile world, feel threatened on all sides by penury and want. The nuclear threat hangs heavily over all. The counsel of Maitreya will show men that they have nothing to fear but their fear. That a blessed future awaits man if he will but act in his own best interests. That the Intention of God is man's greatest good. He will show that men must act to create the world they want; that He comes not to save but to point the way. He will empower all who take upon themselves the burden and joy of service. He will anoint all who share His burden. The

upholders of the old sense the danger but fight a losing battle. They seek to strengthen the walls of their citadel in vain. Their ramparts weaken as the tide of justice turns. Their buttresses betray them as men strike out for freedom. Into this turmoil Maitreya has come, to put His divine resources at the service of man."

Throughout the world the have-nots are jumping into boats, begging, borrowing, stealing a way to get into the developed countries. Refugees from all the underdeveloped nations are finding their way into the developed world legally or illegally, and this will continue. As my Master puts it: "Their ramparts weaken ... their buttresses betray them." The developed world can no longer close its doors to the dispossessed and expect everything to go forward in a nice cosy way as it always has done.

The G8 nations are meeting now in Okinawa, and among them for the first time are four Presidents representing the developing world. These four will strongly announce the needs of those they represent — not only their own countries but more than 130 developing countries. They are simply representatives and cannot make resolutions or vote, but they can advise, speak and put forward their point of view. This is the first time that this has happened.

Every year the G8 nations meet and pass resolution after resolution to do something for the developing nations, usually very little, but they never do even that little. They never carry out a single resolution. It is all to do with holding up the buttresses, the ramparts, so that people of the Third World continue to be poor and weak, with 17 per cent of the resources, against 83 per cent held by the G8 nations.

Everything that is happening is forcing the developed world to abandon its plans for world domination on a scale compared with which the present would seem beneficent indeed. They do not want development of the Third World. They like it the way it is because it is easier to control countries that are poor and suffering. You can control the price of their produce. You can buy it 'for a song' on the world market, and control almost every cost because you have invested the money in the first place to develop it.

Globalization is making sure that the control of the world is moving away from the United Nations and governments to the great controlling corporations of the world, most of which are American, European and Japanese. They have become more and more focused and expert at what they do, but people are now rebelling. They are saying that they do not want this any more. Globalization is not doing the Third World any good. It is only doing the corporations good.

Actually, globalization, did the large corporations but know it, is making easier of access the redistribution of the world's resources, but they do not think of it that way. They think of it as the means of cheap production and distribution of their manufactured goods. They have built up a great network of distribution methods. The internet and its technology makes their control even more complete. At their mercy, therefore, it would appear, is the Third World.

With the Avatar here this will not work out as they see it.

The Avatar

"Breath held, humanity awaits the appearance of the Avatar. Knowingly or not, millions now stand ready to receive the Teacher, the Revealer of new Truths and the guarantee of men's future and divinity.

"All now conspires to bring about this blessed event. Cosmic and planetary, the Forces of Regeneration reap now the harvest of Their sowing and bring into being the condition which allows Maitreya to appear. Forced by force of law to withhold, for a time, His open mission, He knows that the law is being fulfilled, the debts are being paid, the opportunities taken; and that now in full splendour may He appear, and receive the love and service which, many will avow, they are ready to bestow on Him.

"His Grace already does embrace the world. His Love enfolds the nations, East and West, North and South. None escape the arrow of His Love. Daily, His Ray awakens men to their true destiny, and conjures anew their hope and trust.

"From far and wide the representatives of the people gather at His side, and He endows them with a wisdom altogether new. Soon, this enlightened group of men and women will present their story and experience, and prove past all gainsaying that the Christ is in our midst. Millions then will hearken to this promise and demand to see the Representative of God. Under many names will He then come forward and thus fulfil the hopes of every faith. His call for Justice, Peace, and Brotherhood will then be heard among the nations, avowing God's concern for the well-being of men everywhere. His voice will remind the peoples of their origin and destiny, and bring them, in trust, to the feet of God.

"That His task is well prepared you may be sure. His disciples, inwardly trained, have long engaged themselves in this work of preparation and know well their various roles. Called into action, they will carry the work of reconstruction to every corner of the world and replace misery with joy, separation with unity, hatred and malice with altruistic love. Thus will it be. Thus will the New Time enter its course of splendour, and thus will mankind realize the promise which His presence brings.

"That not all will testify to His Glory is certain; for some, the Mantle of God has too brilliant a light. But most will see in Him the fulfilment of their hopes and dreams for justice and love, for sanity and freedom. And to Him will they turn their eyes and hearts, seeking guidance and comfort, inspiration and purpose, enlightenment and love. These in abundance will He bestow upon the world. A vast River of Truth is He, nurturing all who from these waters deeply drink. A Fountain of Love is He, enclosing all within His heart. An Avatar like none before is He, come to lead men into the realization that they, too, are Gods." (*Share International*, October 1988)

With such an Avatar working openly, sounding out His call for justice and sharing, you can imagine that this world will quickly change for the better and that humanity will respond. What will drive them to that realization is the collapse of the stock exchanges, for which Maitreya is waiting. When the stock markets crash, we will have no option but to regenerate our lives, reconstruct our political and especially our economic structures, and create that simple right relationship of each to each which will fulfil the Plan in the Mind of the Planetary Logos, the Plan known to Maitreya and the Masters.

You might wonder what Maitreya is like to meet. I do not mean in *Share International*'s Letters to the Editor. There He is a funny man indeed. He is young and old; a woman, a man, a child. He is playful. He is serious. All of these things. But how is He in Himself? How will He appear to humanity, because He will not go through the antics of the familiars He creates? Let us see what my Master says about it. It is quite extraordinary.

The Blueprint of the Future

"When men see Maitreya in full and open view, they will find much to admire: His grace and joy; His modest wisdom and all-inclusive love; His readiness to share all that He has and is with men of every station. His humility will astound, His knowledge, vast and deep beyond measuring, will reveal to men the paucity of their own. Thus will they turn to Him for guidance and, sure of His concern, become again the students and earnest seekers they once were. Thus will it be, and thus will the Great Lord present to men the Blueprint of the future. That future holds for men such wonders that few today could comprehend them.

"Imagine then a future where no man lacks for aught. Where the talents and creativity of all men demonstrate their divine origin. Where war has no place in their thoughts and where goodwill casts its benevolent net over the hearts and minds of all.

"Imagine cities of light lit by Light Itself; nowhere to be found the squalor and deprivation of today; imagine transport, fast and silent, powered by light alone, the far-off worlds and even the stars brought within our reach. Such a future awaits the men and women who have the courage to share.

"Such a future awaits those brave ones who love Freedom.

"Such a glorious future awaits those who long to understand the meaning and purpose of life.

"Maitreya, too, awaits His opportunity to emerge and to begin, openly, His Mission. He, too, grows impatient with the long wait. But the Law rules all and Maitreya abides lovingly by its wisdom. Nevertheless, the time is very near when the Great Lord can emerge and speak directly to men. This being so, those whose task it is to prepare His way have but little time in which to do so. Make that then your first priority, leaving all else aside.

"As always, the free will of men may not be jeopardized. Thus it is that His name will not accompany His first appearances, allowing men themselves to ascertain His worth. As a man among men will He appear, voicing aloud His brothers' needs and thoughts.

"In time, so many will respond that His true identity and stature can be confirmed. This time is expected to be short but the pace of recognition lies in the hands of men themselves. The present phase of miracles, now worldwide, will continue and accompany this process until no one can deny its significance at this time.

"Thus the world will be won over and prepared for change. Thus the call will go out from the people of all the nations for the Avatar to speak, and thus will Maitreya answer that call and declare His mission and purpose.

"That silent declaration will announce the start of the New Era: of peace, of sharing, justice and freedom; the awakening of men to their divinity, and the creation by men of a civilization wrought in the form of God's Plan." (*Share International*, October 1999)

The Way Masters Work

"His humility will astound," your Master says. What could the humility of the "Master of all the Masters and the Teacher alike of Angels and of Men" possibly be like? And how can it serve as an example to us? What can we learn from it? (January/February 2001)

You have not seen, at His level, the qualities of divinity. One of the major qualities of divinity is humility because the major expression of divinity is lack of self or ego. There is no one to be proud. It is as simple as that. It is not as if Maitreya goes around being humble. You are humble if you have no ego. It is the ego that produces the vanity and glamour of pride. Maitreya does not have any glamours; He has no pride. He says: "Do not worship Me.... If you worship Me you are trying to lower yourself. I do not want this. I want you to be equal. You are a spark of the Supreme Being. Do not think you are below Me." People may find this hard to believe but it is the truth. There is only one divinity and that is shared by everyone — by you and Maitreya and everybody else. On that level of divinity there is neither up nor down. There is simply divinity. There is a difference, of course, between us and Maitreya. We have not *demonstrated* the divinity which is only potential within us. He has fully demonstrated it and so there is nothing left to alter the instinctive, natural humility of divinity. The opposite of humility is pride, arrogance. If there is no ego to be proud or arrogant or vain, then what is left?

Humility is left when pride and self-love are not present. It is a natural given state, not something you acquire. You acquire arrogance, conceit and glamours of all kinds, but you cannot acquire humility. You can acquire a humble attitude, but that is something quite different. That is the [Charles Dickens's] Uriah

Heep type of humility which is totally unreal. It covers all the glamours of its opposite.

When you see a Master, you will realize it is the given state that you see because He is not assessing Himself. It does not occur to Him to say: "How am I doing in relation to this? Am I getting across? Am I making myself felt? Did I impress them when I said that?" It would never occur to a Master to do that; He has no sense of the separate Self. There is no person in the way of the higher Self. You are seeing a person Who is the Immortal Divine Self, and therefore what we would call humility is the totally natural expression of that Self. Humility is the natural expression of the soul. If the self with a small 's', the ego, gets in the way then you see something false. His is the natural state, and people will be astounded that He does not place Himself above humanity. That is why you will probably be absolutely awed by the simplicity, the utter, holy simplicity of that Being. That could be an example. Examples are great, but do not just imitate.

What does it mean to be anointed by Maitreya?
(January/February 2001)

To be anointed by Maitreya is to receive the blessing of Maitreya, the Christ Principle, through the heart.

What is meant by the Masters' Plan to link the three centres —
Shamballa, Hierarchy, and humanity? (January/February 2001)

It is not the Masters' Plan. It is the Plan of the Lord of the World that eventually the three Centres — Shamballa, the Centre where the Will of God is known, Hierarchy, the Centre where the Love of God is expressed, and humanity, the Centre where the Intelligence of God manifests — will one day be one integrated Centre. Stage by stage, the Centre we call Hierarchy and the

Centre we call humanity will come together. The start is being made. In a sense it has long been made, but it will take place openly, outwardly, from now on. People will enter the Hierarchy through the door of initiation until so many people are consciously working in the Hierarchy that the Masters will judge that the two Centres are integrated.

Then these two integrated lower Centres will link with the highest Centre, which is Shamballa. Then the Will, Love, and Intelligence of God will be manifesting potently and correctly through these three integrated Centres.

What are the mechanics of how the Masters will give forth the blueprint of the Plan? (January/February 2001)
The Plan is in the mind of the Logos. The task of the Masters is to bring it into manifestation through humanity and its work with the lower kingdoms. They do this by stimulating the self-consciousness of all Beings and the consciousness of the lower kingdoms. Eventually the relationship between the human kingdom and the animal, vegetable, and even the mineral kingdom will evolve to a point where you would not recognize it.

Humanity is in charge of the evolution of the lower kingdoms. It will have to set to rights its own world, clean house and mature, in order to do it, but humanity will be stewards for the evolution of these kingdoms. The mind of humanity has a big impact on the animal kingdom, and this will increase as the age proceeds. A telepathic rapport will be established between humanity and the animal kingdom and many of the animals will be herded, grouped and put to work by telepathic communication. Certain animals will demonstrate an extraordinary response to this and will become mediums, bringing in information from the subtle worlds. We will stop experimenting on animal bodies and end the terrible conditions of factory farming. All of that will go, and quickly, and this will create a far better karmic relationship between the human and animal kingdoms.

(1) How do the Masters go on after the fifth Initiation? (2) Do They die or do They stay in that body? (3) Can They decide freely if They want to live in Their dense-matter body or in a body of light? (4) Does this depend on Their future task? (April 1997)

(1) Many Masters continue to live in the body in which They took the fifth Initiation while (2) others retain only an etheric body, appearing, when They do, in a self-made *mayavirupa* vehicle. (3) Some Masters go to higher planets or directly to Sirius, and so discard the physical vehicle, which, in any case, is *now* a body of light. (4) Their individual destiny decides the matter.

*The Masters demonstrate the Love of God. Do They always actually **like** Their disciples?* (March 1998)

The Masters have total, unqualified, unconditional love. Do they *like* everyone? I think the Masters must find it very difficult to *like* some disciples (my Master calls me His karma!). They must shake Their heads and say: "I wish I could like this one. Oh, I wish I could like him. But I love him, I love him."

Why do the Masters not prevent wars? (May 1997)

They do try — They tried very hard to prevent the First and the Second World Wars. But They may not infringe humanity's free will. They try to work through world leaders. If a leader, like Gorbachev, for example, responds, then we can have the ending of the Cold War, but They can only do so much within the Law of Karma. Humanity's free will is sacrosanct and governs Their actions.

We have the right to do anything up to the point of destroying the planet. We could destroy *ourselves* but not the planet. However, this is a message of hope. Maitreya knows already that we will accept the principle of sharing and, therefore, create justice and peace. Maitreya has not come here to waste His time and go back into the Himalayas; He is here to stay, and for the whole of the Age of Aquarius.

According to Benjamin Creme's Master, Jesus will be working with the Christian churches. (1) Will other Masters be working with some of the other great world religions? (2) Will the goal be to unify them into one soon, or (3) will these traditions (Hindu, Roman Catholic, Buddhist, etc) most likely continue through the Age of Aquarius? They seem to have some near-insurmountable major differences. (December 1999)

(1) Yes. (2) No. (3) Yes, but a new approach to the divine will emerge and people will come from all the existing traditions into that.

Can you be more specific about what fields the Masters are working in at the present time? (January/February 2001)

In all departments, depending on the particular Master. Above all, in the political/economic field.

Individual Masters

*In Alice Bailey's book **Initiation, Human and Solar,** it states that the Master Morya and the Master Koot Hoomi are "well known figures to the inhabitants of Shigatse", a village in the Himalayas, and that Djwhal Khul "occupies a little house not* *far distant from the Master KH". (1) Is this still true today? If so, (2) if we went to Tibet, to Shigatse, would we be able to see Them?* (January/February 1999)

(1) No. The Masters have moved since the Chinese invasion.

(1) I have read that the Masters Koot Hoomi and Morya frequented, and perhaps lived in, Shigatse. This puzzles me. Shigatse even then was a good-sized town/city. It was hardly a "remote mountain fastness". (2) Were They taking the first short steps of externalization there? (October 1999)

(1) The Masters did not actually live in the town but in the outer area. They were, nevertheless, well-known figures in the town. (2) No.

Is the Master Who has been in Tokyo since 1975 a man or a woman, and how old is He/She? (September 1999)

He is a man. All the Masters are in male bodies at the present time. He is roughly 200 years old, which is young as the Masters know age. His work will emerge in time. He acts really as the stimulus, the inspirer of groups of disciples who live in Japan but not only in Japan, also in Asia, north and south.

Are there any disciples in Japan like Abraham Lincoln who will come forward to offer their power, insight and vast experience to the group? How does the Master in Tokyo work? (May 1997)

You may have heard of a new group in the world called the New Group of World Servers which was formed in 1922 by Maitreya. This is made up of men and women of various degrees who are dedicated to the betterment of humanity along their particular line of work. It is very large, and divided into two groups. There is a large outer group making up some three to four million people who are in all the countries of the world without exception. They work under the inspiration and guidance of their own souls. They usually have no conscious experience of Hierarchy or of having any conscious role to play in relation to Hierarchy. They are in all fields: political, economic, religious, social and scientific. They work under soul impression. There is also a much smaller inner group who work directly under impression from certain of the Masters. They are aware of their connection with Hierarchy as disciples and seek to carry out the Plan in so far as they know about it. They all have in common an altruistic desire to serve the planet.

In 1975, a Master came into Tokyo. One came into New York, one into London, one into Geneva, one into Darjeeling, and one into Tokyo. Since 1975 the Master in Tokyo has been working with the New Group of World Servers in Japan, and indirectly with those who are open to His mental impression, but in a lesser way, in the outer group, with those who can only respond to that impression through their own soul. He works with a few directly and with other larger numbers indirectly, through their own souls.

Abraham Lincoln was a human avatar, a third-degree initiate. In Tokyo there is not yet that stature of initiates, but there are higher firsts (1.5 up to 2), and seconds and thirds who are working in the same way in all the centres. There are disciples in Japan similar to the ones in various other centres who are working either directly or indirectly with, and have been trained by, the Masters.

When we have several requests, can we ask the Master in Tokyo, and will the request be answered? [Questioner from Japan] (September 1999)

Well, you can try. I do not know whether you will be answered or not. I suppose it depends on your karma and the nature of the request. I mean, if it is for a bigger car, I doubt if that would be given. If it is for more enlightenment, then you might be answered. Maitreya Himself has said: "My help is yours to command. You have only to ask."

I know many cases in which people have prayed to Maitreya for help of some kind and have received it in a very definite way. Prayers are often answered, but you have to recognize the answer, and you may not like the answer. If you ask a Master for help, that Master may well give help, but you might not like the nature of that help. The help will always be for your good, for your betterment, but that is, perhaps, not what you are really wanting. People usually ask for material help from Masters. That is not the line of business that They are in.

Do the Masters dispense 'grace'? For example, if one were to pray to a Master briefly, requesting 'grace' to improve one's ability to do effective Transmission Meditation: (1) Would the request be heard? (2) Is the Master capable of said blessing? (3) Is He likely to bestow it? (September 2000)

(1) Yes. (2) Yes. (3) Yes.

Can you say something about the Master in Moscow? (July/August 1999)

The Master in Moscow has been living there since 1923 but absolutely occult, not known, behind the scenes, working to mitigate the totalitarian effects of the regime in which the Russian people lived since 1917. In 1975, five Masters came into the world, and later two more: one in Moscow and one in Rome, the one in Rome being the Master Jesus. The Master in Moscow was already there but He became much more 'open' in 1978, working directly with certain advanced disciples in Russia whom He could train personally and impress mentally, and also those who were open to astral impression. I cannot give you His name.

Could He possibly have inspired some of Gorbachev's actions?
(July/August 1999)

Actually no. It was Maitreya Himself Who appeared to Gorbachev and inspired him to go to America and talk peace with President Reagan and to open Russia to *glasnost*. The US claim it was the triumph of Capitalism over Communism that ended the cold war but it was in fact Maitreya Who brought that 'war' to an end — an event He had predicted in 1988.

Can you tell us about the work of the Master Serapis?
(July/August 1999)

The Master Serapis is a very advanced, an 'ascended', Master, a sixth-degree initiate, head (Chohan) of the 4th-ray ashram in the Hierarchy. (There are seven major ashrams and, stemming from each, six subsidiary ashrams, so there are 49 ashrams altogether.) The Master Serapis is one of the Masters very actively engaged in the reappearance of the Christ, and works with the angelic or devic evolution. He has contacts with the human evolution, to be sure, but His main work is with the devic or angelic evolution, a huge parallel evolution to the human. He is also a great inspirer of art and music.

Angels, or *devas*, range, in evolution, from sub-human to the human to super-human. Everything in cosmos is becoming human, is human, or has gone on beyond the human; we are the midway point where matter and spirit meet, and through which all evolution goes.

There are billions of *devas* of all kinds, higher and lower. Maitreya has been called by the Buddha, and later by St Paul, "The Teacher alike of angels and of men". He is the World Teacher, He has brought into the world certain great angels who eventually will work with humanity. Many people imagine that they are in touch with angels. My information is that this is not correct. Angels do not work as yet with humanity; they work for humanity but not with humanity. In the future, as humanity advances and its vibration is raised, more and more people will be able to work with the *deva* evolution and much healing will be learned in this way. That is the major aspect of the work of Serapis at this time.

*It is said in **Initiation, Human and Solar**, by Alice A.Bailey, that by the intermediary of the **deva** kingdom and the Master Serapis, a great revelation will be given to humanity in music and painting. Presently, there's a great trend towards electronics and computers. (1) Do you think these media will become extremely dominant in the future? (2) And are these media a preparation for the great revelation?* (July/August 1998)

(1) In relation to music and painting, no. (2) No. The revelation will be about the true meaning and purpose of art and music, and the Art of Living.

Is it allowed for you to disclose what country the Master connected with Islam will appear in? (May 2000)

Egypt.

(1) Is the Prophet Mohammed now a Master? (2) Is He in a physical body? (3) Does He have responsibility for Islam? (January/February 2000)

(1) Yes. (2) Yes. (3) No.

(1) Is Mary Magdalene now a Master? (2) Does that Master now work with Jesus and the Lord Maitreya? (January/February 2000)

(1) Yes. (2) Yes.

Can you tell me if there is a Master in Slovenia? (March 1997)

According to my Master (Who should know) there is no Master in Slovenia. Of the 13 Masters [now 14] now in the world (apart from Maitreya) one is in London and three in the mainland of Europe: Geneva, Paris and Rome (the Master Jesus). There are no plans for a Master to be in Slovenia.

(1) Are there any Masters in Holland? (2) If not yet, are there plans for a Master to enter Holland? (3) Would this only happen after Declaration Day? (January/February 2000)

(1) No. (2) No. (3) No.

*In **Share International** October 1998, you answered a question about how the South Indian sage Amma [Mata Amritanandamayi] fits into the circle of Masters of the South Indian Lodge. The answer was that she is a disciple of one of the Masters of this Lodge. Why is so much known about the Masters of the Trans-Himalayan Lodge and its structure and work, while so little information is provided about its southern counterpart?* (June 2000)

The Masters of the Trans-Himalayan Lodge have lived esoterically for millennia and it has taken the writings of H.P.Blavatsky and Alice Bailey to bring Their work to our notice. The Masters of the South Indian Lodge, on the other hand, have lived and worked openly, giving Their teachings to, and through, a large number of well-known disciples.

(1) Are the Masters of the South Indian Lodge part of the Spiritual Hierarchy? (2) Are they part of the 63 Masters of the Hierarchy who are involved in the human evolution? (3) Are

182

they Masters of Wisdom who have taken fifth initiation and more? (4) If the answer to the above is no, what is their relationship to the Masters of the Trans-Himalayan Lodge?

(1) Yes. (2) Yes. (3) Yes. The Masters of the South Indian Lodge have worked more openly, but a degree of openness is a relative thing. They are not known to the general public. Some of Them are still working but no longer in the physical body. They choose Their pupils carefully and some of these become well known, such as Maharishi. His master, Guru Dev, is a Master of the South Indian Lodge.

Could you say something about the debate as to whether the works of William Shakespeare were written by Francis Bacon, and in any case was Francis Bacon the Master 'R'? (March 1998)

Francis Bacon *became* the Master 'R'. He was Francis Bacon the philosopher and statesman and He is now the Master Rakoczi. In the 18th century He was known as the Comte de St Germain. He is in a Hungarian body, His base is in the Carpathians, and He is the Regent of Europe. He is one of the Masters coming out into the world now. He could be called the 'Managing Director' of the Hierarchy; He seeks to put into effect, through humanity, the plans of the Masters. My information is that William Shakespeare, who was a great initiate, and is now on Sirius, was, indeed, the writer of the Shakespeare works; they have nothing to do with Francis Bacon.

The Master Jesus

I was taught that the one and only God was Jesus Christ. Is that true? (September 1999)

Well, Jesus Christ is usually called the one and only Son of God rather than the one and only God. The Being Who was Jesus in Palestine 2,000 years ago is now one of the Masters, a very advanced Master, Who works with Maitreya moment to moment. The Master Jesus, as He is called today, has been living in the outskirts of Rome for several years. If you were to ask the Master Jesus: "Are you the one and only Son of God or the one and only God?" He would say: "No, there is no such person." There is no such person in the whole of the universe as the one and only God or the one and only Son of God. Everybody without exception is a Son of God. The difference between ourselves and the Masters, like Jesus or any other Master, is that They know They are sons of God. They experience that divinity and They demonstrate that divinity. They demonstrate the intelligence, the love, and the will of God whereas we do so to a tiny degree. But every Master was an ordinary human being just like us. They have gone through the evolutionary process ahead of us and demonstrated the divine potential, which all of us have, so that one day we shall be like the Masters. It is inevitable.

Humanity is very badly educated. I do not mean only by the schools but by the churches, the religions. The purpose of the churches is to teach and to heal. They have taught very badly and healed almost not at all. Most have taught about God as a great transcendent Being Whom we can never know, that we are miserable sinners down here, and we are hardly worthy to lift our head to God. That is not true. It is the opposite of the truth. Every single human being is potentially a God. The Masters are the guarantee for us that one day we shall express our divinity as They express Their divinity. That is why we are here. That is the purpose of our life.

The spiritual crisis hanging over humanity, focused through the political and economic fields, is the crisis of identity. We do not know who we are. We do not know why we are here, the purpose of life, where we are going. We do not know therefore how to relate to each other. If we truly, inwardly, recognized ourselves as divine and every other human being as divine, obviously we would relate to them in a different way. We would not allow the destructive separation which characterizes the world today.

In an interesting section on the externalization of the Hierarchy in A Treatise on Cosmic Fire, Alice Bailey has the Master Djwhal Khul stating that "The Master Jesus will take a physical vehicle ..." (p.759). Would this be a 'slip of the pen' on her part, in view of your information that the Master Jesus is, in fact, in a Syrian body by now 660 years old? (April 1997)

It is not exactly a 'slip of the pen'. It means He will appear physically.

Is it possible that anybody can get in touch with the Master Jesus? (April 2000)

Certain people do, but I have no control over this. There is a very interesting African nun, Sister Anna, who lives in Rome. I have not met her but I have met her Bishop who is one of the Cardinals in Rome. She has written a book entitled *The Divine Call*, and in it she shows photographs of the Master Jesus which He allowed her to take. She sees Him every Thursday and on Wednesday night she begins to get the stigmata. On Thursday He comes and visits her. One of the other Sisters lent her a camera and she asked the Master Jesus if she could take a photograph. He nodded that she could, and she took the photograph in the book. (A good Catholic bookshop will have it.) The Masters, in particular the Master Jesus, visit people all the time. They are not aloof from humanity, They really do turn up in people's homes. I know people who have seen the Master

Jesus or Maitreya many times, usually in disguise but not always. It happens all the time.

Please explain: the Master Jesus, a 6th-ray soul, is a disciple of, and was overshadowed by, Maitreya, a 2nd-ray soul, 2,000 years ago. (May 1999)

The 2nd-ray energy of Love, the Christ Principle, was released by Maitreya – Who embodies it – through Jesus. The energy of Pisces – inaugurated through Jesus – is essentially the energy of the 6th ray.

*In the New Zealand book **Song of Waitaha**, by Barry Brailsford, the Waitaha claim that a being, whom they call Rongo Marae Roa, planted the seed of peace among their people. That is, they gave up the ways of war and lived harmoniously as a confederated nation of tribes. Was this "God of Peace" the Master Jesus?* (December 1998)

Yes.

Recently a member of our Transmission Meditation group discovered a reproduction of a painting by the German artist J.R.Wehle (1848-1936) bearing a strong resemblance to the picture mentioned in the July/August 1996 issue of **Share International** as manifested by the Master Jesus as a black-and-white negative on a colour film roll. Does the fact that you described it as a self-portrait by the Master Jesus imply that Wehle was impressed or inspired by the Master Jesus when painting the picture?*

* Title: ' *"And they followed him" — Jesus and His disciples walking through the corn'*. (April 2000)

J.R.Wehle was impressed by the Master Jesus while painting the picture. The Master Jesus used the painting as the basis of the thoughtform in black and white which appeared on the colour film roll.

Avatars

*On page 63 of your book **Maitreya's Mission Volume Three**, you say that "... Avatars are not actually members of this planet's Spiritual Hierarchy. They 'come in' from outside the planet". Yet on page 147 of the same book, you describe Moses as "... not an ordinary man but a (human) Avatar". (1) How can someone be "human" and an "Avatar" at the same time? I thought being human means coming from this planet. And yet you say being an Avatar means coming from outside the planet. (2) If Moses was a (human) Avatar, what planet did he come from?* (April 1999)

Moses 'fell' from Mars to Earth and so became one of Earth's humanity but also a (human) Avatar.

Reading about Helena Petrovna Blavatsky I understand that she was constantly accused of fakery and her character was often slandered. Today there are similar criticisms and accusations made of two great avatars — Sathya Sai Baba and Swami Premananda. On the Internet many of Sai Baba's long-time devotees have come out to accuse him of fraud and sexual molestation, even murder, documented from the 1970s onward. Why does this happen to such evolved beings? (June 2000)

It is a perennial problem. Many of the great Teachers have been slandered and attacked in this way: for example, Gautama Buddha, Jesus, Mohammed, Shirdi Baba (the previous incarnation of Sathya Sai Baba) and probably others before them. It seems to be an occupational hazard.

187

Sai Baba is a Cosmic Avatar, as Maitreya is a Planetary Avatar. He comes into the world under the Law of Avatars, the Doctrine of Avatars, and comes under the aegis of the Lord of the World, that One Who stands for our planetary Logos. He is brought in under law. Now do you think such a law has brought in a molester of children, a trickster, a conjurer, a fraud, a sex molester or a murderer? Do you think that the Lords Who organize the incoming of avatars, Who know Them, Who see them as great cosmic entities in Their own right, Who sacrifice Themselves to come onto this planet for so many years in order to help the evolution of the planet, would do such a thing? It is not only unlikely, it is actually literally impossible. It is impossible for an avatar, any avatar, especially an avatar of the stature of Sai Baba, Whose exact stature would astonish you, if you knew what it was. It is impossible for Him to do what has been claimed about Him, the creator of all sorts of fraud, conjuring tricks like the production of *vibhuti* by the half ton out of nowhere. You show me the conjuring trickster who can do that and you will make me think again.

There seems to be a law that the greater a being is, the more they attract the villainy, envy and caprice, the unwholesome negative desire for power, of others who seek to bring down the great. It happens time after time. The Buddha suffered from the same thing, so did Jesus, so have all the great teachers who have come to the world. No doubt, people will find that Maitreya is a molester of children and a conjurer, a trickster, just because He can disappear at will.

There is an old saying that the tallest and best trees, bearing the very best fruit, are precisely the ones which receive the most stones. Stones are not thrown at little ordinary trees where the fruit is all right but not very good, or is over ripe, or sour. It is the big trees, the great trees, with splendid fruit, that are really worth going after. These are the ones that collect the stones;

likewise with the great teachers. Those who have something great, something unique and wonderful to give to the world are the ones who attract this calumny.

Today, incarcerated in prison is another avatar, Swami Premananda. He has been in prison for years, accused of exactly the same things; sexual molestation, murder, fraud of all kinds. He is as innocent as the daisies and likewise is Sai Baba. It does seem to be a law. Sai Baba Himself has said it will get worse before it gets better. So look for more of the same. Small people seem to hate greatness — I suppose it makes them feel even smaller.

A guru in South India called Bala Sai Baba is the spitting image of a young Sathya Sai Baba. (1) Is He an Avatar? (2) What is His relation to Sathya Sai Baba? (September 2000)

(1) Yes. (2) Pupil.

Is it the Planetary Logos Whom we mean when we say "God"? (October 1999)

In the immediate sense, yes. There is a 'God' at every level. Our immediate God is the Planetary Logos. Jehovah of the Old Testament, the Ancient of Days, is the etheric physical-plane reflection of the Logos. He is a young man, Sanat Kumara, the Lord of the World, Who came from Venus 18½ million years ago. He is our nearest equivalent of God. But the Solar Logos, at the centre of the solar system, is God: we are part of His consciousness, too. The Solar Logos relates to the system of Sirius. The relationship of this solar system to that of Sirius is similar to that of our personality to our soul. As we are reflections of our soul, so this solar system is a reflection of Sirius. Then there is 'God' at the centre of the Galaxy.

I heard that Sai Baba has said only a person who believes in God is protected by God. Is this true? If it is true, does God not, therefore, give all people love equally? (October 1999)

Well, you have to understand what Sai Baba meant when He said that. It is a question of what is meant by belief. It is really a question of experience and not of belief. Belief really does not do anything; experience does all. As you experience, you become aware, and it is awareness of God that protects you. It is easy to say: "I believe in God," but that has got nothing to do necessarily with the experience of God. Most religious people will say: "I believe in God, or I believe in Allah," or "I believe in the Divine Source," but unless that belief is an experience it will change nothing in the person. God is everywhere. There is not anywhere that God is not. In a sense, and to my belief, there is not anything else but God. That is all that there is in the whole of Cosmos. And everything we see, including ourselves, is a form that that divinity takes to express itself at a particular level. The closer you are to God the more you are going to know about and experience God.

The second part of the question is: "If this is true does God not give all people love equally?" God gives love, but you take from that what you can. You take a lot or a little.

In the Christian Bible, Jesus has been said to have said: "To them who have will be given. To them who have not even that little which they have will be taken away." (Matthew 25:29) This has been completely distorted in meaning to enable the greedy and selfish people in the world to say: "Oh, it says in the Bible, 'To him who has will be given more'. So the more I have the more I will be given." But that is on a material level which is not meant in the saying of Jesus at all. Rather it means, where the love of God, the Christ Principle, is active in you then more of That can be given. And the more it is in you the more can be given because like attracts like. If you have a large amount of love it will attract an even greater amount of love. If you have a tiny little bit of love in you, then it can only attract a tiny amount of love. The love is boundless, and you just take from it in relation to what you already have.

Who is the Mother of the World? (September 1999)

The Mother of the World is the '*Shakti*' (female counterpart) of the Lord of the World. She is the Female Principle, manifesting down through the ages as Mary in the Gospel story, as Ishtar of Assyria and Babylonia, and as Isis in ancient Egyptian times. Throughout history, the Mother of the World has taken outer manifestation as the Divine Female Principle. Our God is male/female, and those two aspects of divinity functioning together create the universe.

The Historical Jesus

What kind of preparation did Jesus undergo to fit Him for his task of being the vehicle for Maitreya? (November 1998)

Gradual overshadowing by Maitreya.

How do you know that Maitreya overshadowed Jesus? (July 2000)

It is basic to the Ageless Wisdom teachings which were, in the case of the Alice Bailey teachings, given out by the Master Djwhal Khul. He expressly said that, for the three years from the baptism to the crucifixion, Maitreya overshadowed Jesus. I know more from my own Master that the overshadowing began when Jesus was aged 12, when He began credibly to dispute on an equal level with the rabbis in the temple. This continued until he was 24. His mission began at age 30. For the three years from

30 to 33 the overshadowing was not simply an on/off overshadowing but was a perpetual process. He was there, not every moment of the day, but constantly.

Some of the time Maitreya alone was in the body of Jesus. At other times Jesus was alone in His body. At other times and most times Maitreya and Jesus were in the same body together. Jesus's consciousness became aware of all that happened around and through Him. He knew with total knowledge and consciousness that it was Maitreya acting through Him. Of course, it happened with His complete co-operation and free will, which is never infringed by the Masters.

The Bible records that Jesus directly asked some of his disciples, like Peter the fisherman and Matthew the tax collector, to be his disciples. It indicates that none who were asked declined. (1) Were there any that were asked and declined? (2) Was it the plan to have exactly 12 disciples (the number of completion), or (3) would Jesus have taken more if he were able to get more? (December 1999)

(1) No. (2) Yes. (3) No.

(1) Did Jesus actually say he'd be with us to the end of the age? (2) If so, which age? (3) Exactly what did he mean? (4) Was that promise from Jesus or Maitreya or both? (December 1999)

(1) Yes. (2) The Piscean Age. (3) He would not leave the world. (4) Both.

Apparently there were many people performing miracles or tricks in Jesus's time. (1) Was something obviously different about his? (2) Why did he do them? (3) Why did he ask his disciples not to tell others about his healings and miracles? (December 1999)

Not miracles but conjuring tricks. (1) Many of the "miracles" said to have been performed by Jesus were symbolic only. Some were genuine miracles. (2) Each has its own purpose. (3) Because they were not all "miracles", and He did not want undue publicity.

Did Jesus in Palestine actually walk over the water or is this only some kind of symbolic statement in the Bible? (April 1997)

No, the statement is symbolic. He could, nevertheless, have done so but did not.

I find it confusing with the two St Johns. People refer to John and you don't know if it is John the Baptist or John the Beloved. (1) Why did Jesus particularly love John? (2) Which Master was John the Beloved and which was John the Baptist? (January/February 1997)

(1) John the Beloved was one of the more advanced of the Disciples around Jesus and one of the "inner three". (2) He is now the Master Koot Hoomi, Chohan of the second-ray Ashram in the Spiritual Hierarchy. John the Baptist is now on Sirius.

Does Daniel's vision, as described in the Bible (Old Testament, Daniel 7:13-14), speak of Maitreya: "I saw in the night visions, and, behold, one like the Son of Man came with the clouds of heaven, and came to the Ancient of Days, and they brought Him near before Him. And there was given Him dominion, and glory, and a kingdom, that all people, nations and languages should serve Him: His dominion is an everlasting dominion, which shall not pass away, and His kingdom that which shall not be destroyed." (January/February 1999)

Yes. It is, of course, a spiritual kingdom which is meant here: the Spiritual or Esoteric Hierarchy of which Maitreya is the Head.

When Daniel speaks of the Saints in verse 18, is he speaking of the Masters of Wisdom: "But the Saints of the Most High shall take the Kingdom, and possess the Kingdom for ever, even for ever and ever." (January/February 1999)

Yes.

What happened to the Turin Shroud immediately after Jesus's death? (January/February 1998)

It was retrieved from the tomb in which Jesus had been laid by three of His immediate followers and hidden for two years. Subsequently, it was shown, irregularly, to Christian pilgrims to Jerusalem. In the 6th century it was fairly well known as the authentic burial shroud of Jesus and a holy relic.

*In a recent **Time** magazine article about the Turin Shroud it mentions another shroud: "According to the Gospel of John, Jesus left not just his shroud behind in the tomb ... but also a 'napkin, which had been on his head, not lying with the linen cloths but rolled up in a place by itself.' In a silvered cedar chest in the Cathedral of Oviedo, in Spain, there is a cloth, measuring 83cm by 53cm [c.32 x 21 in], that some believe to be the napkin. Records say the Cloth of Oviedo was spirited out of Jerusalem around 614 when the city was attacked by Persia, then travelled through North Africa to Oviedo, where it has been housed since 1113." Did this napkin/shroud really belong to Jesus?* (July/August 1998)

Yes.

Various sources indicate that the biblical Jesus was a composite assembled at the time of the Nicean Council. How much of what Jesus is recorded as having said in the New Testament is an accurate version of what He did in fact say/do/teach? (March 1999)

Sixty per cent.

It has also been indicated that Jesus was not from Nazareth, that the town of Nazareth did not even exist during his lifetime, and that the confusion stems from the fact that he belonged to a mystical order, a group known as Nazarenes or Nazarites; is this correct? (March 1999)

Yes.

Who was Jesus after His incarnation as Apollonius of Tyana and before He took the Syrian body in which He lives now? (April 1997)

He retained the name Jesus, and in the 6th-7th centuries visited and taught the Native Americans and the Polynesians of the Pacific. This fact is known to the Mormons.

Would you please comment concerning the life of Apollonius of Tyana: did he die naturally or did he discard his body and at what age? (October 1998)

He discarded His body at age 400 years.

I would like to know just how important is baptism — as far as Christian experience is concerned. Is baptism by water as Christians perform it necessary for one's spiritual growth? (October 1998)

Baptism is a symbolic ritual and its effect is purely psychological. It symbolizes the purification of the astral nature necessary to take the second of the five initiations to Mastery on this planet. It is certainly not — as a water immersion —

necessary for one's spiritual growth. Otherwise millions of non-Christians would be unable to achieve that growth — which is certainly not the case.

Mary, the Mother of Jesus

I've seen claims as to where Mary, the mother of Jesus, was buried, including such places as Jerusalem (Chapel of Dormiton, Israel), Glastonbury (England) and Mari (Pakistan). Would you tell us where she was actually buried? (December 1997)

In Egypt.

Mary, the mother of Jesus, must have been quite extraordinary for those times. (1) Did she know consciously that her son was to be the Messiah? (2) Did she and Joseph treat their son accordingly and teach him with that consecrated future in mind? (3) Could you please describe something of their natures and characters? They are always pictured in such an idealized fashion but perhaps it is an accurate depiction in their case? (June 2000)

(1) When told, yes. (2) Yes. (3) The descriptions given are pretty accurate; they were members of the Essene community and took the religious life very seriously.

Will the Master who was the Madonna be seen and known as one of the Masters emerging with the Lord Maitreya? (June 2000)

No. Not for some 200 years, when He/She will incarnate as the first Master using a female body.

(1) Is the Master who was the Madonna the head of an Ashram? (2) Does He have disciples working in the world? (3) What sort of field of service do these disciples work in? (June 2000)

(1) Yes. (2) Yes. (3) Mainly in the religious and humanitarian fields.

Were any of the other incarnations of the Master Who was the Madonna well known? (June 2000)

No.

Externalizing the Masters' Ashrams

How can we directly apply the information from this talk in our Reappearance work? (January/February 2001)

One way I would suggest is to teach. Make it known, spread the word of the Reappearance. The Reappearance of the Christ is hard to talk about, but it is also the Reappearance of the Hierarchy of Masters. It is not the Christ alone, great event as that is. It is the return for the first time in nearly 100,000 years of the Spiritual Hierarchy of our planet, that inner group Who really controls the destiny of the planet. This is momentous, and the world does not know about it. It is your task, if you take it upon yourselves, to make it known. Every time you mention the fact of the World Teacher or the Christ coming, remember that He is not coming alone but with a large group and that Their influence will be *crucial*.

The actual externalization is not simply the Masters coming out openly, waving to the populous and being very chummy and friendly. It is to do with the externalization of the inner ashrams onto the outer physical plane. What is being attempted, and will be carried out, is the replication on the outer physical plane of the ashrams which have existed for millennia, still exist and will continue to exist on the inner planes. It is creating a replica so that the two areas work simultaneously. The disciples working in the ashrams in the outer world will be the same people who are already in the inner ashrams. They will still gravitate to their own Masters.

The ashrams are the focal points for the energy of the Master, the energy of a particular ray. There will be seven major ashrams and 42 subsidiary ashrams on the outer plane just as there are on the inner planes. Everyone will find their relationship with an ashram, but now, openly, on the outer plane, and the goal will be the taking of initiation. At the moment, the goal for a lot of people is to have a wonderful holiday, go around the world and see things they have never seen. These are worthy goals, there is nothing wrong with them, but can you imagine that becoming the goal of taking the first initiation? They will go to schools and colleges for training, then to the mystery schools, and thus find their way to the door of initiation. This will eventually become the common goal for millions of people. That is what the externalization of the Hierarchy is really about. Make it known. Tell the people what you know.

Will disciples eventually have conscious contact with their ashrams for training and service? (January/February 2001)

Yes. As I have said, it will be a replication on the physical plane of the ashrams which already exist on the inner planes.

Can you clarify? You said there are now 14 Masters plus one Lord of Compassion in the world. Who is that? (January/February 2001)

Maitreya is one of the three Lords of Compassion. He is the One Who is in the world, and so there are 14 Masters of various degrees — fifth and sixth, and the Lord of Compassion Who is Maitreya. Eventually there will be about 40 Masters in the world.

Control of the Forces of Destruction

Your Master said: "Never before has so much depended on Maitreya's coming." Are there any circumstances in which Hierarchy would infringe our free will in order to move things along — such as making the stock market crash happen quicker? (January/February 2001)

No, that would infringe our free will. What the Master meant when He said: "Never before has so much depended on Maitreya's coming," is that never before in the history of the world has humanity had control of such forces of destruction. The discovery of atomic fission has altered dramatically the position of humanity. It has given it a destructive power without the discipline and peaceful intentions that would guarantee harmony. In fact the very opposite. Even the possession of those weapons is done on a system — a group of elite, powerful countries and a number of smaller countries all having them, and others barred from having them.

The US makes a huge song and dance about North Korea's atomic facility, but why should it be excluded? Why should America, Russia, China, France, Britain, India, Pakistan and many others have it but not North Korea? It is a travesty of logic. The US decides who will have the bomb and who should be prevented from having it. So it makes an enemy of those who want the bomb, and those they would rather did not have the bomb. They are not concerned for a moment that North Korea will send a ballistic missile into Washington or New York. It will not attack the United States. It would be suicide, and they know that. They are concerned that it will give the North Korean Government parity with the South Korean Government, which is underwritten by the United States. It is an internal problem, not an international problem. The United States has made it an international problem. They are making the problem of who holds nuclear missiles and who does not more complicated than it need be.

There is a club, but they either have to close the club altogether and get rid of all the weapons, or admit as many people as want to waste their time, money and energy in creating these weapons. A few more nations would want them, but some nations would refuse to build them. They are sensible nations who will never seek to have atomic bombs.

That is the 'logic' of international relations. America is a young nation. It is only a very short time ago that it was born as a nation. It is like a big 18-year-old with huge, massive forearms, telling the others what to do. The US cannot go on doing that and then wonder why it is not liked. America is feared and disliked all over the world. I do not mean by every country — Britons like America — but all over the Arab world, because of its support for Israel; by China and others, by the ex-communist world, America is disliked and distrusted because it is big, strong and a bully. It has invaded more countries than any other nation since the Second World War. It believes that it has been the upholder of the 'free world' but it is not the only 'free' nation in the world. America sees itself as the only country that works and fights for freedom. It is not true. Among others, Russia fought for freedom and lost 25 million people fighting for that freedom, but as soon as it succeeded, it became the enemy of the United States. It is as my Master said: the world is being presented with the absurd choice between freedom and justice. Choose which you are going to have. Choose the modern, developed, American-type competitive world and you get a degree of freedom. Never mind about the justice, it is not important. That is a travesty of the truth. You cannot have freedom unless you fight and work for justice. That is what

America has to do. That is what you have to do. That is what Maitreya will do.

Humanity, as a whole, will have to go back and start all over again. Where did we go wrong? Start from the beginning of the Industrial Age, for example, and think again about the distribution of food and raw materials. Think about how we can do it more equitably. The advice will be there, the techniques are ready to be given. All we have to do is say yes. But I think Americans will find it quite difficult.

*In the **Externalisation of the Hierarchy** by Alice A.Bailey, the Master Djwhal Khul enumerates as follows: "The time of the end. The judgement of people. This period of judgement is a group interlude to the full emergence of the New Age influences." (1) Does the "wilderness experience" mentioned in **The Reappearance of the Christ and the Masters of Wisdom** refer to this event? (2) Is this event close? (3) Is Y2K [the so-called 'millennium bug'] a part of it?* (September 1999)

(1) No. That will be the result of the correct 'judgement of people'. (2) We are in the middle of it. (3) No.

Are we already in the 'wilderness experience'? (January/ February 2001)

No. For America, the 'wilderness experience' will probably be harder than for anyone else because it has become used to so much comfort, so much overuse and misuse of resources.

The developed world, in particular, has to learn to live more simply. Quite apart from the disparity in living standards around the world, we cannot sustain the assault on the world's resources at the present pace. If we do, the ecology will completely break down on this planet. It will become denuded of trees, water will be even more polluted, the air and soil likewise, and we will die of poisoning. My Master says pollution is already the number one killer in the world. It breaks down the immune system and leads to deaths from various illnesses as a result. In 10 or 15 years this planet will become almost uninhabitable, so deadly is the misuse of resources — unless we change direction.

America is more to blame than anyone else because it is big and greedy and has the resources to do it. It has 250 million people and the majority live at a higher level than anyone in the world *en masse*. (I do not mean every individual; America has 30 million people living under the US poverty line.) There are places in Britain, France, Germany and Japan where people live as extravagantly as people in America. The highest levels of living, however, are in the US, highest not in quality but in the use of resources. The US uses more resources than any other nation — 40 per cent by a population representing 5 per cent of the total.

Worse than that, the resources are stockpiled. In the mountains of the US there are tunnels leading into caverns where stockpiling of goods goes on incessantly. All the so-called 'strategic reserves' are stored away in literally indestructible chambers in the middle of mountains where even an atomic bomb would not penetrate. There are all the chemicals, the various metals, like titanium, and scientific materials which could be used in an emergency. That emergency is not going to arise, but the government does not know that. They have put trillions of dollars into these reserves which could long ago have changed the lives of the starving millions and given them clean water and regular food. These goods are sitting there in huge amounts which will never be used.

If there were a war in the future, it would be a very short one indeed. You would not need a strategic stockpile. It would probably be over in a couple of weeks, and the world would no longer be habitable. We would all be killed, if not in the first nuclear strikes then in the toxic clouds of chemical and biological warfare which would accompany or follow the first atomic blasts. It would be total, utter devastation of all life on this planet. That has threatened several times. We have been saved from it a couple of times by the Space Brothers.

I do not doubt that if that threatens again, the Masters, and if necessary the Space Brothers, would intervene to prevent that catastrophe. The information to construct the atomic bombs which were dropped on Hiroshima and Nagasaki was given by the Hierarchy and released to the scientists on the Allied side. The authority to do so was given by Sanat Kumara, Lord of the World, and was given to end the war and ensure an Allied victory. The two sides were running neck and neck for several months in 1942 for the secrets which control the atomic process. Sanat Kumara was approached by Hierarchy and He gave His assent. So Sanat Kumara, Lord of the World, would be involved in any such use of atomic energy.

If there were some country or countries or groups who threatened the world with atomic terror, would the Hierarchy intervene? (January/February 2001)

My information is that the Hierarchy would intervene. The threat would not be allowed to run that far. Steps would be taken to prevent its detonation. I do not know how it would be done, but it would be done.

The danger is the destructiveness that humanity has at its control. That is why it is so imperative that Maitreya makes Himself known and leads us back from the precipice. He has never been so needed as He is today because the problems, which are the problems of life or death, have never been so concentrated as they are today.

You have described three previous revolutions which turned bloody despite the Masters' interventions to soften the changes. (January/February 2001)

No. I think you took that wrongly. The Masters did not intervene before the bloodiness took place. It was to limit the degree of bloodiness that the Masters intervened, not to soften the changes.

Will the Masters do anything differently this time to intervene when the tensions between the 'haves' and 'have nots' accelerate? (January/February 2001)

They are intervening all the time. They are speeding up this whole process. You could call that intervention.

The three wars of revolution were inspired by the Masters and got out of hand. At the time of these coming changes, will there be more bloodbaths? How can we help prevent it, keep a balance between progressive forces and maintain the usefulness of the system? (January/February 2001)

That is the Masters' task. I doubt that you are quite equipped to do that for the world as a whole. You can probably do it in your own domain, in your kitchen. We do not want bloodbaths in the kitchen!

How to Communicate to the Public

Your talk emphasized the profound impact on all aspects of our lives that the emergence of Maitreya and the Masters will have. How can we better communicate and express this profundity in our publicity efforts? The reaction of most people is: "How will it affect me and mine?" (January/February 2001)

You can only treat people at their own level. You can say that this will have a profound impact on all aspects of life and try to answer their questions. You cannot know all the answers, you cannot speak for every single person's reaction. When they say: "How will it affect me?" you can say that it will affect people in many ways. We in the West have to simplify our lives so that all people can live. It will eventually completely change educational systems, and this will affect all our children. It will have an effect on every aspect of life.

If they have any imagination, they can see that a Master like the Christ, like the other Masters Who are similar, if not quite so extraordinary, must have a profound effect, a steadying note on humanity. People will think twice before being profoundly greedy and selfish and, consequently, destructive.

The Christ Principle will begin to work more and more in our hearts. This will reorient us to a deeper, more respectful, view of life. We will treat life and people with more esteem, and begin to see the people that we do not know, people on the other side of the world, as more truly a part of ourselves, as brothers and sisters. This will create our readiness to share, seeing it as a common-sense way of dealing with the world's resources. Intelligent self-interest demands the sharing of resources. It has to be this way because it is commonsense and more and more people will see this.

You can help to express this in the way you approach the public. Do not undervalue the general public. Maitreya is in the world because He has been invoked. The world has invoked the Christ, brought Him into the world. He did not do it against our free will. The masses of people (including yourselves) have called Him into the world, but you do not own Him. He has come for everyone, and everyone has a right to express their readiness for what He has to say. Each one is a soul. You have to learn to see people as souls and reckon them higher than perhaps they reckon themselves at the moment.

Please elaborate the comment you have made in the past that we should act 'as if' we know Maitreya and the Masters are in the world, and prepare the way. (January/February 1998)

If you are acting 'as if', it is rather like taking it on trust that Maitreya and the Masters are in the world. You have the inner intuition that this is so, or if your mind tells you that with so many outer expressions and illustrations of it, it must be so. Perhaps Creme does not know it all, but there must be something in what he is saying that makes me believe this is so. What do I do about it? Do I just wait until it is proven? If you are going to do any good, you have to make a decision. My advice (and this is the advice of the Masters in any point relating to this type of trust) is to take it on trust for the time being, as a hypothesis. "It could be true, it seems possible." Take it at that level for the time being until proven otherwise, and then *act* on the hypothesis that this is so. Act, therefore, 'as if' this is so; not lessening your activity in case you are overdoing it and it is later proved not to be the case, so you have wasted all that time and energy. That is something a lot of people do. They hang back and say: "Well, if I really knew, I would be right out there, but I cannot bring myself to give it my all because it might not be true after all." They are not fired. If your intuition fires you, you really know, even if you cannot prove it. Knowing and proving are two different things.

I remember at the time, in March 1959, when I was spoken to by Maitreya and He told me: "You will have a role to play in My coming, if you accept it," my Master said to me: "You have heard something today that has changed your view of things. The time is coming when you will be expected to *act* upon it and affirm His coming." A day or two later He gave me a long dissertation on faith, the need for faith — not blind faith, but true, inner faith, *faith in your own experience*. He ended up by saying: "For lack of that one ingredient, faith, many promising disciples have failed. Have faith, and affirm His coming."

So great is the need for faith that without it you will never do anything. If you have no faith in yourself, you will never do anything personal or original. If you have no faith in the reality of your outlook, you will never achieve anything. Even if you are later proved wrong, it is better to act with faith, make mistakes, and learn from them, than not to do anything at all because you do not have the inner conviction of your faith. You think: "It might be, it might not be. Oh, I don't know. I don't know what to do," because you do not have faith. If you have faith in yourself, even if you are later proved wrong, it is better to act than not to act. You can only make mistakes, and mistakes can be remedied. Unless you make them, you do not know whether they are mistakes or not.

My painting teacher used to say: "The worst paintings you ever do are those that you do not do." I have never forgotten that. If you do not do something, nothing happens in life, you are just coasting through life. It is better to make really bad mistakes and learn from them, than not to make anything at all. (I mean within reason. I am not asking you to rob banks!)

To act 'as if' is, precisely, to act with faith — faith in your own judgement — not doing something if you really think it is wrong, but if you think it might be right and it is worthwhile, like preparing the way for Maitreya, for example, without outer proof or personal experience. If you simply wait for the proof to come you may have missed the opportunity of all your lives. As Maitreya says over and over again in His messages, this opportunity to serve is the greatest gift that has been given to you in all of your lives. [Message 26 & 27] And remember, it is short-lived. It will not come again for another 2,000 years; even then it will be different. In 2,000 years' time you may be involved in organizing groups of disciples, preparing the way for the next World Teacher. Of course it will be a very different humanity, unbelievably more advanced, in every respect a new world, but the way will have to be prepared. Act as if you know it is true, and prove it in the doing.

Do you have any advice on how best to approach or deal with people we meet who embody the conservative Piscean energy which is so resistant to change? (January/February 2001)

If you mean the fundamentalists — Christian, Jewish or Muslim — then I know what you mean. Probably it will take the first 50 years of Aquarius for many of them to change, to recognize Maitreya. I say probably, I do not know for sure. Maybe it will be only 25 minutes. People are where they are, and there is no single way of approach.

Approach people intelligently. If you are intelligent, you will not go up to a fundamentalist and say: "You are so wrong. You are so stupid. How can you go about believing the things that you believe? I will tell you where you are wrong" — and then tell them about Maitreya. You cannot do that, it is crass and unproductive. That is what they do to you and show their lack of tolerance and common politeness, to put it mildly. You have to be more diplomatic.

"Those who embody the conservative Piscean energy." Few are all one thing or another. Everyone is a bit progressive and a bit conservative. Some are so conservative they are beyond the pale, and some are so progressive, with a capital 'P', that they are absolutely unbearable in any context. Meet people halfway and be respectful of their rights, their right to hold on to their ideal, because it is the outcome of their experience and their ray-structure. They would tend to be older than the average, although not all — there are some very young conservatives. It is the young conservatives I find most difficult; I wonder how young people like that can believe the things their grandfathers hardly believed in. But they do more and more. As the pressure of change takes place, inevitably there is a reaction, a counter-thrust, and so there is a swing to the right.

There is a strong fascist-type element in the US who are watching events and waiting for their opportunity. That opportunity would come when the changes are taking place to a certain degree, but they will find that the more educated elements of the public will take sides which they would not expect. They will take the side of change. You will find in the event that the soul quality of America, which is the second-ray of Love-Wisdom, will be evoked by Maitreya, and will come into effect as it did after the Second World War with the Marshall Plan. The Marshall Plan is the greatest achievement of modern America, bar none. Unfortunately it stopped when it had done its immediate work in Europe, and it was changed into the CIA plan, which was to maintain the status quo, destabilize left-wing-oriented countries, and keep the US ahead. It is still a very powerful agency, but it too has an end-time.

When Maitreya is more accepted and world public opinion is being galvanized, those who resist change will find themselves becoming the minority. Millions of Americans of goodwill will side with Maitreya for change and justice. A new

Marshall-Plan type of action will be created which will save the starving millions in the world. A great, dramatic aid effort such as has never been gathered together before will be organized and distributed through United Nations agencies. This will have a profound effect on world opinion including American opinion. Those against change will find themselves more and more limited, more and more pushed back into their strongholds which not for long will be able to withstand the decisions of the majority.

You made an interesting comment in a lecture about the difference between preparing the public and simply giving information. What is the main distinction in these two similar acts? If people give others the information about the Emergence of Maitreya the World Teacher, is that not sufficient? Do you mean a difference in the type of information? (January/February 2000)

One can give the basic facts of the events and one can also outline the problems facing humanity and how they can be met and resolved by certain actions, thus preparing the public for *their* role in world transformation. The changes needed will come from the changes occurring in the hearts and minds of humanity. This takes long preparation. The information remains the same but the implications arising from it must be grasped and acted upon by everyone.

The Effect on the Reappearance Groups

Will the externalization affect the activity and work of this group as a whole, and will it affect the group evolution and group initiation? (January/February 2001)

It will affect everything that happens in the world, all the people in the world, to a profound extent, including this group, the work of this group, and the eventual possibility of group initiation. But the possibility of group initiation does not depend so much on the externalization of the Hierarchy, but on the overcoming by the group itself of their individual and group glamours.

That is holding back the creation of a group fitted for group initiation. It is not to do with the Masters returning or the work of the Masters at this time. There is ample stimulus, guidance and information given which can help us reorder our priorities and come into correct group relationship. We have gone over them many times and individual groups study them. They are in the works of the Master Djwhal Khul. The trouble is that the groups do nothing about it. There is not one single group that gives any real energy, effort, intelligence and work to the overcoming of their group glamours. Very few people in any group make an effort towards overcoming their individual glamours which are so set, the fog so dense, that they do not even see them. They do not understand the reasons for these rules of conduct to be accepted, acted upon, made part of the group relationship. They do not see the necessity. It is all to do with that, nothing to do with the externalization of the Hierarchy. That would not make it easier or less easy.

It is simply that the groups do not do what they can and should be doing for themselves, people individually, and the groups as a whole. It is to do with impersonal group relationships; with the ability to use the energies of destruction in a constructive manner; to do with the ability to work as a miniature hierarchy, and to learn the law of occult silence. Practically nobody in any group in the world takes these seriously to the point of working intensively at it. They may think that they do, but my information is that they do not, and no group is any further along the path towards group initiation than they were when that subject was brought up years ago. It has been studied, presented in *Share International* (and in *Maitreya's Mission Volume Two*), outlined and gone through in detail many times. Some people even pretend that correct group relations are unimportant and work against them.

So the answer to the question is that the externalization would certainly not have a bearing on group initiation unless the groups change and take it seriously. As for the effect on the group work, this group's work, at this time, is preparing the way for the Emergence of the Christ and the Masters into the world. That task is almost over. The Masters are going to emerge in the very near future, so that part of the work will be done. What is required is an interpretation of the work of the Masters, an explanation of Their reasons for returning and for the particular relationship They make or do not make with humanity. That is something which you should already know or be studying and be able to interpret for the general public. I would see that as an ongoing work of this group.

The fundamental work of all disciples, not just this group, is to overcome their glamours, to become mentally polarized, and if possible spiritually polarized. It is to relieve some parts of the astral planes of the dark, dingy cloud which saturates them, which is caused by the glamours of all of us. Glamour, illusion, creates this cloud, this non-reality of humanity, which includes the disciples up to a certain degree. It is what holds humanity back.

The coming into the everyday world, openly, of the Masters will help to some extent to thin that dense cloud of glamour. But what will do it most potently of all will be the outflow of the Christ energy. The Reappearance of the Christ essentially is the manifestation of the Christ Principle in the human heart, in individuals, including the individuals in these groups. In so far as that energy is anchored in your heart chakra, Maitreya can work through you, and through you He can change the world to some degree. That is how He will work. He can only do it if the Christ Principle is active and potent in you. The less glamoured you are, the more pure will be that reaction, the purer the vibration of love from the heart, and the more useful you will be, together with, one would hope, the education which most of you have had over a number of years, either from meetings like this or from your reading of the teachings.

The answer to this question of how it will affect the groups very much depends on the activity of the individuals in the different groups. Tackle your glamours. Get rid of them, the glamours which never seem to go away, which seem to get stronger rather than weaker; relationships getting more torn and ragged at the edges, instead of a simple harmonized working together for the need of the work. It is altogether too personality-ridden. Even those who do work, do so from a growing level of personality identification. You have to get rid of 'you' in front of 'yourselves'.

The work should be in front of you and you nowhere to be seen, simply doing what needs to be done. But as people work and get some response from others, perhaps a degree of acclaim, it tends to foster their ego, and instead of becoming less egotistical they become even more so, more imbued with the glamour of achievement. This happens in all the groups, wherever they are, who feel that they are succeeding.

People are looking for a result from what they do. How successful was it? It is not a question of "How successful was it?" It is a question of "Was it worth doing?" And having done it, stand back and let it do its work. If it was worth doing, it will carry the energy of its worth. You do not have to look for a success rate, how many people applaud you for doing it, or how many people went home in tears. It is a question of doing the work because it has to be done, because it is there, like climbing Everest because it is there. The work is there; it has to be done. If you want to be a disciple at all, that ought to be enough, without identifying with it, without applauding each other, without bringing personality reactions into it at all.

It is not the first time I have said this, but it is always at the basis of achievement. Achievement is like non-achievement. It is the achievement of the invisible. The invisible is the cement which you create in the group which binds the group together but is never mentioned, never talked about, never emphasized to any degree. It is the invisible outflow from the group in contact with the public, imparting information, carrying a light, illuminating certain areas of thought. That is the achievement. You cannot measure it, and you do not have to measure it. Let the Masters measure it if They are interested. All you need to know is that the work is being done.

How much does Transmission Meditation facilitate the Approach? Do the energies of Transmission Meditation improve the environment for the Masters? (January/February 2001)

I wonder what is meant by "improve the environment". Improve the air quality, the weather or the amount of moisture in the air? Does it mean just generally make it nicer for the Masters to be in the world? If that is the question, then the answer is no, it does not.

Transmission Meditation does bring the energy from Hierarchy to the general public on a mass scale, primarily to the New Group of World Servers. They are the ones, above all, who respond to these energies distributed by Maitreya and the Masters. Highly potentized, these energies impact the minds and hearts of the several million people working in the New Group of World Servers, which was formed by Maitreya in 1922.

They are most stimulated, most galvanized, by the energies which the Masters transmit through Transmission Meditation groups. They are the first to receive and use them. As a result, their work and impact on society is heightened and intensified, so it has a real bearing on the masses of people.

Every department of life — political, economic, religious, scientific, cultural, educational, and social — has members of the New Group of World Servers representing it. In their various lines of work, they respond to these energies although they may not know the energies are there. They may never have heard of Hierarchy but either directly, as part of a small inner group, or indirectly, in a much larger outer group, they are responding to the impress of the energies and the ideas of the Masters, through their own soul. They do their work because they believe in it, because that is their ideal. They are putting forward sets of values that they believe to be needed by the world, the only things that will set the world to rights. To a large extent they are correct in their assessment. In individual cases there may be too great an emphasis on one way or another.

None of these individuals are perfected Masters. They are ordinary people, somewhere from 1.5 up to third-degree initiates, so it is a broad spectrum. In every case they are motivated by altruism, by a sincere devotion to the needs of the world as they see them. They are in all political parties and none, not only in the progressive parties, certainly not so well represented in the conservative groups. Some are powerfully political; others are powerfully non-political. Some are religious; some are anti-religious. They represent their own particular line of work to the best of their abilities, and it is through them that the world is being changed. The ideas, the thoughtforms, of the future living conditions are being presented to the general public, who are more and more taking sides.

Does Transmission Meditation facilitate the Approach in that respect? Yes. Does it facilitate the Approach in the sense of speeding up the day on which the Masters actually set up the ashrams on the physical plane? I do not think that would be the case except in a very broad general sense. Does it make it easier for Maitreya to come forward? No. He is waiting, as we are, for the stock exchange crash. Maitreya does not need the shortening of the date by some work on our part before He can come forward. Our work in Transmission Meditation produces its effect in the world mainly through the New Group of World Servers, and less directly on the mass of humanity. But if that conditions the speed of Maitreya's emergence, it does so through events in the world and above all the big event, the one for which He is waiting, which is the major stock exchange crash which He predicted in 1988.

How can we bring the oneness we feel in the group overshadowings into the world? Please talk some more about how we can break down the barriers to our knowing that we are one and one with God. (January/February 2001)

This is something you have to find out for yourself because you are you. You would do it in a different way from everyone else including me. Become more of what you are. You know you are a divine soul in incarnation. Try to be it. Try to show it. Meditate more, retain the results of the meditation. Do not immediately turn on the television to find out what is going on in the football match or the ball game. There is no simple answer to this. This is like asking: "How can we become spiritual? How can we come closer to God?" Meditate more and serve more, but do it without ego. Do it with yourself out of the way, behind you rather than in front of you. The only thing that keeps anyone back is their own ego. Everything else is possible if you take your ego out of the way. If you take your ego out of the way, what are you left with? Nothing, some people think. That is the fear. "If I take out myself, I am nothing at all. I am just a drone doing all the work and not getting thanks for it, not getting any pats on the back."

Do you appreciate other people's appreciation? Do you appreciate being just and being good? Is it all to satisfy the ego? So long as it is doing that, you are not serving. Service only begins when the ego is not in it, when there is no judgement being made about the result, when you are not identifying with it, when you are not attached to it. You have to be more detached about everything you do. If you did it with detachment, these questions would never arise. They would not enter your mind.

I was saying last night to a little group: "Everybody asks me 'Why?'" And I suddenly realized that I never ask my Master "why?" I have the opportunity to ask my Master most things, and the question I never think of asking is 'why?'. He does not usually say anything, but if He says something, I never say: "Why is that?" But when I say something, everyone says: "Why? Why do you think that, why was it that and not something else? Why are things different from what I thought they might be? Why?"

It is a never-ending question. Why, why, why? Leave out the "why" and just do as you are asked — or not, you have free will. It would never occur to me to question the wisdom of the Masters in doing a particular thing. So I never ask why. I just accept it. They say it and the work gets done because it is, from

Their higher point of view, the right and necessary thing to do. That is how you should approach it. If a Master suggests that I should read a certain book, I would never say: "Why?" I know it would be for my benefit. I would just read it, and not wonder why I had to read it. If I read it, something would happen. I would be changed in some way from reading the book. If it were suggested by a Master to read it, then He would obviously have a good reason, and I would not question it. I would not want to know it. I do not need to know. I just need to do the work. That is how you should see this work, just that it has to be done. The world has to be informed. You are creating the thoughtform, the climate of hope and expectancy. Stop asking why you are doing this or why you do not do this and why, why, why. Put "why" out of the dictionary!

Do we as a group have a role to play in lessening the fear, chaos, etc that may ensue from an economic crash? (January/February 2001)

Yes, if you can do it, but not as a group. It is not our role as a group. It is your role as an individual who thinks he or she knows how to lessen the fear, the chaos, etc that may ensue. You cannot do much about the chaos, but the fear you can foresee and mitigate, by all means.

PART THREE

THE COMING OF A NEW LIGHT

Let there be Light

by the Master —, through Benjamin Creme

Each century brings mankind closer to his goal; the demonstration, in all its perfection, of the Light of God. In this way man becomes what he potentially is — a living God. Each incarnation marks a step cut in the mountain of ascent. With each such experience man adds to his vehicles a modicum of light, subtly changing thereby the vibration of his bodies. When all his bodies are thus vibrating to the frequency of light, the task is completed, the journey ended. From the point of view of man, the journey is over; from the point of view of Those Who have achieved, the journey has but begun.

Thus each man and woman makes the metamorphosis from man to God. Out of the chrysalis of matter, with all its limitations, emerges the liberated Master, radiating the Light of God.

Formless

Across the vastness of the universe, this Light persists; through all dimensions and planes it expresses its nature, conditioned only by the forms in which it shows itself. These forms give access to the Light to those whose consciousness rests in the world of matter, but essentially Light is formless, needing no structure to sustain its Being.

Deep within each one of us dwells such a light, awaiting the opportunity to shine forth. Within each glows the potential of all Cosmos. Within each, too, is the will to bring forth that light and thus make manifest the nature of God. That Light and that Will pertain to the soul and come into activity as a result of soul alignment. Seek, therefore, alignment with the soul and bring into manifestation the purpose of God. Search within and find the source of all knowledge and love. Reveal to the world the Light of the soul and join the ranks of those who serve.

Era of Light

The world stands ready for more light. The peoples everywhere are thirsty for new knowledge of themselves and of God. Because of this readiness, the Masters have prepared Themselves to inaugurate a new era of Light. Limitless opportunities for progress will be offered to mankind: man will marvel at the discoveries which will open the door to mastery of natural forces; he will stand amazed by the wonder and beauty thus revealed; he will know for certain the fact of God and his relation to that divinity, and will enter willingly into co-operation with the Divine Plan.

All of this awaits humanity as it stands at the threshold of the Aquarian Age. This will be an age in which the Divine Plan will flourish once again, bringing man at last into conscious acceptance of his destiny.

Many today would doubt this, as they survey a world of cleavage and tension. The problems seem too complex, the divisions too extreme. But precisely then, at the moment of greatest need, comes the Teacher, ready to bring new Light. Such a One is now among you, waiting in the wings, patiently, for the invitation to serve.

Release the Light that He brings and enfold all things in holiness. Embrace His Teachings and bring succour to all in need. Manifest His Light and create anew this world. (*Share International*, December 1983)

221

Nature of Light

The following article is an edited version of the Keynote Talk given by Benjamin Creme at the 1998 Transmission Meditation Conferences in San Francisco, USA, and Kerkrade, the Netherlands. The talk was based on an article by Benjamin Creme's Master, titled "Let there be light", which is printed above.

"Each century brings mankind closer to his goal: the demonstration, in all its perfection, of the Light of God. In this way man becomes what he potentially is — a living God."

It is interesting that the Master says "each century". The Masters think and work in 2,000-year periods and in 25 and 75-year periods. A 25-year period, four in a century, is like a couple of weeks to a Master in time scale, although They have no sense of time at all. They work outside time. They do meet together and discuss various possibilities and assess the achievement of particular lines of work every 25 years. The 25-year mark and the 75-year mark are crucial points of focus for the Masters and for the incoming and outgoing of great cosmic energies.

For example, the energy of Pisces began to recede in 1625, not 1624 or 1626, and the energy of Aquarius began to make its effect on this planet in 1675. These are crucial pointers to the way the Masters work: They assess the forward work and the achievement of the past 25 years. Every century, They meet again and assess how well Their Plan has worked out to bring humanity a step forward; to assess how many disciples are consciously working with the Plan — in this way finding the best possible means of achieving Their Plan, Their hope for humanity. The Master says very clearly: "Each century brings mankind closer to his goal, which is the demonstration, in all its perfection, of the Light of God."

The spiritual triad

People ask: "Why are we here? What is the purpose of our reincarnational cycles?" They provide the soul with the opportunity of serving the Plan of God. It is the soul which incarnates over and over again in a series of vehicles which it gradually invests with its own nature, its own Being, until the man or woman is totally soul-infused and can work consciously and intelligently with the Plan. The soul makes the great sacrifice of descending from its state of perfection on the causal plane to working on the physical, emotional, and mental planes through the vehicles which it provides for itself for that purpose. The soul brings the Light of God from the Spiritual Triad, the Self, the Spiritual Being which is reflected through the soul, and from the soul to the personality. The Spiritual Triad embodies *atma* (will), *buddhi* (love/wisdom), and *manas* (mind). These three aspects of the triad are focused in the soul, and one by one — starting usually with the *manasic,* then the *buddhic* and finally the *atmic* or will or purpose aspect — become powerful elements in the life of the personality by building in the Light of God. Gradually we become what we are potentially: a living God.

The long journey of evolution

The Master says: *"Each incarnation marks a step cut in the mountain of ascent."* That is a very broad statement. It is true in essence, of course, because even a useless incarnation, relatively speaking (and most of us will have had plenty of these), is at least a resting point in that long journey of evolution.

Although it is probably true in the Master's mind that each incarnation "marks a step cut in the mountain of ascent", that has to be taken, I believe, as a relative statement of fact. All of us waste incarnations. It does not seem to be inevitable because Maitreya never wasted an incarnation. That is why He is the Alpha and the Omega, why He has never failed in an incarnational endeavour. That is why He is the Christ. That is why a man on Earth, a not very evolved planet, has been able to embody the Christ Principle. This planet Earth has created a Christ, which is something that, for instance, Mars has never done. Although Mars has a technology and a conscious awareness of the meaning and purpose of life that as yet most of the inhabitants of this planet do not have, it has not achieved the creation of a Christ.

"With each such experience man adds to his vehicles a modicum of light, subtly changing thereby the vibration of his bodies."

The natural substance of our vehicles, physical and etheric, is atomic matter. This physical body is made of atomic matter. Our etheric physical counterpart body is also made of atomic matter, and has its own vibration, its own light. There is nothing which is not light. With each incarnational experience, if there is no backsliding or treading water, if there is a modicum of effort, a forward and upward movement, we add to our vehicles a little substance of subatomic particles, which is light, thus raising the vibration of the vehicles. This increases until it equals the vibrational rate of light itself. When that is complete and all the bodies are vibrating at the same rate, the task is done. You are the liberated Master. This, of course, takes time; it does not happen overnight. It takes countless incarnations to come to the beginning of the process.

The Christ Principle

For long ages incarnations proceed without the soul paying much attention to its vehicle, the man or woman, because there is nothing in the life of the individual to warrant its attention.

Eventually, by the process of life itself, the vehicles — first the physical, then the astral, and then the mental — gradually change their quality. More and more subatomic matter is attracted magnetically to that which is there, and so a light begins to shine. When this reaches a certain frequency, the soul turns its attention downwards. Until that time the attention of the soul has been turned upwards to the Monad, or Self, or Spark of God, of which it is the reflection. The soul changes the direction of its attention — not permanently but more and more frequently — gradually investing its reflection with its own nature. The Christ Principle is born as a light in the cave of the heart, the heart centre at the right side of the body, at the same level as the physical heart. It stimulates that centre until it begins to radiate. The person then changes dramatically.

There comes a point when everything that he knew, everything that he enjoyed, begins to lose flavour. The old life begins to seem boring, useless, going nowhere. His ideas broaden. He becomes interested, perhaps, in various spiritual teachings — whatever will lead him out of the stalemate of what, up till then, constituted his life and consciousness.

The soul is the first Master in this respect. When a certain point is reached, a certain attainment of light absorption, a Master might become involved in the furthering of that individual's life endeavour. This proceeds until the person is ready for the first of the five planetary initiations which cover the last few lives of the evolutionary process.

Initiations

The first initiation becomes possible when there is established control, to a real degree, of the physical elemental, of the tiny, devic elementals whose activity constitutes our form or body. They create the form of humanity, and control, through their activity, the desire-nature of the individual until we, ourselves, reach a point of discipline and control where we can control their action. This conflict eventually brings to the force-centres, the chakras of the initiate, the light from the Initiatory Rod. At the first two initiations it is the Lesser Rod that is wielded by Maitreya. At the third and higher initiations, it is the Flaming Diamond, the Great Rod, activated by light from the sun, and focused into the chakras of the individual by the Lord of the World, Sanat Kumara, Himself.

At the first two initiations, this is an extraordinary transforming process. It is so dramatic that the entire life of the individual becomes transformed. Almost always he or she becomes vegetarian. Think of all the young people around the world who spontaneously become vegetarian. This is part of the light purification of the physical body. Light works in several ways: it acts as a great purifier, and also as a great life-giving stimulus to evolution because it is our nature. Light is evolution, and the nature of life is light or electricity.

Electrical universe

We know many forms of light. In the far distant past, before there were switches, there was nothing for early man or woman to do but keep a fire going. In this way they had some light. That light allowed them to see each other, showed the path outside the cave and kept wild animals at bay. There was always a large fire kept going in early, primitive societies. That pertained for many thousands of years. In all the caves where it is known that humanity lived, there are traces of fires which they had to keep burning to heat themselves. Heat is another form of light.

Heat is the light of the physical sun. There are really three suns, each emitting a different kind of light. From the *physical sun*, there is light and heat by friction; heat is produced by friction. The radiation from the sun, combining with, or acting in friction with, the infra-red radiation from the Earth, produces heat. If you go to the top of Mount Everest, you will find that instead of being hotter (because it is nearer the sun) it is the coldest place on Earth because it is so far from the Earth/Sun vibrational meeting-point in the atmosphere where friction takes place. If the atmosphere is very thin, as it is on Everest, it is colder because there is a lack of friction. The *Heart of the Sun* radiates Solar Fire; and the *Central Spiritual Sun* radiates Fire Electrical. We live in an electrical universe; the nature of the universe, all cosmos, is light or electricity.

When we switch on the electric light we are actually tuning into the lowest, physical-plane, level of the light of the world. The discovery of electricity has opened humanity's eyes to the possibility of knowing who we are, of becoming the gods that we essentially are. When we understand the true inner nature of electricity, we will gain control of the forces of the universe. We have only, as yet, touched the surface of electricity. We handle it more and more adeptly as time goes on; we can make it do all sorts of things. It has created our technology. We use it for heat, light, the creation of motion, and so on. But still we have missed the inner mystery of electricity. That, when discovered, will lead us to the control of light itself.

Electricity has these different levels: electrical fire of the Central Spiritual Sun, Fire Electrical; Solar Fire from the Heart of the Sun; and electrical fire-by-friction of the physical sun. In each of these lies a great mystery. At the core of that mystery is the nature of light and therefore the nature of life itself. Humanity is coming near to a point where it will begin, under the stimulus of the Masters, to investigate the nature of life, demonstrating as the light from the sun. We have been told that Maitreya will eventually introduce a new technology, the Technology of Light. That will allow us to understand and use the secrets hidden in the nature of electricity.

God-realized

"When all his bodies are thus vibrating to the frequency of light the task is completed."

227

When all our vehicles — physical, emotional, and mental — are vibrating to the energy of light, at the same frequency, and the link with the soul is total and complete, there comes the link between that of which the soul is the reflection — the Monad, the Spark of God, the Self — and the physical-plane man or woman. The need for the soul as the 'Divine Intermediary', as it is called, is no longer present, and the soul is reabsorbed by that from which it emanated, the Self or Monad. This occurs late in the evolutionary process and demonstrates as the fourth initiation. The fifth initiation follows from the complete union of the now totally soul-infused personality and the Self or Divine Spark. The individual is then a Perfected Being, God-Realized, Self-Realized, as are all the Masters. They no longer need further experience on Earth. They can, if that is Their destiny, leave the planet and go to higher planets or even out of the solar system, to Sirius.

Perfection

"From the point of view of man, the journey is over."

That is the end of the journey on Earth — the purification of all the vehicles and the heightening of the vibration of these vehicles to relate perfectly to the vibration or frequency of light. From the point of view of the Masters — Those who have achieved this perfection, this liberation from Earth, this consciousness and control on every plane (which is what makes you a Master) — that is only the beginning of the journey.

Can you imagine what that means? The Master sees stretching ahead of Him vistas of Being that we cannot even imagine. It is not simply that you get better and better at doing something, as you get better at typing if you practise, or better at painting, if you have any talent, as you go on doing it. You would hope that that would be the case. The nature of life for the Master changes utterly. Having achieved perfection on planet Earth, He might, for example, go to Venus. Each planet has

228

seven incarnational experiences or rounds, as they are called. The Earth is in the middle of the fourth round. Venus is in the last of its incarnations; it is to Earth as an *alter ego*, our Higher Self. This solar system is to the next system — the one just over the hill, Sirius — as our personality is to our soul.

Sirius

As individuals, we are a dim, limited reflection of the colossal Will, Love, Intelligence and fiery nature of the soul. Are we all of that? Of course we are, but not until we become a Master do we register that Will, Love and Intelligence perfectly, radiating the Light of God so that we can stimulate thousands of disciples with that Light. For the Master, this changes if He goes to Sirius: He is like a beginner, a first-degree initiate. Many Masters do go directly to Sirius from Earth on the 'Path to Sirius', one of seven paths of the Higher Evolution. The speed of evolution there is, to us, unbelievable.

For example, the painter Mantegna was 2.2 degrees initiate in the 15th century. That, today, is quite advanced, but it is not even the beginning of spiritual polarization. When He became a Master a few lives later, He went directly to Sirius. We are now only at the beginning of the 21st century. That is no time at all in the evolutionary sense, but if He were in this solar system now, He would be at the same level as Maitreya, so great are the opportunities to achieve which await the person who goes to Sirius, so high is the vibrational rate of the Light which emanates from Sirius.

Sirius is one of the Seven Sacred Solar Systems that surround the "One About Whom Naught May Be Said", the Supreme Logos of our galaxy. Our system is the next-door neighbour, and the reflection of, one of the Seven Sacred Solar Systems. That must stand us in good stead!

Although this solar system is not particularly important in itself, and not very evolved (and this planet is not particularly evolved either), we are in the fortunate position of receiving a Law from Sirius. What we call the Law of Cause and Effect stems from Sirius. It is the result of the light emanating from Sirius. When it reaches this, lower, solar system, a reflection of Sirius — like the personality in relation to the soul — it acts out as the Law of Cause and Effect, or Karma, which is the fundamental Law of this system and our planet. Everything we think, everything we do, each thought, each action, sets into motion a cause; the effects stemming from these causes make our lives, for good or ill. We create, thereby, the circumstances of our lives, in relation to the Law of Rebirth set in motion by the Law of Karma. These two great Laws work together bringing us into incarnation over and over again as karmic need, and the need of the world, determine at any given time.

The Plan

The Masters control the entire process of working out the Plan of evolution which is in the mind of our Planetary Logos, the Heavenly Man, Who is seeking to bring His Light into perfection on planet Earth. His Plan is related to the Plan of the Solar Logos. Each planetary Logos is contributing His degree of Light to the greater Plan of the Solar Logos. Our Solar Logos, likewise, is seeking to relate His Plan to that greater, higher Plan emanating from the Solar Logos of Sirius.

What we should understand is that what we call life and what we call light are one and the same. Light is a manifestation of life, and life is a manifestation of light. That is Being. We are used to talking in terms of consciousness. Each area of awareness brings us to a higher and more inclusive state of consciousness. We include into our consciousness more and more of what is possible, in our solar system, to know. When you know, you can do. When you do, you manifest. When you manifest, you make real the Plan of the Planetary Logos. The more of that Plan we understand, the more intelligently we can work with it. The Masters know the Plan. They are living gods and can work intelligently with the Plan through humanity and the lower kingdoms. We are not quite as inert as the lower kingdoms but pretty inert, and our difficulty has been that for at least 100,000 years we have lost touch with the Plan. We have lost our way.

Technology of Light

Mars and the Earth are more or less at the same level, each in the middle of the fourth round. They have perfected Beings, middling-to-perfected Beings, and people who are not nice to meet on a dark night. The beauty of Mars, if I can put it this way, is that they have *not* lost their way. They have not lost sight of the Plan; they are still working within the Plan. That is why they have an extraordinary technology. The Technology of Light for them is commonplace. They are finding ways to go beyond that, or to use that for galactic transformations which we would boggle at if we could even imagine them. They have put a great ring of light around our planet, for example. It keeps the Earth in balance in the system. The stories of the poles reversing and the north becoming south are a nonsense. The Space Brothers — in particular the Martians with their advanced technology — have placed this ring of cosmic light around our planet, which holds the Earth in its axis, intact. The Martians have the ability to use light like that because they have not made our mistakes.

Atlantean era

About 100,000 years ago, during the late-Atlantean civilization, there was a great war between the Forces of Light and what the Masters call the Lords of Materiality. We call them the forces of darkness, those beings from a previous solar system whose task

231

it is to uphold the matter aspect of the planet. The Masters were working with the Atlantean root race for 12 million years, and humanity was advancing rather well and along correct lines. There were successions of great civilizations. The Masters worked openly, and gave humanity great gifts of science that we have lost — science much more evolved than ours is today. They had the Science of Light in those days but it was given as a gift to humanity by the Masters.

The humanity of the time was learning to perfect the sensitive, emotional, feeling apparatus, the astral body. So well did they do it that it is still the most powerful body of humanity. That was the achievement of the Atlantean root race. That is why, until we are halfway between the first and second initiation, we are 'polarized' on the astral plane. Astral polarization means that the astral plane is the seat of our consciousness.

Towards the end of that long period, the Masters were guiding humanity forward to become more and more perfect in its astral expression but also to gain some level of mental ability. There were those who could think, but a very small number compared with the number of people in the world. Anybody who could think gained a measure of power. A person who could think would today be like a farmer with his cattle. The cattle cannot think; they can emote, they can feel pain. You do not have to go to a slaughterhouse to see that. They cannot think in the way that humanity thinks but they are beginning to respond to the human mind. Dogs, for example, show quite a degree of astral telepathy and response to the mind of humans, those to whom they are close. Horses, elephants and camels also.

Average humanity at that time became like chattels, the vassals of those powerful people who could think and who began to get very rich, and to be greedy and separative. They responded more to the forces of darkness, the Lords of

Materiality. If you think that commercialization of life today has produced a deadly emphasis on materiality, it is nothing to the time in Atlantean days when there were people richer by far than the wealthiest man on earth. I do not necessarily mean in money, but in terms of what they controlled.

There was a great war then between the Forces of Light, the Masters of that time, and the Forces of Materiality, who were very strong. They had a great following because people loved this materiality. Those who could think forced droves of people to build the empires that they created. The result, in the end, was a stalemate, and the Masters retreated into the mountains and deserts of the world: the Andes, Rockies, Cascades and, later, the Himalayas, Carpathians, Urals, Atlas, the Gobi and other deserts. They became retreats where many Masters waited for the time when They could come out again into the world. They buried the records of these previous civilizations deep in the Gobi desert, the Himalayas, Rockies and the Andes – very beautiful examples of the thought and creative ability of the Masters of the time. They were not made by Atlantean man but by the Masters and Their immediate initiates and disciples.

The Light of Knowledge

For 100,000 years we have lost the outer example of the Light of Hierarchy. It has always been there behind the scenes, but necessarily, since it has been hidden, humanity as a whole has forgotten its heritage. We have had to battle seemingly alone, although never actually alone, because always, at the time of greatest need, the Hierarchy has sent one of Their number into the world to act as a Teacher for the time, age after age, cycle after cycle. For the last 100,000 years, that has been the case. Never has there been a time without that help; the Light has always been available.

In more recent times, that Light was brought fully into the open with the writings of Helena Petrovna Blavatsky (HPB),

Helena Roerich, and Alice A.Bailey. That has enlightened the world in a very definite sense by introducing the Teachings to hundreds of thousands of people who have reached the stage where they are responding to the Light of their soul and awakening to the Light of Knowledge. The Light of Knowledge, the awareness of what lies behind appearances, what constitutes the world of meaning and the nature of Beingness, is now available for all humanity when they are ready to absorb it. No aspect of this teaching, this Light of Knowledge, is ever withheld from humanity if we are ready to receive it. We ourselves limit by our receptivity, our readiness, the degree to which the Light is released.

With the return to the world of the Masters as a group after 98,000 years, this Light of Knowledge will galvanize humanity in the most extraordinary way. There will be a dramatic increase in knowledge along many different lines — particularly in the Science of Light and the nature of Being. The Masters go on to explore and develop Being while we have, up to now, and for a long time to come, to confine our activity to the nature of consciousness, the awareness of what it means to be a conscious human being.

New livingness

"Across the vastness of the universe, this light persists. Through all dimensions and planes it expresses its nature, conditioned only by the forms in which it shows itself. These forms give access to the light to those whose consciousness rests in the world of matter, but, essentially, light is formless, needing no structure to sustain its being."

For most people, not only does light need a form to be recognized, but also the degree to which it can be recognized, known and used depends on the level of attainment of the individual. The Masters can contact, absorb and redirect light from far-off cosmic entities like the constellations. For example,

234

today we are entering the Age of Aquarius. That means the Light of Aquarius in the form of its cosmic energy is transmitted daily, hourly, moment to moment into our solar system. That is the new Light, the new livingness which will galvanize humanity in this coming time.

We imagine there is just living, and there is just so much that we can call living. When we are dead, we are not doing it. When we are not dead, we are doing it. But there is living and *living*. There are degrees of livingness just as there are degrees of knowledge. Livingness has its own different levels that depend on the state of awareness of the person who is doing the living. For a Master, Beingness is something altogether different from what it is for us. For a child, Beingness is probably being happy, doing all sorts of things that come spontaneously to its eyes, that stimulate its brain, and that it gets a 'kick' out of doing. It does not do things that depress it. The child does things that enliven and stimulate it, which satisfy its need for movement, action, knowing — for livingness. The livingness of the child is different from ours. We also include depression, inertia, unknowing, in our livingness. They are part of our sense of living. If we are wise, we accept that we do not know everything and try to make up the loss by reading or going to lectures. We try to make the best we can of what we have. It is natural and intelligent to make the best of it.

The Light through which we understand the nature of Cosmos, Livingness, Being, does not need a body. In its own Being it is formless because it encompasses everything. In order to see it, however, to come close to it, register it, we need it to have a form. If our consciousness is on the physical plane, then what we call the light of electricity is meaningful. But have you ever thought that electricity has a higher aspect which we do not know about, which we have not seen and cannot touch because there is no form for it? We only know the light of electricity because it can light up the room. We can switch it on and off. We can do this until the bulb goes, and then the electricity has no form any more. We can put food in a plain box and it does not get any warmer. But put it into a box and turn a switch and suddenly this formless electricity becomes heat. That is giving form to what is essentially formless.

Since it is formless, we do not know yet how many levels exist of that formless state. Is it one total, simple, formless state that is everywhere, but invisible, or are there different levels of it? With electricity there are different voltages, and these are different levels of power: fire-, heat-, or light-power of that 'thing' we call electricity. But essentially the electricity itself is formless; it does not need a form to be. It only needs a form for us to recognize it. Likewise with the new Technology of Light. Light itself, being electricity, has no form, but with the advancing technology called genetic engineering we can use particular qualities of electricity. Electricity works by binding together form. It holds together the molecules of the body, for instance, and this being so, it can be used.

Maitreya has told us that it will be used to create new organs, that organ transplants will eventually become redundant because the Technology of Light will allow us to create these organs.

I am quoting here, from the Master Djwhal Khul, what He wrote about light or illumination which, I believe, is to do with the Technology of Light, although He does not call it that. He says: "One of the imminent discoveries will be the integrating power of electricity as it produces the cohesion within all forms and sustains all form-life during the cycle of manifested existence."

You may wonder why our body keeps its shape. Our chin and jaw line remain pretty well the same from birth to death, although there are subtle changes like the skin getting slacker

236

and wrinkled. But the bone structure, relatively speaking, remains the same. The heart, liver and kidneys may sometimes malfunction but they may remain perfectly functioning until we die, at whatever age that is. That is extraordinary. Even the etheric body has a shape although it is a subtle shape that moves and changes. There is a mechanism whereby, once created, the human body, unless it is hit by an automobile or drops down a cliff, retains its shape and its inner functioning power, the organs intact.

The secret is electricity. The energy of electricity, at a higher level than a light bulb allows us to see, "produces the cohesion within all forms and sustains all form-life during the cycle of manifested existence". It produces also the coming together of atoms, and of the organisms within forms, our organs, so constructing that which is needed to express the life principle. That is a fundamental, deep-seated mystery of electricity, and it is going to be discovered in about the next 40 to 50 years. That will revolutionize medicine, particularly surgery, to an extraordinary degree.

Soul alignment

"Deep within each one of us dwells such a light, awaiting the opportunity to shine forth. Within each glows the potential of all Cosmos. Within each, too, is the will to bring forth that light and thus make manifest the nature of God. That light and that will pertain to the soul and come into activity as the result of soul alignment."

Without soul alignment none of this would be possible. Life on Earth is so constituted that soul alignment inevitably comes about because we are souls in incarnation.

Each one of us has this Light, the potential, of all Cosmos, and everything that that means: the awareness which registers in the human being perfected in the nature of God — the Will,

Love and Intelligence of God — or whatever other aspects of God that we can realize. We do not have names for more than these three. There must be dozens of qualities of the nature of God that as yet we do not recognize but which remain to be revealed. All of that, extended out and out to the whole of Cosmos, into infinity, makes up our potential. It is an extraordinary thought. It would be daunting if we had to do it all at once, but it does not happen all at once. It is a slow, gradual unfolding over aeons of time, so we have plenty of time to get used to the idea and to practise. From practice comes perfection. When the Masters talk about perfection, it is simply practice. We just practise living correctly.

" ... within each, too, is the will to bring forth that light and thus make manifest the nature of God."

"Nothing happens by itself; man must act and implement his will." [Message 31] This statement is by Maitreya, and I am sure it has been said a thousand times before. It takes the will to bring into manifestation even the Plan of God. Each one of us is endowed with that will aspect whether we know it or not, whether we use it or not. At whatever level of endowment we have in any given life, as human beings, gods in incarnation, each one has that Will aspect of the divine, which embodies the Purpose; the Will manifests the Purpose. When we know the Purpose of God, we can be God.

What all of this is emphasizing is the fact that we are not separate from God. There is not anything else but God or Light in the whole of the manifested and unmanifested universe. And we are all of that. We have all of that in potential, and all we have to do is recognize it, become aware of it, and manifest it. It is not easy but obviously possible because the Masters have done it.

"That light and that will pertain to the soul and come into activity as the result of soul alignment."

We have to bring about soul alignment. We have to align the personality, with its vehicles, to the soul. Gradually the will, love and intelligence of the soul become manifest in the physical-plane personality and the work gets done in this way.

Spiritualization of matter

"Search within and find the source of all knowledge and love," which are there already in the perfected soul. The soul is not perfecting itself. The soul is perfecting the series of vehicles and spiritualizing, from its own nature, the matter of this planet. The aim of the incarnational process for the soul is the spiritualization of matter. As it incarnates over and over again, it magnetically draws to itself more and more light, matter of subatomic quality, until the whole body is light.

The 4th-degree initiate, not yet a Master, has a body which is already three-quarters light. Every incarnation adds to the light to some degree. Each initiation adds tremendously to the radiatory capacity of the individual. This is the result of the Rod of Initiation which throws its light into the chakras of the initiate, producing a tremendous change in the radiatory capacity of the individual.

We recognize where people are in their evolutionary development by the radiation of their activity. (However, I know people who think that they are on the verge of the fourth initiation but who are actually about 1.2.)

People seem to have a very vague idea of what constitutes being initiate. All the great actions of the world have been made by initiates of some degree. Every major change in the world has been the result, in the first place, of Hierarchical stimulus working through Their initiates and disciples of various degrees. The initiates enunciate the great ideas. These ideas become our ideals. We put the ideals into effect, and the civilization grows. That is how it has always been.

It could not be any other way because only those with light can absorb light. That is the meaning of the biblical statement: 'To them that have shall be given.' It does not mean you should get more money because you are already rich. It means if you have the light of spirit, the Light of Beingness, in your Being and are radiating it, you can attract more. It is axiomatic. The higher can only be attracted by an instrument high enough to attract it. What we are really doing in our evolutionary journey is creating an instrument — each life, hopefully, a better instrument — which will be more subtle, more sensitive, its 'antenna' better equipped to realize the light, understanding and consciousness that is there for all to absorb and use if we have the instrument to do it. It is a question of creating an instrument, and it is for that that we are in incarnation.

Service

"Search within and find the source of all knowledge and love. Reveal to the world the light of the soul and join the ranks of those who serve."

As soon as you make contact with the soul, inevitably you want to serve in some way. It is automatic because it is the nature of the soul, not the personality, to serve. The soul seeks to bend the personality into a true reflection of its nature, and that is why the stages of soul absorption and infusion are difficult; the personality is always in rebellion. It does not want to make the effort, or when the effort gets really hard it runs away.

I have found this over and over again when people talk about their problems. Their problems nearly always result from the fact that they are running away from the very thing they should face. Everyone is fine so long as life feels easy, we are making progress, we can see results — especially seeing results. But come a time when we do not see results, when we are meeting what seems to be a big obstacle or difficulty in life, the tendency of many people is to run away from it, not to face and overcome it. We do not realize that these obstacles are put there to bring out from us the strength to overcome them.

We never will become a Master if we do not have the strength to overcome whatever we are faced with, however unpleasant or difficult, however a challenge to our self-esteem. Our Being will never demonstrate itself to any great degree until we put it to work in overcoming such obstacles. The obstacle might be practical, on the physical plane. It might be purely psychological — nearly always it is psychological in advancing people — but even on the physical plane, whenever an obstacle is met, many people run away from it. They think: "If I am over there, it will be better than here, and I will not have to face this particular problem." Until they face it, however, it will keep coming back, especially a psychological challenge, because they have not dealt with it, not equipped themselves to deal with that problem whenever it arises. If we are equipped to deal with it, it tends not to arise, or, if it does, it is no longer a problem.

It is like learning to do our job in the office or factory. The first days are terrible. We do not know where we are. (I say this as one who has never worked in an office or factory, but I have imagination!) It is too much for most people, at some time in their lives, to face the very thing that life is presenting them with to make them grow. The first thing, I think, is to make an inner decision that we will solve every problem, overcome every obstacle, before we try to go on. Instead of running away, we will try to solve it, give it our best to overcome, and if we do that, it will, by strengthening us, weaken every problem that we face after that. The bigger the obstacle, the bigger the challenge faced, the more we are fitted to become initiate and eventually a Master.

It is the only way. We have to do it because as a Master we are alone. There comes a time when we will realize that we are absolutely alone, without any help whatsoever except from our

241

own Being. Our own Being is God, not less than all cosmos. We can only tap into a tiny little bit of that at any time. But if we do not tap into it and bring it to bear, we can never use it. We have to learn to tap into our potential and not ask other people what to do. Some people are always asking others: "I have this problem. What do you think I should do about it?" Unless we face the problem, unless we make our own decisions, we will never grow. We will never become a Master. We will never even become 2nd-degree initiates, let alone Masters. (I am assuming you are 1st-degree initiates!)

The restoration of the Plan

"The world stands ready for more light. The peoples everywhere are thirsty for new knowledge of themselves and of God."

If that is the case, then it will be given. As soon as humanity sets up a cry for help — for more light, more information, more technology, more awareness, in a word, of its own nature and purpose — then that is given. The cry is heard by Hierarchy, and the word rings out: "Open the gates" — the floodgates of light, knowledge, inspiration, guidance. All of that pours out from the Masters in answer to the cry. That is what happened in 1875 with the publication of *The Secret Doctrine* and *Isis Unveiled* (H.P.Blavatsky). That is what happened before the war through the Agni Yoga and Alice Bailey teachings: presenting new light and knowledge for the exploring minds of those ready to absorb and respond — *and to do something about it to serve the Plan.*

The Plan is being restored. The Plan was interrupted by the great war between the forces of Light and Darkness in late Atlantean times. The Plan, from the Masters' point of view, has still gone on. Humanity has evolved, slowly, but the Plan was definitely interrupted. Humanity had to be left to find its own way. And, finding its own way, it is stronger. We are much stronger now than was Atlantean man. Atlantean man could not think. Millions now are thinking. Mass education has changed humanity profoundly.

"Because of this readiness, the Masters have prepared themselves to inaugurate a new era of Light."

This is an extraordinary thing to be saying.

"Limitless opportunities for progress will be offered to mankind: man will marvel at the discoveries which will open the door to mastery of natural forces." All these forces are there. We think we know about them, but we do not. We do not really quite know what gravity is; we have only thought about it. We do not really know what electricity is. We know one physical-plane level of electricity, and we can use it if we are careful. We can use it fairly adequately for the time being, but we have not touched the essence of electricity. It is altogether different from what we think.

"Man will marvel at the discoveries which will open the door to mastery of natural forces; he will stand amazed by the wonder and beauty thus revealed."

Every discovery of reality, or aspects of reality, is beautiful. It is a beautiful unfoldment of the riches of life, the natural system in which we live, which we call nature. The only problem is that we separate ourselves from it. We see nature out there. We think God is up there and that we are here. There is actually no separation between any of these. We are not separate from nature; that is why we should not despoil the natural environment. We are not separate from what we call God. It is imminent in every aspect of our Being. And we are not separate from each other, which is the great thing we have to discover.

The great heresy of separation brings us to that misery which we call glamour. Glamour is the result of separation, believing in the supreme heresy that we are separate. As soon as we realize that, glamour will end. For the time being, however, it is at the source of every misery, unhappiness and limitation which we can know and impose on our lives. It is that which lies behind the appalling fact of the starving millions, the unbelievable waste of resources, the inequalities, the injustice, the cruelty of life. All of that is glamour, and is the direct result of the experience we have that we are separate.

The One Life

We will find that we are not separate, and that we cannot for long maintain that glamour with impunity. We now have the forces that can destroy all life. We also have free will, and so it is up to us to change direction. When we do, we will be amazed. We will "marvel at the discoveries which will open the door to mastery of natural forces", "stand amazed by the wonder and beauty thus revealed," "know for certain the fact of God". When you realize God in yourself, God in the machine, God in the light that is streaming from the light bulb, which is creating the marvels of the new science, then it is a fact. You realize God is not an old man with a beard up in the sky; that is an old symbol that we have to put out of the way. We have to realize that *we* are God. Everything around us is God. The space between all in cosmos is God. That life, and there is only that One Life, is us, in us and around us. We call it God but we could as easily call it ourselves. We could call it nature. We could call it any other person we know. That is the One Life which is God. It is not up there, out there, separate from us. It is inherent in every aspect of our Being.

Different Levels of Light

It seems the Master's article talks largely about the light of the soul and manifesting that, our light. But in the last line of His article, where He is talking about Maitreya, the Master says 'Manifest His light.' Why does He switch from the light of the soul to Maitreya's light — to emphasize that they are the same? (January/February 1999)

They are the same at different levels. Maitreya is the embodied soul of humanity. He embodies in His own Being what we call the Christ Principle, the Christ Consciousness. The Christ aspect is the soul aspect. When it is lit in the human heart, the contact with the soul grows and deepens. That is the light of the soul which you radiate as you serve. What the Master means is that into this lighted domain, with all its problems, has come Maitreya with His greater light. It is the same light, only of greater intensity, naturally, because He is the embodied soul of the world. Awaken that light in yourself. What He means is, respond to Maitreya's ideas and make them your own. As Maitreya says: "Take Me into yourselves and let Me work through you. Make Me part of yourselves, and show Me to the world." [Message 10] It is to take the light of Maitreya, the soul, the consciousness aspect, and make it your own. As it grows in you, so will you attract more light from Maitreya. You become a magnet. As you act and serve, the magnet gets more and more powerful, and as it attracts more of that light, so you will become more perfect in serving the world.

Can you describe the relationship between light and love? Is there a difference between the two? (January/February 1999)

Light and Love are the same but there are different levels of light. There is the Light, Fire Electrical, which comes from the Central Spiritual Sun. Then there is Love, Solar Fire, which comes from the Heart of the Sun. They are different aspects of one light. Fire by friction comes from the physical sun; again, that is light. Fire Electrical includes soul light but soul light does not include fire electrical; just as will includes love and intelligence but intelligence does not include love and will. Love does not include will; these are three different aspects.

There are other aspects for which, as yet, we have no name. One of these is brought in by the Avatar of Synthesis, a quality that the Master Djwahl Khul says we may think of as "the Principle of Directed Purpose" which is related to the will aspect. It is the Will which nothing can thwart, which carves a path through all obstacles to carry out the Purpose of God. Flowing as it does now through Maitreya, that Cosmic energy clears many levels of apathy and resistance from our lives so that the Will of God can manifest. That is what is happening now. This will be an age in which for the first time humanity, of itself, awakens to its divine nature. I do not mean in a mystical sense. I mean in the actual, practical sense of knowing that we are divine and demonstrating the divinity.

I have read and heard it said that love is something like the binding energy of all reality. You stated in the keynote speech that electricity, at one level or another, is the energy that binds all form. Are these notions one and the same? Or is there some differentiation that it may be valuable to understand? (January/February 1999)

They are one and the same at one level but there are different levels of that manifestation. We call it electricity at one level, we call it love at another. Both are necessary. The basic energy of life itself is electrical, electrical force coming from the Central Spiritual Sun. It relates to the spirit aspect of reality. The love energy comes from the Heart of the Sun.

The energy of the life force from the Spiritual Sun binds together all forms; it creates the relationship which makes forms possible. It makes organisms within forms, molecules within the organisms, tiny atomic structures of a certain pattern — all of that is conditioned by the activity of light, the spirit aspect. It is that which creates phenomena. The love aspect, the second aspect of that same light, coming from the Heart of the Sun, sets up a magnetic relationship between all these created forms so that they are all bound together. Every atom is bound together with every other atom in the whole of cosmos. Both are necessary, and they function at somewhat different states of matter — creating matter, then binding together the atoms of that matter by a magnetic, cohesive drawing together. That is what we call Love.

Do these energies serve the same purpose, just at different levels? (January/February 1999)

They serve the basic purpose of the Lord of the World — bringing the material world into manifestation, creating all forms that make up that manifestation, and holding the forms together so that they do not fly off into another solar system.

From the Alice Bailey teachings I learned that darkness has to be changed into light. My conclusion is that darkness is potential light. Then one could say that in reality darkness does not exist. There is only light or potential light existing. Is that right? (May 2000)

Yes.

Science has already discovered that there is light in every living cell, which is called biophotons. (1) Could we call this light consciousness or principle of life? (2) Is this light the same as that called Fohat by H.P.B. or Primal energy in the books **Supermundane** *(Agni Yoga)?* (May 2000)

(1) Yes. (2) Yes.

There are seven chakras and seven rays. Is there any connection between the two? (January/February 1999)

Yes, indeed. The Master Djwhal Khul (Who gave the Alice Bailey teachings) has written that when we accept the reality of, and understand more about, the etheric body, more light can be thrown on the chakras and those aspects of electricity that we call the seven rays.

Inner and Outer Light

My father was blind, with atrophied optic nerves. Towards the end of his life he often spoke of a brilliant white light in his head. He could sometimes locate physical objects around him by the light's location in his head. He often winced from its brightness. Would this have been soul light, a reflex caused by his disability, or an illusion? (January/February 1999)

There are different kinds of light which may be seen. There is the light of the atomic particles of the brain itself. Then there is the light of the etheric body, the etheric counterpart of the brain. There is the light of the soul, which is usually seen as a brilliant sun in the head — very brilliant, so bright that it is difficult to look at. In this particular case, it is a combination of all three: the light of the atomic structure of the brain, the etheric light, plus the light of the soul. I do not think it is light throwing itself outward and producing an awareness of objects outside the individual, so much as the heightening of the awareness by the growing light in the head, in particular the soul light, that gives an unerring sense of where objects are.

Yesterday during the blessings before and after your talk, there was a sensation of golden creamy specks of light raining down inwardly. Was this real, or an illusion? (January/February 1999)

It was no illusion. It was real but it was not only seen inwardly — it was also in the room. It was the energy of Maitreya which gave this shower of golden light seen inwardly but also filling the room.

The air seems to be swarming with tiny dots of light that swim around and disappear. These aren't floaters in the eye. What are they — light? etheric energy? molecules of air? or bad eyesight? (January/February 1999)

They are not bad eyesight. They are light — specifically, etheric light. They would normally be of the 4th-etheric, the lowest etheric level. They are everywhere you look. Go down to the seashore and look just above the waves, you will see the swarming, moving, particles of light. You can learn to steady them, to pick one out and follow it until it disappears. Then its place is taken by another, and you can hold it. Hold your eyes very steady and trace one. Usually they are so fast that you just see swarms of light, you could not separate one. But you can slow them down, and you can make this little journey that it makes with itself, around and around, spiralling; they go in little spirals and then disappear. Then another one appears, and you can literally slow the movement down with your eye. The more relaxed the eye the more you will see the etheric counterpart body around everything.

When you are being overshadowed by Maitreya at your lectures and Transmission Meditations is it always Maitreya's energy of Love which He releases or are other energies released, too? There seems to be some controversy about this. (March 1997)

Maitreya's Love energy — what is called "the True Spirit of the Christ" — is always released, but not necessarily alone, or during the whole period of the Transmission. While Maitreya is overshadowing me, He, Himself, is overshadowed by a great Cosmic Avatar — the Spirit of Peace or Equilibrium — Who works with the Law of Action and Reaction. Maitreya relays the energy of the Buddha — Cosmic Wisdom — and the Shamballa Force — the 1st-ray energy of Will and Purpose. Together with these, He releases the four-fold energy of the mighty Avatar of Synthesis: Intelligence, Love, Will, and another for which we have, as yet, no name but which is related to the Will aspect. All of these Cosmic energies are released for the benefit of the audiences, Transmission Meditation participants and the world.

Everyone likes the 'feel', the experience, of Maitreya's Love energy — it is so uplifting, warm and easy to absorb — and for this reason I sometimes ask for it to be released alone and separate from the blend of all the energies, which is more usual. I hesitate to do this too often, however, so as not to interfere with Maitreya's energetic plans.

Quite a number of people, especially those who are predominantly along the 2-4-6 ray-line, find the other energies, particularly the Shamballa Force and those of the Avatar of Synthesis, very disturbing, alien to them, difficult to absorb and 'handle'. It may take time (sometimes a long time) for such people to accept these forces as beneficent in the way they accept the Christ energy of Love. As usual, it is a question of knowledge and experience.

It is certainly possible to conceptualize a distinction between light within and light from outside oneself. As a group, we are flooded with outside light, especially on weekends like this. How does the light of Transmissions, overshadowings, and blessings actually affect our form and consciousness? How do the inner and outer lights differ and interact? (January/February 1999)

When you are in a Transmission Meditation group, work at fairs and give lectures, and so on, you are sending out the light of knowledge. You are taking in light and sending out light. Transmission Meditation, plus your activity in relation to this work, or any kind of spiritual work, has an immediate effect on the chakras. It intensifies soul activity and therefore the soul light. This intensifies the light flowing in and out of the etheric body, so that the chakras themselves are stimulated. All of this together, especially in a group situation, creates a state of spiritual tension. Each individual has a greater or lesser degree of spiritual tension. Their worth in the world at any given time, their worth in this work, is measurable in relation to that state of tension. The greater the spiritual tension, the greater the creativity of the individual, the greater their spiritual worth to the world as a whole.

We have to create spiritual tension. Nothing happens without tension. It is as if you have inside yourself a spiritual spring, and everything you do of a spiritual nature (including, of course, Transmission Meditation) winds up the spring, like a clock. It winds to a point where it cannot any longer be wound without snapping. Then it unwinds, and you have a change, a shift in consciousness. Every human being undergoes this same process. Before every expansion of consciousness there has been a period of spiritual tension. The spiritual activity — the overshadowings, the blessings, the Transmission Meditations, the work in the world of a spiritual nature — is enhancing the spiritual endeavour, winding up the spring. Then comes a time

251

when it cannot be wound any more, it lets go, and your consciousness expands. That is how you advance. That is the key to the whole process of expansion of consciousness, and therefore of evolution. The more you transmit (if aligned) the more you act in a spiritual sense, the more you are an educator, the more you are spreading the light of knowledge, of the soul, of wisdom, of the intuition — these lights are all part of Light, and pertain to different aspects of your Being — all of that winds up the clock, increases the spiritual tension.

It is the same for every group. Every group is using a certain proportion of soul energy in its activity and a certain proportion of personality energy. These vary in different parts of the world. Most of the groups that I know and work with use a large proportion of soul energy and a small proportion of personality. This group (I mean the groups around the world, except for one or two) is functioning at a very high level of soul energy because it is inspired by the idea of the Christ being in the world. Their soul has responded to that great, magnetic idea, the return of the Christ and the Hierarchy of Masters. That has kindled the fire of their soul. It has brought about, throughout the world, this growing number of groups who are reaching, stage by stage, a point where the light gets so intense, the tension build-up so intense, that it unleashes itself, it unwinds. This unwinding is not a loss of energy but actually a shift in awareness. That happens before every initiation. Each initiation is the result of that manifested spiritual tension. It is only that which makes it possible to stand the Light from the Rod of Initiation.

Does this not put a strain on the nervous system? (January/February 1999)

The answer to that is both yes and no. It depends on the toughness or otherwise of your nervous system. It depends, to put it very broadly, how more or less neurotic one is. I mean that

252

in a serious sense — how glamoured, or otherwise, one is. How more or less directly we can approach this process without glamorous reactions which hold us back and do not allow us to act directly. That weakens the nervous system. But for those whose fire is strong and whose mechanism of response is direct, the effect on the nervous system can be very invigorating.

*The Agni Yoga book **Supermundane** (Agni Yoga Society), page 34 (and there are many other references), refers to Primal Energy. "Man's good fortune is his access to Primal Energy, and his misfortune that he does not accept this blessed power, but usually condemns it. What a dreadful thing it is that man refuses to accept his best treasure." What exactly is Primal Energy? Having read the Alice A.Bailey books what term might I be familiar with?* (September 1997)

Etheric energy, charged with psychic power.

Astral Light

Is there such a thing as astral light? Is the astral nature all glamour? What's the difference between astral light and soul light? (January/February 1999)

There is such a thing as astral light. There is only one light, and of course that flows through all planes, including the astral plane. The remarkable thing which is happening now is that there is an intensification of the astral light of the planet and a downward movement of that light onto the physical plane. This was begun by the rupturing of the web between the physical and the astral planes during the prolonged bombardments in the First World War and then again in the Second World War. The dropping of millions of tons of bombs, the bombardment by

253

hundreds of thousands of huge guns, created enormous noise all over Europe (and different parts of the world in the last world war) and in Russia and so on. This has ruptured the web between the physical and the astral planes of existence.

This is also making it possible for a realization of life after death because the astral planes are the planes on which most people spend their sojourn out of physical incarnation. The vast majority of people are, of course, astrally polarized — that is, the astral plane is their focus of consciousness — and, necessarily, a large part of their sojourn will be in what the Tibetans call the '*bardo*', the astral planes. This can last a very short time if the person is more advanced, or, in average humanity, a very long time indeed. Of course, on that plane there is no time; there is no time outside our physical brain.

In the '*bardo*' of the astral planes, life goes on as desire which is the major principle governing activity on the astral planes. Whatever you desire is there. You want an ice-cream, you have it. You want a new house, you have that too. There are people there who go down the mines every day — get up (there is nowhere to get up from but they get up), get dressed, go down the mines, work hard all day hewing coal, and come up again. They are dirty and thirsty so they go to a pub and have a few pints of beer to get the dust out of their lungs, and then they go home and have something to eat and go to bed. They do this every day. It is extraordinary. There are no mines on the astral planes, but whatever you think of, whatever your desire is, becomes possible. That is the illusory nature of the astral planes.

The astral light is something quite different; it is the light of the astral atoms. Just as there is the light of the soul plane, there is the light of the mental, the astral and the physical planes. There is physical-plane electrical light; your physical body is itself vibrating as particles of light, the light of the physical plane, which can be seen in the head as the resonance, vibration, of the atomic particles making up the physical plane. When a person is responding to the light of the mind, the light of the soul through the mind, this throws a light on glamour. He becomes aware of glamour and can overcome it. To quote the Master Djwhal Khul again: "When one has found the lighted centre within oneself, one is in a position to become aware of the light within all forms and atoms. One knows what needs to be done then to dispel glamour in one's own life, using the light of the mind, which is the light of knowledge." [*Discipleship in the New Age, Vol I.*]

As I have indicated, the astral light is awakening humanity to the awareness of life after death, of the subtle planes of matter, to the existence of entities on those planes. From these levels a great deal of new information and revelation will come in relation to working with the higher forms of electricity. It has to come from the subtle side. That is why I cannot answer questions on the Technology of Light from the strictly physical-plane point of view. Not only do I not know enough about it, since it is not here yet [1998]; but it will not come like that, it will be so different from anything which you have thought of as science up till now. It is the science of the psyche, and that is the new psychology.

The astral plane is so powerful, can it provide experiences of light? I am thinking in particular of religious zealots. (January/February 1999)

Well, yes and no. It is not the light, of course, which is glamoured. It is the individual, whose focus, polarization, is on the astral plane. If you are polarized on the mental or spiritual planes, you do not have that same problem in dealing with astral light. You simply see it for what it is, astral light. It is an area of consciousness and an area of activity for humanity for a certain time. Better to be out of it quickly and on to the mental planes,

255

and if possible, through them, on to the spiritual planes. Astral light is a reflection, at a lower level, of the light of *Buddhi*, intuition.

The Master Djwhal Khul mentions that the survival of consciousness after death will be proved through photography — could you explain this? I know of experiments with tape recorders recording the voices of the recent dead; would it be similar? Are such experiments happening now? Would one need special film? (March 2000)

All living things are created by light. Cameras and film which are sensitive to astral light will be developed. These will allow 'dead' people to be photographed while moving, smiling, speaking, etc. Sound will later be added which will allow astral communication without using a medium.

The Atlantean Race — Wrong Use of Astral Energy

What caused earth's humanity to lose its way? The wrong use of astral energy at the end of Atlantean times? Or misuse of free will? The withdrawal of the light of the Masters 100,000 years ago? (January/February 1999)

The growing power of the materialistic forces caused humanity to lose its way. Two groups work in synchronous activity: the Masters of Wisdom on the spiritual planes and the Lords of Materiality, upholding the matter aspect of the earth. There came a time when more and more people began to think. The majority could not think, they were concerned with vitalizing and perfecting the astral-emotional-feeling body; thinking for most people was a long way ahead. And so it was for countless millennia until a few who were more advanced began to think. So powerful were the Lords of Materiality of the time, so rampant was black magic (white magic, of course, was used by the Masters), that great divisions grew up among the people.

Many of the great myths are really records of that time, and the stories of kings like Midas, and so on, reflect the extraordinary focus on materiality which developed in late Atlantean times. Before that, there was no word for 'thief' — no one would thieve or steal. It was not until, with the growing power of materiality, some people waxed rich and got very greedy; then, inevitably, crime began. Today the Western, developed nations wonder why there is so much crime. It is because there is so much division. Through market forces, it is inevitable that a few people get very rich and a large number of people remain poor. The gap gets wider and wider, and, as Maitreya says: "The rich parade their wealth before the poor" [Message 81]. This brings envy, hatred, resentment, and crime. If the world had a more equitable distribution of goods, there would be very little crime. Crime is not innate.

The time came when these two forces were so polarized that there was a great war. The war ended in a stalemate; nobody really won. It ended in a decision by the Masters to retreat, for a time, to the mountains and deserts of the world, where Their successors are, for the most part, to this day. After 98,000 years, the wheel has turned and enabled the Masters to come out again: because of Their own evolution, and also because humanity, at last, has come to a point where it can, on the whole, think and make decisions, respond to advice and suggestions and can use their minds to analyse situations. Eventually, they will agree that the only way is the just redistribution of resources. Then they will come back to the point where they left off from following the Path of Light, the evolutionary path. The Plan can start again. Not that it has ever been absent, but with the Masters out of the world, necessarily, an aspect of the Plan has been suspended for all those years.

257

"Wrong use of astral energy?" Yes, certainly, because astral energy at the time was the dominant energy; all but a few were astrally polarized.

"Our misuse of free will?" True, the misuse of free will, through taking the wrong direction, the path of materiality. Materiality is not just the worship of lots of goods; it is also the misuse of power. Hitler was, personally, probably not very rich, but he totally misused his power and was, therefore, deeply materialistic, so he could be obsessed by two of that group of the Lords of Materiality. The Masters use overshadowing, which can be just an occasional impression of the mind, or can go all the way to a moment-to-moment overshadowing which stops just short of obsession, so that the disciple's free will is never infringed. The dark forces, on the other hand, take that same process all the way to obsession, and Hitler was, literally, obsessed. That is why he was so powerful, but it would not have been possible had he not been deeply materialistic. We have to widen our sense of what is materialistic. It is not just wanting 'abundance' (with many people abundance is the number-one call for the future). It also means power, dominant power.

Were the ancient Egyptian and the civilizations of Central and South America originally founded by escaping Atlanteans? (December 1997)

The Mayan and other cultures of Central America were debased successors to the Atlantean civilizations, not necessarily escaping. The Egyptian civilization was the result of colonization from Poseidonis, a large island remnant of Atlantis where the Azores are today.

Did the ancient Egyptians use psychic powers or Atlantean technology to move the giant blocks that make up the pyramids? (December 1997)

Yes, psychic powers and the use of sound vibration.

Did black magic really turn people into pigs? (January/February 1999)

You have not read your Greek myths! Do you not know the story of Odysseus? He wandered for 20-odd years on his way back from Troy and had all sorts of adventures, one of them on the terrible island with Circe, the unpleasant sorceress who turned everybody she disliked into pigs. There were a lot of swine there who originally had been men. Yes, it is a fact!

It has been reported in **The New York Times** *that the lost Ark of the Covenant, the ancient Israelites' most sacred object, could be in the holy city of Aksum, Ethiopia, in the care of Orthodox Christian monks. It is described in the Bible as a gold-plated chest which Moses built to contain the tablet of the Ten Commandments. Is the relic in Aksum the lost Ark?* (June 1998)

No. My information is that the Ark exists but has, since 597 BC, been hidden in Egypt.

Can you tell us anything about the crystal skulls, surely the product of a great previous civilization? (January/February 1998)

They were common in the civilizations of later Atlantean times, connected with their religion which today we call Spiritualism. Most of those we see today are of Mayan (Mexican) origin — the inheritors of much of the Atlantean culture.

Educational Behaviour

The Master said: "The world stands ready for more light. The peoples everywhere are thirsty for new knowledge of themselves and of God." How does this relate to this group's work in the "educational endeavour vast in scope" which He also said we are involved in? Is this educational endeavour one of the ways in which we are bringing light to the world? (January/February 1999)

I hope so! Yes indeed! If it is written in words that everyone can read and understand, yes, it will bring the light of your knowledge, your awareness, to the world. That is light; knowledge is light. Anything that heightens our awareness of the nature of Reality — whether that is physical, etheric, astral, mental or spiritual — is light, is worthwhile, and should be taken up. That knowledge brings light.

As teachers, we need to pass on these teachings to humanity. This is accomplished through simplicity of words and action? (January/February 1999)

Yes indeed. Of course, if you can do it simply so that everyone can understand, that is best. Above all, not so much simplicity of action as the demonstration of the right action. Nothing achieves powerful educational impact more truly, more immediately, than example. If you can show by example the qualities that you are talking about — the nature of light, of life, and so on, then you are well placed to teach. If you are actually living it, you will demonstrate it. People will say: "I can see it, I know what he means."

This is what the Masters are counting on in the demonstration of Their Being to humanity. They know it will show an extraordinary blueprint of future possibility. We will say: "Can we become like that? They are wonderful, but They are men." People will see that 'mere men' can become Masters, like Maitreya. If They can do it, we can do it. They are not different, only more developed. Everything that we go through, They have gone through. If we see, by example, that the total, unconditional love, extraordinary wisdom, unbelievable intelligence of the Masters are not so far away from us that we can never aspire to them, this will awaken the aspiration of humanity to achieve these qualities. It will show what can be done.

If you have the true instructor, the really great teacher, it is not a question of imitating but thinking as he (or she) thinks, looking at life in a new, awakened way which he has given you. You are shown that it is possible by his demonstrating its nature. That is the beauty of it. It is not just the words, but the nature of the life.

In the Letters to the Editor about Maitreya's experiences, it seems that in the majority of them Maitreya, or one or other of the Masters, just smiles or waves, and it makes such a difference in the person's life. The obvious reason for this is because He is a Master. But I think He is demonstrating for all of us how we can very simply transmit our soul's love and light by smiling, and it can help create a climate of joy. (January/February 1999)

Yes, I agree. But there are also those delightful 'New Age types' who go around the world smiling all the time until you want to bash them. There is the smile of genuine love and joy, and there is that false, sentimental smile that says: "I understand the meaning of life, and harmlessness, and that all is One, all is God, and I am one with all. Do you not think I am lovely?"

261

"Yes, oh yes, you are. You are also a pain in the neck! Be real, be yourself!" If you cannot help but smile, if the joy wells up in you and you are smiling when you are just going to the corner shop, or the dentist, then smile, by all means.

What comes first, the experience of light or the actions that express that light and make it manifest? Or perhaps they work together and support each other. (January/February 1999)

The experience comes first. They work together and support each other but you have to have the experience before you can have the action.

Is fear not a major inhibiting factor in demonstrating our divinity? (January/February 1999)

How true. One of the roles of Maitreya after the Day of Declaration will be precisely to rid humanity of fear and guilt. Fear is the most inhibiting factor of our psychological makeup. To a great extent, it prevents the manifestation of the life principle. We could manifest much more of our innate divinity if we were not riddled with fear and guilt, much of which has been inculcated by the various religious groups. They have a lot to answer for. Guilt and fear are basic now in the thought-formation of humanity. Maitreya will act to rid the world of the fear and guilt which are the result of wrong education, conditioning of the worst kind, mainly by the churches of all religions.

In the struggle to understand the scientific explanation of light, electricity, etc, I become frustrated in the attempt to sort it all out in my mind. During that process I tend to lose sight of what I feel in my heart — that we are all aspects of One. When living a level of life from that understanding and thereby living light and love, is it absolutely essential to busy my mind with something that feels so foreign? Or am I really missing an important part of the whole? 'We are not separate' sums it all up for me. (January/February 1999)

Quite right. If you have an intuitive type of mind, that is generally the way that you will approach this kind of subject. On the other hand, if you continue to approach everything exclusively from that intuitive point of view, you will probably take a little longer to become a Master of Wisdom. A Master is a *knower*. There are two paths: the path of the *bhakti*, the heart-oriented devotee (and that is a perfectly valid approach); and there is the path of the occultist, the one who searches for meanings and acts out of his understanding, the *jñani* in Sanskrit terminology (and that is also an absolutely valid path). Eventually these two paths come together; the Master is both the *bhakti* and the *jñani* together, otherwise He would be incomplete.

An avatar can be one or the other. For example, Paramahansa Yogananda was a *Bhakti*, He wore His heart on his sleeve. Sri Ramana Maharshi, Who was a *jñani*, approached life in a different way and taught differently. In fact He taught silently. His is the path of Self-knowledge, of understanding 'Who am I?' The *bhakti* does not worry with 'Who am I?' He just demonstrates his intuitive understanding that all is love, all is God, all is light, and all is One. The *jñani*, in the sense of being the knower, is the scientist.

The scientist approaches life from a less simplistic, if I can put it that way, view of relationships. If you think of it as 'all is One', you miss out on the area of relationships. If you act as a scientist, even if not a physical-plane one, you see correspondences. Even if these require an intuitive leap to do so, you are making correspondences with different aspects of reality. In so doing, you can build ships that will go to the end of the galaxy. You cannot do that just by knowing that all is love, all is One.

This is the interesting thing about the different ways in which rays act. If you have a 2nd-ray mental body, for example, which will give an intuitive view of life to the individual, then you will probably find all that we talked about unnecessary — the relationship between this or that kind of light, the Light of Knowledge, of Wisdom, of the intuition, soul light — and ask why we need to separate them.

We do so because they have different functions. As we advance, certain capacities make their presence felt in our life: first of all, the light of knowledge, the light of the mind. And as we further advance, we touch some aspect of the soul and bring in the light of wisdom from the soul. Then, blending the light of knowledge, which is the personality light, and the light of wisdom, the soul light, we have the light of the intuition, which is both knowledge and soul light. This light is so bright, it puts all the other lights out through its radiance. Then we get the synthetic awareness of the intuition, which is what the questioner is talking about. That is the natural way for the 2nd-ray mind to work. It does not like science, it finds all that frustrating and difficult. Of course, it is a synthesizing quality for one life; this particular person might well have a 5th-ray mind in their next life. Then they will be saying: 'What do you mean, synthesis? We are really going to find out, we are going to look through the microscope and find what it is all about!' It takes all sorts.

Can you advise how to study Master Djwhal Khul's teaching intelligently? Many people seem to find it dry and academic. (March 1998)

Intelligent study involves the use of the intelligence and intuition. That is difficult, because intuition is a soul quality. It also involves a serious approach which most people do not have. They often have only an interest and their interest comes and goes.

You have to have an interest in it, and you have to study it not as "a dry academic study". (I do not know if Djwhal Khul's work could ever be that but let us assume that it might be.) I would suggest that people might study the Master Djwhal Khul's words in the way that they might listen to a talk by Krishnamurti. You can listen to Krishnamurti in two ways: to what he says, taking it in intellectually, and say: "That is very good. I agree with all of that. I understand 100 per cent, and I agree with it. I think he's a very fine and wonderful old gentleman." Or you can listen, and as he is speaking, apply it to yourself. When he says: "Ask yourself 'Who is experiencing this fear?'", do it as he is talking. Who is? I am. Well, who am I? Find out who is doing the experiencing. Am I separate from this experience? As he is talking, go through it. At the end you will find that you are a different person.

Technology of Light

You say that the Technology of Light will make great advancements in the field of medicine. How does it translate into other fields of endeavour, such as the economic and political? (January/February 1998)

It seems obvious that if the Technology of Light is going to give us unlimited power, heat and locomotion directly from the sun, and everybody has it, then no one will be able to own it, as today the oil sheikhs have untold riches under the desert. The Technology of Light is obviously going to have a powerful effect on the economy of the world. Nobody owns it, yet we all use it. What happens to General Electric and their counterparts all over the world? They are out of business. In the political field, so much power is wielded by people who are lobbying governments, controlling big industry. All of that will be out of the window, too. It is obviously going to simplify the political and economic structures of our world profoundly, quite apart from its application to medicine. Anything that gives unlimited, unpolluting power will change every aspect of life.

There is a lot of research going on in science concerning the utilization of particles of light as compared to the already-developed use of particles of electricity. Is this new scientific field, called photonics, the beginning of the Technology of Light? (April 1999)

No, it is not. They are still dealing only with physical-plane light.

For 50 years scientists have been trying to discover a nuclear fusion process. (1) Have the Masters chosen not to enlighten researchers concerning nuclear fusion? (2) How can humanity become worthy to receive nuclear-fusion technology? (June 1999)

(1) No. The delay in using nuclear fusion is mainly a result of the obstructive action of vested interests — namely the present nuclear-fission agencies. (2) It is not a question of "becoming worthy". We simply have to develop the technology.

Genetic Engineering

Scientists have just announced that they have finally got all the information possible about the human genome — 'the genetic book of life', it is being dubbed. Some are saying this

266

breakthrough surpasses other developments such as splitting the atom or landing on the Moon. What is its significance for future health and treatment of disease? Is this the beginning of what you describe in your books as the ability of medical science to grow organs on the same genetic pattern as the patient and replacing diseased organs relatively easily? It also raises very basic ethical questions. (October 2000)

Yes, this is the beginning of the information which will make transplants redundant. It also solves very basic ethical problems.

What do you think of genetic engineering? (July/August 1999)

Genetic engineering can be either good or bad. It is an appalling thought that experiments are actually taking place in various laboratories of the world in an attempt to create half-human and half-animal creatures. Genetic engineering in the hope of creating clones of people is, I think, a misuse — it is useless anyway, as clones are not really human beings because they are not souls. Our science has focused more and more on the materialistic aspect to the extent that most people have lost sight of the spiritual basis of life, and the economy is the dominant 'god' to worship in the world.

Genetic engineering as applied, on the other hand, to the animal and vegetable kingdoms will give us altogether new and better plant and animal species, and it will increase the vitality of animals to a point where they can respond more and more to the human mind as they themselves evolve. When they respond to the energy of the human mind in a heightened way, we will get a tremendous increase in the intelligence of the animal kingdom. Many animals who live or work closely with humanity — dogs, horses, elephants, camels and so on — already demonstrate a level of intelligence but this can be speeded up, just as human intelligence has its stimulus in the higher, spiritual kingdom made up of the Masters and Initiates. Genetic engineering is part of that process. Many animal diseases will die out. Many animals will go out of incarnation altogether. Their own kingdom is being purified, brought 'up-to-date', by taking very ancient animals out of incarnation that have no further role to play in our civilization. It is a sentimental attachment of the wrong kind to foster looking for white rhinos and keeping them in parks, spending millions of dollars doing so, when they are being deliberately taken out of incarnation by the Masters. They have served their purpose long ago. They are redundant and that goes for many others. We will create new types of animals which will have certain, almost human, faculties.

Another very important way in which genetic engineering will show its value is in combination with the new Technology of Light, which will give us unlimited power directly from the sun and fulfil all our needs — for industry, heating, lighting, and so on. There is nothing remotely like it in our world today, and in conjunction with an advanced form of genetic engineering it will do away with organ transplants. Instead of going into hospital and waiting a few months or so for a transplant one will simply go into a clinic for a few hours and come out with a new organ, built exactly to one's own genetic pattern.

Once Maitreya has emerged, how long would it be before humans could go to clinics to have their organs made, if one needed a kidney transplant for instance? (December 2000)
It is impossible to say. I have been told that there are early experiments being made in the direction of the Technology of Light but it requires things that are not yet created, quite apart from the genetic engineering which is still in its infancy as far as this is concerned. It will take time. My Master has said that we should look for the first signs of this technology, not necessarily the actual opening of clinics, in 10 to 15 years after the

emergence of Maitreya. That is a very short time but things could move very fast once certain things happen. It might be nearer 20 years before such transplants become possible.

*Do you think genetic engineering is following the Law of Evolution, which the Master Djwhal Khul describes as "the perfecting of form expression"? (**The Externalisation of the Hierarchy** by Alice A.Bailey, p.109)* (April 2000)

The answer to this question is both yes and no. The vociferous debate and controversy which is being waged by the dogmatic stance of those who promote (for whatever reasons), and those who oppose the very idea of, genetic engineering, is based largely on ignorance. Genetic engineering will prove to be one of the most potent means of developing, for the better, both animal and vegetable forms and, in combination with the coming Technology of Light, will transform the use of surgery, making the transplantation of organs — heart, liver, kidneys, etc — a thing of the past.

However, there is genetic engineering and genetic engineering. Much greater care, and much more extensive experiment, is needed before the results, in the form of modified crops and animals, should be offered to the public. At present, the lure of financial rewards and over-enthusiasm has created a difficult situation for both sides, the promoters and the objectors. In time, a more rational and more strictly scientific approach will lead to a wiser understanding. In the meantime, the fear of genetically modified food has stimulated a tremendous expansion of organic farming and produce which is much to be welcomed.

Can you comment on the issue of cloning humans? (December 2000)

The major governmental authorities in the world and the highest scientific agencies have come down firmly on the side of no cloning of human beings. It is possible, but it is not as easy as you may think.

Human beings are souls in incarnation. You cannot clone a human being as a soul. You can clone the human body, that is all. Since it has no soul, it has nothing to direct it. It has no purpose. You can only make a kind of mechanism, a non-ensouled body. The idea of a cloned human being is a nonsense unless you can bring in the soul.

Who can do that? Who can bring in a human soul to incarnate in an already perfected human body? You could clone a foetus, a few weeks old. Why you should want to I do not know; we already have plenty of people in the world, too many. But you could do it theoretically. I am sure in many laboratories and clinics hidden away in all the major countries where this work is taking place, there are such experiments going on.

It is said that there are experiments in which people are making half-man, half-animal births. Women are willing to give the use of their womb to carry a gorilla or monkey. It is a monstrous idea. It goes back to Lemurian times. I am sure with the Masters in the world that idea would never get very far.

There will not be cloning of humanity. It is the very individuality of every person which is the interesting thing. That is the basis of our free will. We are individuals, each one unique. The only thing that could be manufactured by the engineering method is a cloned physical body. How long would a physical body last? How useful would it be without the soul — and the energy, purpose and will of the soul — to infuse it and condition its actions?

I would like to know how genes affect people from lifetime to lifetime. Are the structures of them altogether changed from life to life? (1) In essence, do people get completely different physical bodies, thus genes, every life? (2) Are genes constantly transformed, thus transcended, from life to life so that you're continuously working with essentially the same genes from life to life? (3) If this latter is the case, then what is the procedure and/or rate of development for this process to occur? (November 1999)

(1) No. (2) Yes. (3) The transformation takes place as the vibrational rate of the atoms is heightened. The rate is self-regulated.

Science and Religion

Can religion and science ever see 'eye to eye'?
(January/February 1999)

The separation of religion and science is a false one. Those who are scientific think: "I do not want to get involved in that mystical stuff. I like to know where I stand. I am interested in the physical plane, in working things out for the betterment of humanity." The mystical person says: "I do not like science, it is cold and hard. I just *know* that God is love, and I feel it within me." That is fine but each is related to the other, neither has the whole picture. It is not a question of one being a better way or a colder or a warmer way. It is simply that different types of minds, governed by different ray energies, incline to understand this and not to understand that; different rays produce different types of people in any incarnation. In a particular incarnation we incline to one or other. We have to integrate these different aspects.

The religious path is one of mysticism. Intuitive awareness and mystical experiences will prove for that individual that God exists. The scientist, whether he is the psychological scientist or

271

the technical, experimental scientist, will, by his own methods, come to the same understanding. In fact, science has revealed more about the nature of Reality in the last 2,000 years than has religion.

Religion has added little about the nature of Reality since the 6th century; in that century we Westerners abandoned most of our understanding of Reality such as reincarnation and the law of cause and effect. The early Christian teachers, Origen and others, taught the fact of reincarnation — as did Plato, Socrates and Aristotle before them. In the 6th century it was removed from the Bible and lost to Western man and woman. This is a terrible deprivation. It removed from our awareness one of the great laws governing our lives. It was a calamity, nothing less. The Emperor Justinian forced it on the church fathers.

We have to approach Reality from as many angles as we can, because there are seven different types of human being under seven different rays and mental equipment. They will inevitably tend to approach Reality differently, and they are all valid. If they are accurate, they are valid. In the immediate future time there will be a congruence of what until now has been mysticism and science. The scientific mind will explore from an awakened consciousness the nature of Reality. We cannot get to the higher aspects of electricity by the old, purely physical-plane methods. We need the insight from a level where that insight is already a reality. That will come through the astral light, from the 'other side'.

The Soul and Incarnation

Don't human souls incarnate in bodies which are subject to poverty and disease by choice — in order to grow? (March 1998)

No soul comes into the world to starve; it is against the law of life. Not even a worm is born to starve. If you are born in Africa, parts of India, South America, China, you may starve. If you are born in America or the UK you might be hungry but you are probably not starving. Maitreya has said that the only reason people starve is that they have the misfortune to be born in one part of the world rather than another.

No one incarnates deliberately to starve. If you starve intentionally you do it as a spiritual exercise or ritual — Jesus is said to have fasted for 40 days in the wilderness. Fasting has long been known to have beneficial effects on the body and therefore on the emotional and mental aspects as well. That is very different from a life in which you are born into total degradation and misery, in which there is no food or work, in which you have to walk perhaps 12 miles for water or firewood. That is the daily grind of millions of people in sub-Saharan Africa today, but they did not come into incarnation to experience it. We come into incarnation in groups; these groups have probably been incarnating in that area for centuries. They are the inheritors of a colonization process which has now ended. Much of sub-Saharan Africa belonged to the British, and when we left them to fend for themselves, we did not educate or train them in the ways and means of doing so. Nor did the French, Belgians or Portuguese. The people are left with the results of our colonization. In some cases that has been completely acceptable; in others it has been a miserable tragedy, especially in those parts which are not naturally well-endowed. That is the reality, and no amount of theorizing that they *chose* it explains it away. They do not choose it, they find it when they are drawn into incarnation by the magnet of the group of which they are a part. We all incarnate in groups in any part of the world: you have probably been your mother's father, or mother, sister or brother many times over; perhaps you were in sub-Saharan Africa last time.

In terms of incarnation, what happens to a person who does no harm but does not do any good either? (November 1999)

A person who leads a mediocre kind of life, is neither hot nor cold, makes little progress. A life in which you are very destructive holds you back because you have to resolve that destruction under karmic law. A life in which you do much good pushes you forward along the path of evolution, lightens your karmic 'burden', but a life in which you do neither good nor bad, which is really rather tepid, is for the soul rather 'useless'.

The soul usually has three main goals in any particular incarnation, and it sets the circumstances and difficulties of our lives to bring out the qualities which will take us forward in evolution. If we run away from these and try to get round the obstacles rather than overcome them, we have to come back to the same point again and again. Many people want to be somewhere other than where they are; they think that 'over there' the grass is greener. They admire 'that person', and want to be 'that person' instead of themselves. The reason they want to be the person they admire is so that *they* can be admired. But the only interesting thing is our own unique Being — every one of us is unique. In the next life you will be different: you will look different, you may have different qualities because you will be given different rays, which will colour your personality expression and so on, but essentially it is You. At any given time you have the opportunity to develop that 'you'-ness, that individual unique quality which you have, not by imitating but by thinking for yourself and making your own standards, your own valuations: being true to yourself. When you are true to yourself you are true to your Divinity, and no one can take that away from you.

Is it possible in any incarnation to achieve transcendence of thought and therefore of speech? (November 1999)

The Masters make it known that, during the coming age of Aquarius, humanity will reach transformations of consciousness on such a scale that speech will gradually disappear; we will become telepathic. Everyone is naturally telepathic; the Masters always use telepathy among Themselves and with Their disciples if the disciple has it developed. Eventually, telepathy, which we all share with the animal kingdom, will become the norm. It is really a soul aspect, to do with what is called *buddhi*. When the *buddhic* level of consciousness is reached, contact will be continuous, at will, and over any distance.

Can you say something about how creating one's own reality relates to destiny and the Law of Karma? (November 1997)

Both are taking place simultaneously. What we are really doing is expanding our awareness, and that becoming aware is creating our own reality. You can be mad and create your own reality, as madmen do, but it is a reality which pertains only to them. The thing about 'non-mad' creation is that it is a touchstone for other people as well.

In the case of Leonardo da Vinci, for example, — he was a 4.4 degree initiate, almost a Master — his reality was so much greater than that of anyone around him at the time that it might as well have been a madman's reality. And yet, with time, and

275

the evolution of consciousness which has taken place since the 15th century, we now have an understanding of the laws of gravitation and various mechanical principles which Leonardo demonstrated for the first time but which no one in his day could apply. He was creating his own reality, but it is a real reality not a madman's reality.

Blavatsky and Alice Bailey tell us that the permanent atoms of the physical, emotional and mental bodies remain after death. These atoms contain all the experiences of past lives, albeit not completely available to us when we reincarnate. (1) Where do they go until they are ready to enter a newly incarnated person? (2) At what point do the permanent atoms of these vehicles enter a new body? (May 1999)

(1) They do not 'go' anywhere. The three permanent atoms are of etheric matter and remain in the etheric background of all matter until needed for the next incarnation. The soul magically builds the new vehicles (in etheric matter) round each permanent atom, using the vibrational rate of these atoms as the 'key' for the new bodies, so that we recommence physical-plane life at exactly the point reached in the previous incarnation.

(2) The permanent atoms do not 'enter' the new body, which is constructed around them. The physical foetus is a precipitation of the etheric counterpart body.

*In **Share International** you say: "You start your new incarnation **exactly** at the point reached at the time of your previous death." (1) Are you talking about the state of the physical body? In that case what can be said about a person who died from a serious disease and whose body has suffered a lot? (2) Can a disease have the purpose of burning up and purifying karma? (3) If yes, can a person who has died* *undergoing great suffering from a disease be reborn in good health?* (July/August 1997)

(1) No, I was talking about the vibrational rate of the atoms of the physical, astral and mental bodies. At death, one permanent atom of each of these bodies remains. Around them the new bodies are formed — at the exact vibrational rate of these permanent atoms. The rate of vibration of the bodies determines the point reached in evolution. (2) Yes, this is the most common way of resolving karma. (3) Yes. However difficult for many to understand, from the viewpoint of the Masters death is often the healing process, allowing a disease-free body in the next incarnation.

As I understand it, after each incarnation and the dissolution of the soul vehicles (the etheric, astral and mental bodies), the so-called "permanent atoms" are left. These are atoms of physical, astral and mental matter around which the bodies for a new incarnation are formed. I think I can imagine a bit the magical way in which the soul builds first the mental, then the astral and subsequently the etheric-physical bodies, but I cannot understand how the soul makes the connection between all these bodies and the dense physical body that is developing inside a mother's uterus. Is the soul also involved in making this dense physical body, otherwise how can it ensure that this dense physical body will have the same vibratory rate as its physical permanent atom? Can you please explain this matter? (October 2000)

The link between the soul and the dense physical is the nervous system, through which soul energy is carried and distributed. Through tiny channels called 'nadis' the soul distributes its energies as a gas (not yet discovered by science).

How can an individual assess his or her stage in evolution?
(June 1998)

It is a question of awareness, as is everything. The easiest way,
just as a 'starter', is to look in the back of *Maitreya's Mission
Volume Three* and see the various individuals listed there. If you
study that list, it will give you some idea of where you stand.

If you are thinking that maybe you are a third-degree initiate
I would say to you: "What have you done in the world?" You
will find that Gandhi was 2.0, Picasso was 2.4, Cezanne 2.6,
Abraham Lincoln 3.3 degrees initiate. Ask yourself: what has
been your service to the world?

There is a saying with the Masters that the disciple is
recognized by his control of his environment, and the initiate by
the extent and nature of his world service. If you have done
nothing in the world it is not likely that you are a second, third
or higher degree initiate.

It is helpful to read the first of Alice Bailey's books,
Initiation, Human and Solar (Lucis Publishing Company),
which gives the requirements for each initiation. The first
initiation demonstrates control of the physical body (the
physical elemental that makes up the body); the second
demonstrates control of the astral/emotional body (the
astral/emotional elemental); the third initiation demonstrates the
control of the mental body (of the mental elemental); the fourth
releases the individual from the matter aspect; and the fifth
initiation, which is called the Resurrection — and all the
Masters are resurrected Beings — demonstrates a total absence
of any kind of response to the pull of matter.

Study *Initiation, Human and Solar*, and see where you stand
in relation to the requirements for each initiation, realizing that
they are the ideal and the ideal is seldom met. So you could take
the first initiation when you had not perfectly controlled, as you

would see it, the physical vehicle, or the second if you had not completely lost all personal glamour, and so on.

When an individual dies does his evolution stop until he is reincarnated? Per Maharishi, it does stop. (November 1998)

Yes, it does stop.

What happens to the soul and astral bodies of people who let their bodies be frozen after death because they hope that their bodies and they, themselves, will be repaired one day, so that they can go on living? (April 1997)

At death, the soul withdraws from its vehicle and no amount of "repairing" will restore the life — the soul — to reincarnate in that vehicle. In such a situation, the soul returns to its own plane and creates the bodies of its next incarnation. The astral vehicle dissipates and returns to the astral planes.

Most humans are afraid of death. Why? (December 1998)

Because of ignorance about the reality of life, including that phase of life we call death. People fear death because they think of it as the 'end' of themselves. When people realize that death is not the 'end' but the beginning of another phase of life and experience and consciousness, they will lose the fear of death. An understanding of the Law of Rebirth, and of the evolution of consciousness which it makes possible, will free us from this fear.

Will there be no more death? Will we have eternal life in the future? (November 1997)

Gradually, our approach to death will change. The fear of death will go as we realize it is but a phase in the eternal life we already have. When we have (as the Masters and higher initiates have) continuity of consciousness, we will come into and leave physical-plane expression in full awareness of the previous state. The Masters have conquered death — the body of an Ascended Master, for example, is totally indestructible.

*In **Maitreya's Mission Volume One**, you write about the importance of dying consciously (pp.244/245), in order to be able to lift the consciousness as high as possible, through the astral and mental planes. What possibilities exist today (and indeed in the future) in terms of practical preparation for dying consciously — courses, seminars, literature? What can you recommend?* (April 1997)

The writings of the Master Djwhal Khul through Alice A.Bailey; *The Tibetan Book of the Dead*; the writings of Elisabeth Kübler-Ross.

I am intrigued by the concept of "twin souls". I have heard what appear to be conflicting definitions. For instance, all definitions (except one source — which adds to my confusion) state that a person has only one twin for all incarnations. I love that! Is it true, and is this other person truly your "other half"? (June 1998)

Just as physical twinship is not universal (even if not rare), so, too, soul twinship is not universal; not everyone has a twin soul. When it occurs it remains for all incarnations. However, these twins are not necessarily in incarnation at the same time, nor are they necessarily of the opposite sex in any given incarnation.

The Law of Cause and Effect — Karma

Will Maitreya prove reincarnation? (July/August 1997)

Maitreya will certainly teach the *fact* of reincarnation as the basic Law — with the Law of Cause and Effect — governing evolution on our planet. The presence of historical figures (now as Masters) like Jesus, Saints Peter, John and Paul will prove it.

(1) Will the Reappearance of Maitreya resolve karma? (2) Does that mean that every individual soul graduates therefore in this school on earth? (September 1998)

(1) No. (2) They will, but not for that reason. A Master can 'adjust' karma but no one can take away our individual karma. Eventually we learn to resolve our karma ourselves.

What is the relationship between the Law of Love and the Law of Cause and Effect? (July/August 1999)

The Law of Cause and Effect is impersonal and 'scientific' in its action. However, under the Law of Love (especially when wielded by a Master) the Law of Cause and Effect can be mitigated and altered (this is reflected in the Christian idea of 'forgiveness of sins').

Would you say that people have hardship in their lives because they are not in correct relation to their souls? (June 1997)

The hardship of life is the result of the non-carrying-out of soul purpose. We come into incarnation under the Law of Rebirth but also in relation to the Law of Cause and Effect, and hardship is a result of previous misdeeds, personal or racial — we all share in racial karma.

Everything we do, every thought, every action we make, sets into motion a series of causes. The effects stemming from these causes make our lives, for good or ill. If we do harm, inevitably, in the course of time, that harm will rebound. We will call it 'hardship' or we may see it as 'bad luck', but there is no such thing as bad luck. Every painful thing that happens is a result of wrong action in a previous life or in a previous phase of this life; the result of the karmic working out of that past — thus freeing us from its cause.

There are also lives which are very painful — of the fourth-degree initiate like Jesus, for example. The life of the fourth-degree initiate is usually very hard indeed, but we cannot say that it is because He is not in correct relation to the soul — He *is* the soul; the fourth-degree initiate is a living soul, the personality is totally soul-infused, but he/she is working out the last knots of karma before the resurrection experience of the liberated Master.

To what extent are handicaps the result of past karma, as the England football coach Glenn Hoddle was recently sacked for saying? (March 1999)

This is a very complex question and the rather simplistic way that it was addressed by Mr Hoddle (if he was accurately quoted by the media) is what led to his dismissal, unjustly, as I see it. His statement about karma was used by ministers and sports media to hound him out of his post as coach on the premise that it outraged and insulted the disabled. Well, perhaps some disabled individuals might have been offended but the whole incident was lifted to hysterical levels by the political reaction of the Prime Minister Mr Blair, the Sports Minister Mr Banks and head of the Football Task Force Mr Mellor. Their knowledge of the Law of Karma and reincarnation leaves much to be desired and gives them no right to intervene. To answer the question: 25 per cent of born disabilities are karmically related to previous lives' misdeeds; 25 per cent are deliberate handicaps imposed by the soul for its (karmic) needs; 50 per cent are the result of inherited genetic weaknesses. A few are the result of birth trauma or accident.

282

Do these figures include autism?

Yes.

What is your opinion of the group calling itself "Ramala" in whose books the Lords of Karma are reputed to speak? (January/February 1999)

It is my understanding that the Lords of Karma can be contacted only by Masters of the sixth degree or above.

Health and Healing

I have heard that illness is a grace of God. Does the same apply to countries? (May 1998)

Everything that happens is connected with karma. There is world karma, for which we are all responsible, and there is individual karma. Everybody is responsible for world karma because we have all contributed to it over our hundreds of thousands of incarnations. Many of the floods and earthquakes and destructive conditions in the world are due to the effect of the wrong thought and action of humanity, not as individuals but as a whole.

We create destructive conditions because we are not in equilibrium ourselves. Many of us are full of hatred, of competition: always trying to get the better of somebody else, to get ahead of somebody else, to sell our goods before somebody else. The world is filled with competition.

Competition is the result of greed. Greed is the result of fear. Fear results from the sense of separation. If we did not feel separate, we would build the world as it can be, as it is planned to be, as it will be in the future. It is up to us. We are either destructive, or constructive; if we are destructive, we are at war with ourselves and with the society of which we are a part. We must learn to be harmless, to live in equilibrium with ourselves and our environment (which means other people and the planet as a whole) and so create equilibrium around us. When we are greedy and selfish and competitive, trying to get ahead of everybody, then inevitably we create dis-equilibrium. Then the devas who control the weather, the oceans, rain, and so on, go out of equilibrium, and we have the most extraordinary weather patterns, like now, around the planet. It is the result, to an extent, of our own imbalance. We have the illusion that we are separate, but in Cosmos there is no separation. Every atomic particle is related to every other atomic particle everywhere in Cosmos, so there is nothing we can do which does not have an effect for good or for ill somewhere in the world and in our own life.

The present organ transplants are done by recycling organs. When solar energy is used in medicine, will we no longer recycle organs? (May 1998)

No longer will we need transplants of organs from dead people. We shall simply go to a clinic, and, with an advanced form of genetic engineering and light from the sun, entirely new hearts, new livers, new kidneys and so on, will be built into the body in a few hours. You will go home a new person with your own heart, not a transplant.

How can the process of organ regeneration be reconciled with karma? If you go to a hospital today and get a transplant or a medicine that makes you better, does that affect your karma? (May 1998)

If you have somebody else's heart, then, of course, it affects karma, but if it is a regeneration of your own heart, your own liver, then, of course, it does not affect your karma. But it makes you fitter on the physical plane.

Is being a vegetarian required to be a disciple? Does this allow eating eggs, fish, dairy products? (May 1999)

The Master Djwahl Khul has said that eggs are not good for anybody who wants to develop his psychic abilities. They should either be given up altogether or eaten only very rarely. It is up to you. If you know something is holding you back in evolution, it is best to eat it as little as possible. Meat should be

285

dispensed with for anyone reaching at least the first initiation, and I am sure a Master would say for all further initiations as well. The vibration in the blood of animals is inimical to our spiritual progress. It holds back the evolution, and so, if you are trying to heighten the vibrational rate of your vehicles to bring in more light, you are better not to eat meat.

The interesting thing is that aspirants of their own free will often become vegetarians as they approach the first initiation. Many young people are coming up to the first initiation and that is why they have become vegetarians. They may not know that, but the soul is impressing them to give up meat-eating.

My Master says that fish comes under another category. Its vibrational rate is neutral. It does not help, but neither does it hinder, the evolutionary process. If you live in areas of the world where there is little protein, then, of course, fish will provide the protein without lowering the vibrational rate of the body. Jesus and His disciples ate fish and goat's cheese pretty well every day. Fish, goat's cheese and bread was the main diet of Jesus and His brethren.

Dairy products are acceptable but not with too much fat. Preferable are products like goat's cheese (and other cheeses) and milk. Not too much butter, because of the cholesterol, but better a tiny bit of butter than a lot of margarine.

Nobody is made to give up meat-eating but if you are intent on heightening the vibrational rate of your vehicles, then it does become necessary. The Master Dwhal Khul (through Alice Bailey) writes that there is no such thing as a Group diet.

Are dairy products generally counter-indicated? I personally prefer to avoid eating them, but to keep calcium levels up (especially in women) it is said to be advisable to consume a fair amount of dairy products. (May 1999)

There are no fixed rules. A moderate amount of dairy products should be acceptable unless there is a specific allergy to their use.

(1) How detrimental to health is MSG (monosodium glutamate), the preservative sometimes used in Chinese restaurant food? (2) How does MSG affect a person's ability for effective Transmission Meditation? (December 1997)

(1) Slightly. (2) Not at all.

How beneficial are flash-dried, powdered fruits and vegetables? How effective are they as a substitute for fresh fruit and vegetables? (December 1997)

Flash-dried fruit and vegetables are less nutritious.

As I have a few amalgam fillings in the teeth like many other people I am interested to know if this kind of filling is poisonous, because it contains a lot of mercury. Some scientists say it damages organs like the liver and it also damages the brain. It may even be that Alzheimer's disease is caused by these amalgam fillings. Is this true? (October 1999)

No, not true; the amount of mercury in the amalgam is only small.

Could you give a general esoteric cause of allergies? (March 2000)

The cause is not esoteric but is very down-to-earth. The growth of allergies — there are millions of people today with allergies who never had them before — is a direct result of the pollution of the planet. Our air, water, soil, the food we eat, all are polluted by many substances and poisons. The worst of all is the nuclear radiation that spills out from the nuclear power-stations and the nuclear experimentation which is still going on. That is the greatest danger; it breaks down the immune system, and the allergies are the result of this breakdown. These allergic reactions are appearing worldwide. The Masters say pollution, particularly radioactive pollution, is the number-one killer in the world. The sooner we close down our nuclear power stations and all nuclear experimentation of the fission kind, the better for humanity.

What is the advice of the Masters about vaccinations? So many children seem to be adversely affected by them; it is a shame homoeopathy does not promote itself as a viable and safe alternative. Should we not do away with vaccinations altogether? (October 2000)

On the whole, vaccination has been beneficial in eradicating several severe children's illnesses. Homoeopathic 'nosodes' (vaccines) are available for most of these diseases but until homoeopathy is more widely known and accepted (which is slowly happening) vaccination will remain the 'normal' mode. It would be dangerous to "do away with vaccination altogether".

As a schizophrenic I'd like to ask whether there are ways of curing these illnesses, other than those employed at present? Is there a more esoteric approach? (July/August 2000)

Their cure, on a regular basis, depends on a greater understanding of the functioning of the endocrine system and its relation to the body's fluctuating chemistry. This, in turn, depends on an understanding of the etheric body and the chakras or force centres. This will come in time.

Do Maitreya, Sai Baba and the Masters heal people with psychiatric/psychological illnesses? (I myself am such a person, hence my question.) (March 1997)

Yes, if the karma of the person allows.

You have stated that skin cancer is not caused by exposure to the sun. Why do New Zealand and Australia have a high incidence of skin cancer, with their well-documented ozone deficiencies? (December 1997)

White skins lack natural protection. Australian and New Zealand indigenous peoples do not get skin cancer.

What causes "Chronic Fatigue Syndrome"? Some say it is a virus, others that this is a glorified name for depression. (December 1997)

It has an *emotional* origin, usually from an ill-fitting life-style.

(1) Could you tell me what is the origin of dyslexia and (2) is it easy to cure? (March 1999)

(1) There are various degrees of dyslexia, a malfunction of the perceptual faculties in the brain. (2) No. Strategies have been devised to cope with it.

I have read research that ozone therapy cures nearly all diseases, including cancer and AIDS, based on the theory that most diseases cannot exist in an oxygen-rich environment. Would your Master care to comment? (March 1999)

Theoretically true. In practice it is difficult to pinpoint and treat the disease without side-effects on the system as a whole.

(1) Is depression on the increase? (2) If so, would this be due to more people coming up to the first initiation? (3) Or is it because the rise in materialism means that we are more in conflict with our true Self? (April 1997)

(1) No. There is better awareness of this condition today. (2) No. (3) This is true but it gives rise to many other stressful conditions.

What do you think about the effect of electro-magnetic waves on human bodies: (1) Are they harmful to humans? (2) Nowadays they sell a sticker which is said to protect us from these waves. Should I buy one? (July/August 1997)

(1) We live in an electrical universe and these "waves" are everywhere. It depends very much on the voltage or potency, but in normal circumstances they are not harmful. (2) It is up to you, but I would not; I doubt that they would work.

Is ginseng of any value for the health? (July/August 1997)

Yes. It has very definite tonic properties. To my mind it is best used in homoeopathic potency (30c).

In the assistance of healthy birthing, mothers and midwives generally favour home birth and creating a spiritual, peaceful environment for the mother and the child. (1) Do the Masters view the way in which the child enters the world (ie methods of delivery, natural or unnatural, the environment) as impactful upon the personality and having lasting psychological effects, as some people claim? (November 1998)

Yes. Birth is difficult enough and should be as natural as possible.

In a past issue of **Share International** *in the Questions and Answers section, you said men could help prevent prostate cancer by drinking filtered water. (1) Could it also be said that women could help prevent breast cancer by drinking filtered water? (2) What other illnesses could be prevented by doing this?* (September 1997)

Please note that drinking filtered water is not a preventative or cure of prostate cancer. It simply helps to reduce the toxic pollution in our drinking water and so reduces the risk. (1) No, but everyone should drink filtered (by the best method affordable) water. (2) Filtered water should not be seen as a *preventative* of illness but as a common-sense precautionary measure to lessen our intake of pollution — the main cause of illness today.

Does hypoglycaemia have emotional origins? (June 1999)

Yes.

Does brain death mean the death of the human being? (July/August 1997)

Yes.

Results of studies in the UK and the US show that children are reaching puberty much earlier than previous generations. The Bristol University's (UK) "Children of the nineties" study shows that one in six girls in the UK is reaching puberty by the age of eight compared to one in 100 a generation ago; and one in 14 boys aged eight have pubic hair, compared to one in 150 in their fathers' generation. What is the reason for the onset of such early puberty? (September 2000)

(1) Oestrogen in water (from contraceptive pills) 40 per cent. (2) Diet 20 per cent. (3) Early sexual activity (various) 30 per cent.

(4) Natural maturing (with the incoming 7th-ray energy and consequent stimulation of the gonads) 10 per cent.

On Women's Health

Hormonal imbalances and emotionality seem to go hand in hand. (1) Are hormonal imbalances most pronounced in the astrally polarized? (2) Does an emotional, astral nature tend to more pronounced problems with such imbalances? (November 1997)

(1) Yes. (2) Yes.

Do mentally polarized women have fewer imbalances? (November 1997)

Yes.

(1) Do such imbalances impede the life of the female disciple? (2) Do such imbalances have any effect in obstructing soul contact? (November 1997)

(1) To some extent, yes. (2) No.

Does the pouring in of the new energies intensify women's hormonal imbalances? (November 1997)

No.

Are there any physical things that a woman can do to help bring her hormones into balance (other than those things the medical people say)? (November 1997)

Diet has a large part to play in this. A vitamin-rich diet is recommended. Exercise and regulated rest is essential too. The use of Tlacote or Nordenau water (or tablets) is recommended.

Would it help women going through hormonal problems (a) to meditate more? (b) to do more Transmission Meditation? (November 1997)

(a) No. (b) Yes.

(a) Is it occasionally helpful to take hormone drugs? Which ones? (b) Are homoeopathics helpful? (c) Are Tlacote water tablets helpful? (November 1997)

(a) Yes. On individual prescription. (b) Yes. (c) Yes.

What about sex: (a) Does more sex help balance the hormones? (b) Do repressed sexual energies produce this imbalance? (c) Can masturbation help? (d) Is the hormone problem a result of wrong attitudes about sex? (November 1997)

(a) No. (b) No. (c) No. (d) To some extent.

Esoterically, what is the significance of the menopause: (a) Does a person experience the menopause etherically before physically? (b) Do men experience any type of menopause? (November 1997)

(a) No. (b) No — they do not have menses!

(a) Do hormonal imbalances relate to women's higher ability to transmit the Christ's energies? (b) Are such imbalances a resistance to those energies? (c) Are certain physical ray-types more or less vulnerable to these problems? (November 1997)

(a) No. (b) No. (c) Rays 2, 4, 6 are more vulnerable; rays 7, 3, 5, 1 are less vulnerable.

Energy Healing

(1) When Reiki is transmitted to a patient is it true that you are not able to transmit any negative energies from the therapist, or receive this from the patient? (2) Which is the real origin of Reiki in human history? (3) Is it positive for humans to use the Reiki energies in its actual evolutive stage? (April 1999)

(1) No. (2) Late Atlantean. (3) At an early stage, yes.

You once said that Reiki is good for people of a certain level. Please tell us which degree you mean? (May 2000)

Up to the first initiation.

Is there any Master of the Hierarchy working with the Reiki energies? (April 1999)

No.

(1) Some of my friends are using Reiki energies for healing. Could your Master explain where these energies come from and (2) do these energies have any connection with Maitreya? (November 1998)

(1) The sixth Astral plane. (2) No.

Is Tachyon energy, a treatment offered to people in the USA and Germany, really helpful and beneficial? Is it healing energy? (May 2000)

It is astral energy and helpful for healing at an astral level.

Happiness

How can we keep happy? (May 1997)

Serve. The happiest people I know are the people involved in the Reappearance work. What makes them happy is the idea that Maitreya is in the world, and that the ills of the world, the pain, the suffering, the lack of opportunity for millions of people will stop. I do not mean in a day, a week, or even a year. But the process of transformation will take place. That makes them happy; that is what has kept them happy for years.

You are happy because you are cognizant, aware, and experiencing the major events of our time, of any time. Never has there been a time like this. The people involved in the work can experience it at a very purposeful level, which gives them this inner happiness. Most people involved in this work have a kind of inner secret. They know what is happening, and it keeps them alive, vivid, awake, alert — and happy. Also, we have Transmission Meditation.

How can I become aware of my true Divine nature and thus realize inner peace, love and a sense of purpose and belonging? (December 1998)

The age-old, the classic, way is through meditation and service. By meditation we contact our soul — which is our Divinity — and, soul-inspired, turn to service to the world.

Awareness of the Self

What is the most direct way to move beyond the illusion we call life and experience reality, or God, directly? (July 2000)

Maitreya says the simplest way is to identify with who and what we are, the Self or God. He says: "Ask yourself, who am I?"

You will find that you identify with your physical body, your emotions, or your thoughts. "But you are none of these," He says. You identify with them, but they are not you. You are the Self, an immortal being. Our problems, our pain and suffering, are a result of the fact that we identify with everything and anything other than the immortal Self.

Maitreya has given to the world *A Prayer for the New Age*. If repeated daily, the prayer will gradually confer an awareness of the Self. That awareness eventually develops into Self-realization, which is perfection.

The prayer is very simple.

I am the creator of the universe.
I am the father and mother of the universe.
Everything came from me.
Everything shall return to me.
Mind, spirit and body are my temples,
For the Self to realize in them
My supreme Being and Becoming.

Say the prayer with focused attention as many times per day as you wish. Gradually you will become aware of yourself in a different way. You will begin to be more detached. You will begin to see that you are not the body, the emotions, or the mind. You are not this memory which relates you as a person to your job and your family. You will relate more and more to the Self.

In addition to the prayer, Maitreya has said there are three things one can practise: honesty of mind, sincerity of spirit, and detachment. He calls these three practices the simplest way to obtain Self-awareness or Self-realization.

Most people think one thing, say something else, and do something else again. There is no direct line from their thoughts to their actions. This leads to confusion and destructiveness. This is not honesty of mind. Honesty of mind leads to honest speech and honest action. Peace and happiness can be achieved through this harmony.

Sincerity of spirit means not imitating other people, not pretending, not trying to appear different from what you are. Sincerity of spirit is not taking on somebody else's 'garments', not imitating your favourite film or pop star. It is simply being yourself.

If you are an artist, musician, writer or poet, the most interesting thing you can be is you, not somebody else through you. Imitation in art and music is looked down upon. Imitation in life is somehow not looked down upon, but it is just as important. Art, music or literary expression are part of the life expression. This is certainly as valuable and personal, and has to be as original, as you yourself are. Each person is unique. You have to give expression to that uniqueness. That doesn't mean you have to do everything contrary to what is normally known and accepted, but it does mean you have to be yourself.

When you see Maitreya you will find He speaks directly from His heart to your heart. Your heart centre will resonate in response to what He has to say. It will seem so pure, so absolutely, essentially, true. You will have no difficulty in accepting what He says because it will penetrate to the very core of your being. That is why it is expected that once He speaks openly to the world it will not be long before the Day of Declaration occurs.

The third practice is detachment from identifying yourself as the physical body, the emotional body, or the constructions of the mind, the mental body. One day you believe one thing, ten years later you believe something else. There is no consistency in the mind. What you take to be your mind is only memory, experiences that you had yesterday. But this moment is the only moment which exists. You are living now at this very moment in time. That is the only reality that exists. All the rest is memory and is to do with the ability to communicate and work on the physical plane in a way that makes sense. If you agree, for example, to meet somebody at 8 o'clock and take the train to Washington, they will be there at the right platform. Time for us is a convenience. Seen as the Masters see it, the past, the present and the future are all happening at this very moment now. What we call our memory is not the Self, and cannot be the Self.

The Self is something quite different. That Self is an immortal spiritual Being. It reflects itself as a human soul, which in turn reflects itself at this level as the human personality. The path of evolution is the reuniting of the personality with the soul, and the soul/personality together with the Spark of God, the Divine Self. The more detached you become, the more these things can take place. Maitreya says: "When you are detached all becomes possible. Where you are attached you cannot know Me. There I cannot be. But where you are detached there I am always with you."

These three, honesty of mind, sincerity of spirit, and detachment, if practised seriously and consistently, together with the Prayer for the New Age, can bring a person quickly to an understanding and experience of him or herself in a new way: a new freedom, spontaneity and directness, and a growing absence of fear and conflict will gradually make their presence felt.

The political and economic transformation which will be initiated as a result of Maitreya's and the Masters' presence will free humanity from age-old inhibitions and limitations, and galvanize it into a great leap forward in consciousness. Conscious, meaningful living will replace the present confusion, doubt and fear. A confident, courageous willingness to explore both inner and outer worlds will supplant the present weakening cynicism and make possible the evolutionary advance I have sought to describe: the emergence of a new and better civilization and of a new and better humanity.

APPENDIX

List of Maitreya's Appearances

The following is the summary of Maitreya's miraculous appearances to orthodox religious groups worldwide. It is arranged by country in alphabetical order rather than by dates. A water source in the vicinity where He appeared was charged by Him with cosmic energy before the appearance, causing the water to possess extraordinary healing properties. In addition, at each appearance, some of those in attendance were healed of their illnesses.

This information is given to Benjamin Creme by his Master and published monthly in *Share International* magazine.

Country	City	Year	Date	Audience (approx.)
Afghanistan	Haidar Khel	1999	20 Nov	250 Muslims
Afghanistan	Kabul	1993	13 Jun	1,800 Muslims
Afghanistan	Kabul	1996	3 Nov	400 Muslims
Afghanistan	Quandahar	1998	30 Aug	300 Muslims
Algeria	Ouargla	1998	15 Feb	100 Muslims
Argentina	Bahia Blanca	1998	8 Feb	600 Christians
Argentina	Bahia Blanca	2000	30 Apr	200 Christians
Argentina	Buenos Aires	1995	22 Oct	400 Catholics
Argentina	Lake Colhué Huapi, Pat.	2001	21 Jan	No appearance, water charged
Argentina	Mendoza	1997	5 Oct	100 Christians
Argentina	Neuquén	1998	31 May	200 Christians
Argentina	San Juan	1998	8 Nov	200 Christians
Argentina	San Miguel de Tucuman	1997	9 Mar	400 Catholics
Australia	Canberra	2000	30 Jan	150 Christians
Australia	Perth	2000	24 Dec	200 Christians
Australia	Sydney	1995	28 May	300 Christians
Austria	Graz	1998	22 Mar	400 Christians
Austria	Vienna	1992	19 Jul	900 Catholics
Bahrain	'Awali	2000	2 Jul	300 Muslims
Belgium	Brussels	1993	25 Jul	500 Catholics
Bolivia	La Paz	1997	2 Mar	250 Catholics
Bolivia	Oruro	1998	6 Sep	250 Christians

Bosnia	Sarajevo	1993	18 Jul	No appearance, water charged
Brazil	São Paulo	1998	20 Sep	150 Christians
Bulgaria	Varna	1997	18 May	300 Christians
Bulgaria	Sofia	1993	8 Aug	800 Christians
Bulgaria	Sofia	1993	22 Aug	800 Christians
Canada	Baie St Paul, Quebec	1996	1 Sep	200 Catholics
Canada	Edmonton, Alberta	1996	27 Oct	65 Christians
Canada	Laval, Quebec	2000	24 Sep	150 Christians
Canada	Montreal, Quebec	1994	13 Mar	600 Christians
Canada	Ottawa, Ontario	1994	6 Nov	600 Christians
Canada	Quebec	1998	19 Apr	300 Christian
Canada	Quesnel, B.C.	2000	2 Apr	80 Christians
Canada	Regina, Saskat.	1999	19 Sep	100 Christians
Canada	Saskatoon, Saskat.	1995	1 Oct	200 Christians
Canada	Toronto, Ontario	1998	1 Mar	300 Christians
Canada	Vancouver, B.C.	1995	5 Nov	300 Christians
Chechnya		1997	10 Aug	200 Christians
Chile	Puerto Natales	1997	13 Jul	350 Catholics
China	Beijing	1995	6 Aug	700 Buddhists
China	Chungking	1996	8 Sep	300 Christians
China	Shanghai	1997	19 Jan	250 Christians
China	Xiangtan	2000	23 Jul	200 Christians
China	Zaozhuang	1998	12 Apr	300 Christians
China	Zhengzhou	1999	1 Aug	200 Muslims
Colombia	Bogota	1997	2 Feb	500 Christians
Colombia	Bucaramanga	2000	13 Feb	160 Christians
Colombia	Medellin	1998	5 Jul	200 Christians
Congo Republic	Kisangani	1997	17 Aug	300 Christians
Congo Republic	Mbuji-Mayi	1998	26 Jul	200 Christians
Croatia	Osijek	2000	3 Sep	150 Christians
Croatia	Zagreb	1999	22 Aug	100 Christians
Cyprus	Limassol	1998	27 Dec	200 Christians
Cyprus	Nicosia	1993	31 Oct	800 Christians
Czech Republic	Prague	1992	16 Aug	600 Christians
Denmark	Copenhagen	1993	17 Oct	600 Christians
Denmark	Copenhagen	1994	14 Aug	300 Christians
Ecuador	Guayaquil	1997	6 Jul	300 Catholics
Ecuador	Quito	1996	9 Jun	300 Catholics
Egypt	Cairo	1996	14 Apr	800 Muslims
Egypt	Cairo	1997	25 May	1,000 Muslims
Eritrea	Asmara	1999	17 Oct	60 Christians
Finland	Helsinki	1994	6 Feb	700 Christians
Finland	Helsinki	1995	12 Feb	200 Christian
Finland	Kuopio	1996	29 Sep	200 Christians
France	Amiens	1997	27 Jul	200 Christians
France	Lyons	1996	10 Mar	250 Catholics
France	Orléans	1994	24 Apr	500 Catholics
France	Paris	1994	5 Jun	800 Catholics

Gabon	Libreville	2000	29 Oct	150 Christians
Gambia	Banjul	2000	4 Jun	
Georgia	Tbilisi	1992	18 Oct	600 Christians
Germany	Düsseldorf	1992	26 Apr	650 Christians
Germany	Frankfurt	1994	11 Dec	700 Catholics
Germany	Hanover	1992	5 Apr	800 Christians
Germany	Leipzig	1992	22 Mar	950 Christians
Germany	Zittau	1999	28 Nov	100 Christians
Greece	Athens	1994	9 Oct	900 Christians
Greece	Ioánnina	1995	12 Mar	400 Christians
Greece	Thessaloniki	1998	9 Aug	200 Christians
Holland	Amsterdam	1995	26 Feb	400 Baptists
Iceland	Reykjavík	1998	29 Nov	120 Christians
Iraq	Baghdad	1994	18 Dec	800 Muslims
Ireland	Dublin	1995	1 Jan	700 Catholic
Italy	Palermo, Sicily	1994	10 Apr	400 Catholics
Italy	Palermo, Sicily	1995	5 Mar	500 Catholics
Italy	Rome	1993	27 Jun	900 Catholics
Italy	Rome	1993	19 Sep	600 Catholics
Italy	Rome	1994	25 Dec	500 Catholics
Italy	Rome	1996	7 Jan	300 Catholics
Jamaica	Kingston	1994	24 Jul	500 Christians
Japan	Kobe	1996	29 Dec	400 Buddhists
Japan	Kyoto	2001	14 Jan	50 Christians
Japan	Nagasaki	1997	9 Nov	300 Buddhists
Japan	Osaka	1995	29 Jan	400 Buddhists
Kazakhstan	Ayaguz	1996	15 Dec	200 Muslims
Kazakhstan		1995	19 Nov	300 Muslims
Kenya	Nairobi	1988	11 Jun	6,000 Christians
Kenya	Nairobi	1994	6 Mar	500 Christians
Madagascar	Antananarivo	1995	11 Jun	300 Christians
Mexico	Hermosillo	1998	27 Sep	150 Christians
Mexico	Mexico City	1991	29 Sep	600 Christians
Mexico	Mexico City	1992	26 Jan	800 Christians
Mexico	Villahermosa	1998	5 Apr	200 Christians
Mongolia	Ulan Bator	1995	23 Apr	400 Buddhists
Morocco	Bouânane Figuig	1996	26 May	300 Muslims
Morocco	Fez	1999	14 Feb	300 Muslims
Morocco	Marrakesh	1995	9 Jul	400 Muslims
Morocco	Rabat	1997	13 Apr	600 Muslims
Mozambique	Mozambique	1996	17 Mar	200 Christians
New Zealand	Christchurch	1999	24 Oct	50 Christians
New Zealand	Wellington	1994	11 Sep	600 Christians
Nicaragua	Managua	2000	19 Mar	25 Christians
Nigeria	Kano	1997	12 Oct	400 Christians
Nigeria	Lagos	1998	1 Nov	200 Muslims
Norway	Oslo	1993	17 Jan	700 Lutherans
Pakistan	Lahore	1995	27 Aug	900 Muslims
Pakistan	Peshawar	2000	12 Nov	150 Christians

Pakistan	Peshawar	2000	12 Nov	150 Christians
Peru	Lima	1997	5 Jan	500 Christians
Philippines		1994	29 May	400 Christians
Poland	Kraców	1994	21 Aug	600 Catholics
Poland	Kraców	1997	20 Apr	300 Christians
Poland	Lublin	1999	24 Jul	150 Christians
Poland	Silesia	1999	26 Sep	100 Christians
Poland	Warsaw	1993	3 Oct	800 Catholics
Portugal	Lisbon	1995	29 Oct	400 Catholics
Portugal	Oporto	1995	26 Nov	600 Catholics
Portugal	Oporto	1997	30 Nov	200 Christians
Romania	Brasov	1997	11 May	250 Christians
Romania	Bucharest	1992	27 Dec	900 Christians
Romania	Bucharest	1993	7 Feb	Christians
Romania	Iasi	1997	16 Feb	300 Christians
Romania	Vaslui	2000	10 Dec	180 Christians
Russia	Kazan	1998	25 Oct	300 Christians
Russia	Moscow	1992	1 Mar	600 Christians
Russia	Moscow	1995	30 Apr	300 Christians
Russia	Novgorod	1996	11 Aug	150 Christians
Russia	Omsk	1998	17 May	150 Christians
Russia	St Petersburg	1992	27 Sep	900 Christians
Russia	St Petersburg	1994	27 Mar	700 Christians
Russia	Ust Kut	1997	4 May	300 Muslims
Russia	Vladivostok	1995	23 Jul	700 Christians
Russia	Volgograd	1996	2 Jun	800 Muslims
Russia	Volsk	1995	21 May	400 Christians
Russia	Yakutsk	1993	4 Apr	400 people
Serbia	Belgrade	1992	8 Nov	
Serbia	Vrsac	1997	27 Apr	300 Christians
Slovakia	Republic Bratislava	1992	13 Sep	500 Christians
Slovenia	Ljubljana	1996	4 Feb	300 Christians
Somalia	Mogadishu	1996	1 Dec	300 Muslims
South Africa	Bloemfontein	1994	2 Jan	700 Christians
South Africa	Durban	1995	17 Sep	400 Christians
South Africa	Johannesburg	1993	12 Dec	500 Christians
South Africa	Pietermaritzburg	1993	5 Sep	800 Catholics
South Korea	Seoul	1994	28 Aug	700 Buddhists
South Korea	Seoul	1996	17 Nov	450 Buddhists
Spain	Barcelona	1994	1 May	700 Catholics
Spain	La Coruña	1995	24 Sep	300 Catholics
Spain	Santander	1995	14 May	700 Catholics
Sudan	Khartoum	1999	23 May	150 Muslims
Swaziland	Mbabane	1996	8 Dec	300 Christians
Sweden	Malmberget	1999	14 Mar	120 Christians
Sweden	Stockholm	1994	30 Jan	400 Lutherans
Sweden	Stockholm	1995	8 Jan	400 Lutherans
Sweden	Uppsala	1996	28 Apr	300 Lutherans
Switzerland	Baden	1999	12 Sep	100 Christians

Switzerland	Biel	1999	21 Feb	150 Christians
Switzerland	Geneva	1992	24 May	600 Christians
Switzerland	Zürich	1992	28 Jun	700 Christians
Tanzania	Dodoma	1995	13 Aug	500 Christians
Tanzania	Mwanza	1997	3 Aug	500 Christians
Tanzania	Tabora	2000	28 May	250 Christians
Tanzania	Zanzibar	1995	17 Dec	300 Muslims
Tanzania	Zanzibar	1999	5 Dec	200 Christians
Thailand	Bangkok	1994	13 Feb	600 Buddhists
Thailand	Phitsanulok	2000	26 Mar	300 Buddhists
Thailand	Phrae	1997	21 Sep	150 Buddhists
Trinidad	Port of Spain	1994	16 Jan	600 Christians
Trinidad	Port of Spain	1997	31 Aug	250 Christians
Turkey	Ankara	1996	14 Jan	500 Muslims
Turkey	Istanbul	1994	19 Jun	700 Christians
Turkey	Istanbul	1995	5 Feb	700 Muslims
Turkey	Izmir (Smyrna)	1999	10 Jan	200 Christians
Uganda	Kampala	1994	9 Jan	600 Christians
UK	Aberdeen, Scotland	1995	16 Apr	400 Christians
UK	Cardiff, Wales	1994	4 Dec	400 Christians
UK	Edinburgh, Scotland	1992	13 Dec	600 Christians
UK	Liverpool, England	1995	15 Oct	600 Christians
UK	South London, England	1994	31 Jul	400 Christians
UK	York, England	1993	21 Nov	700 Christians
Ukraine	Kiev	1999	10 Oct	100 Christians
Ukraine	Odessa	1999	31 Oct	400 Christians
Uruguay	Melo	1998	25 Jan	200 Christians
Uruguay	Mercedes	1998	21 Jun	150 Christians
Uruguay	Montevideo	1997	7 Sep	300 Christians
USA	Annapolis, Maryland	1999	7 Feb	100 Christians
USA	Ashland, Maine	1996	6 Oct	250 Christians
USA	Atlanta, Georgia	2000	3 Dec	250 Christians
USA	Birmingham, Alabama	2000	5 Nov	250 Christians
USA	Charlotte, N.Carolina	1996	30 Jun	300 Christians
USA	Chicago, Illinois	1996	23 Jun	300 Christians
USA	Chicago, Illinois	1999	25 Apr	500 Christians
USA	Denver, Colorado	1996	25 Feb	300 Christians
USA	Detroit, Michigan	1996	28 Jul	300 Christians
USA	Elko, Nevada	1996	28 Jan	300 Mormons
USA	Flagstaff, Arizona	1996	5 May	200 Christians
USA	Jackson, Mississippi	1999	7 Mar	200 Christians
USA	Kansas City	1995	4 Jun	Christians
USA	Phoenix, Arizona	1995	9 Apr	700 people
USA	Portland, Oregon	1998	4 Jan	400 Christians
USA	Richmond, Virginia	1993	28 Feb	Christians
USA	Salt Lake City, Utah	1997	6 Apr	300 Mormons
USA	San Antonio, Texas	1993	21 Mar	500 Baptists
USA	Washington, DC	1996	24 Mar	600 Christians
Uzbekistan	Tashkent	1993	25 Apr	800 Muslims

Uzbekistan	Samarkand	2000	20 Feb	250 Muslims
Venezuela	Barcelona	2000	12 Mar	120 Christians
Venezuela	Caracas	1995	25 Jun	400 Baptists
Venezuela	San Cristobal	1997	8 Jun	300 Christians
Venezuela	San Cristobal	1999	18 Apr	200 Christians
Venezuela	San Fernando	1996	22 Dec	300 Catholics

THE PRAYER FOR THE NEW AGE

I am the creator of the universe.

I am the father and mother of the universe.

Everything came from me.

Everything shall return to me.

Mind, spirit and body are my temples,

For the Self to realize in them

My supreme Being and Becoming.

The Prayer for the New Age, given by Maitreya, the World Teacher, is a great mantram or affirmation with an invocative effect. It will be a powerful tool in the recognition by us that man and God are One, that there is no separation. The 'I' is the Divine Principle behind all creation. The Self emanates from, and is identical to, the Divine Principle.

The most effective way to use this mantram is to say or think the words with focused will, while holding the attention at the ajna centre between the eyebrows. When the mind grasps the meaning of the concepts, and simultaneously the will is brought to bear, those concepts will be activated and the mantram will work. If it is said seriously every day, there will grow inside you a realization of your true Self.

THE GREAT INVOCATION

From the point of Light within the Mind of God
Let light stream forth into the minds of men.
Let Light descend on Earth.

From the point of Love within the Heart of God
Let love stream forth into the hearts of men.
May Christ return to Earth.

From the centre where the Will of God is known
Let purpose guide the little wills of men —
The Purpose which the Masters know and serve.

From the centre which we call the race of men
Let the Plan of Love and Light work out
And may it seal the door where evil dwells.

Let Light and Love and Power
Restore the Plan on Earth.

The Great Invocation, used by the Christ for the first time in
June 1945, was released by Him to humanity to enable us to
invoke the energies which would change our world and make
possible the return of the Christ and Hierarchy. This World
Prayer, translated into many languages, is not sponsored by any
group or sect. It is used daily by men and women of goodwill
who wish to bring about right human relations among all
humanity.

FURTHER READING

The Reappearance of the Christ and the Masters of Wisdom
by Benjamin Creme

Creme's first book gives the background and pertinent information concerning the return of Maitreya, the Christ. A vast range of subjects is covered, including: the effect of the reappearance on the world's institutions, the Antichrist and forces of evil, the soul and reincarnation, telepathy, nuclear energy, ancient civilizations, the problems of the developing world and a new economic order.
ISBN #0-936604-00-X, 256 pages

Maitreya's Mission — Vol. I by Benjamin Creme

Presents further developments in the emergence of Maitreya and also covers a wide range of subjects, including the work and teachings of Maitreya, the externalization of the Masters, life ahead in the New Age, evolution and initiation, meditation and service, the Seven Rays.
ISBN #90-71484-08-4, 411 pages

Maitreya's Mission — Vol. II by Benjamin Creme

Offers unique information on such subjects as meditation, growth of consciousness, psychology, health, the environment, world service, and science and technology in the New Age. The process of Maitreya's public emergence is updated. Also explains such phenomena as crop circles, crosses of light, visions of the Madonna, healing wells, and UFOs. *ISBN #90-71484-11-4, 718 pages*

Maitreya's Mission — Vol. III by Benjamin Creme

A chronicle of the next millennium. Political, economic and social structures that will guarantee the necessities of life for all people. New ways of thinking that will reveal the mysteries of the universe and release our divine potential — all guided and inspired by Maitreya and the Masters of Wisdom. Includes compilation of ray structures and points of evolution of all 950 initiates given in *Maitreya's Mission*, Vols. I and II, and in *Share International* magazine.
ISBN #90-71484-15-7, 704 pages

Transmission: A Meditation for the New Age
by Benjamin Creme

Describes a dynamic group process of stepping down powerful spiritual energies directed by the Masters of Wisdom. Introduced by Benjamin Creme, at the request of his own Master, this potent world service stimulates both planetary transformation and personal growth of the individuals participating.
4th Edition. ISBN #90-71484-17-3, 204 pp

Messages from Maitreya the Christ

During the years of preparation for His emergence, Maitreya gave 140 Messages through Benjamin Creme during public lectures. The method used was mental overshadowing and the telepathic rapport thus set up. The Messages inspire readers to spread the news of His reappearance and to work urgently for the rescue of millions suffering from poverty and starvation in a world of plenty.
2nd Edition. ISBN #90-71484-22-X, 283 pages

A Master Speaks

Articles by Benjamin Creme's Master from the first 12 volumes of *Share International* magazine. The book includes such topics as: reason and intuition, health and healing, life in the New Age, glamour, human rights, Maitreya's mission, the role of man.
2nd Edition. ISBN #90-71484-10-6, 256 pages

The Ageless Wisdom Teaching

This introduction to humanity's spiritual legacy covers the major principles: the Divine Plan, source of the teaching, evolution of human consciousness, the Spiritual Hierarchy, energies, the Seven Rays, karma, reincarnation, initiation, and more. Includes a glossary of esoteric terms. *ISBN #90-71484-13-0, 62 pages*

The above books have been translated and published in Chinese, Dutch, French, German, Greek, Italian, Japanese, Romanian, Russian, Spanish, and Swedish by groups responding to this message. Further translations are projected. Books, as well as audio and video cassettes, are available from local booksellers.

Share International

A UNIQUE MAGAZINE featuring each month: • up-to-date information about Maitreya, the World Teacher • an article from a Master of Wisdom • expansions of the esoteric teachings • articles by and interviews with people on the leading edge in every field of endeavour • news from UN agencies and reports of positive developments in the transformation of our world • Benjamin Creme's answers to a variety of topical questions submitted by subscribers and the public.

Share International brings together the two major directions of New Age thinking — the political and the spiritual. It shows the synthesis underlying the political, social, economic, and spiritual changes now occurring on a global scale, and seeks to stimulate practical action to rebuild our world along more just and compassionate lines.

Share International covers news, events, and comments bearing on Maitreya's priorities: an adequate supply of the right food, adequate housing and shelter for all, healthcare as a universal right, the maintenance of ecological balance in the world.

Abridged versions of *Share International* are available in Dutch, French, German, Japanese, Romanian, and Spanish. For subscription information, contact the appropriate office below. [ISSN #0169-1341]

Excerpts from the magazine are published on the World Wide Web at: *http://www.share-international.org.*

For North, Central, and South America,
Australia, New Zealand and the Philippines
Share International
P.O. Box 971, North Hollywood CA 91603 USA

For the UK
Share International
P.O. Box 3677, London NW5 1RU UK

For the rest of the world
Share International
P.O. Box 41877, 1009 DB Amsterdam, Holland

INDEX

313

About the Author

Scottish-born painter and esotericist Benjamin Creme has for the last 26 years been preparing the world for the most extraordinary event in human history — the return of our spiritual mentors to the everyday world.

Creme has appeared on television, radio and in documentary films worldwide and lectures throughout Western and Eastern Europe, the USA, Japan, Australia, New Zealand, Canada and Mexico.

Trained and supervised over many years by his own Master, he began his public work in 1974. In 1982 he announced that the Lord Maitreya, the long-awaited World Teacher, was living in London, ready to present Himself openly when invited by the media to do so. This event is now imminent.

Benjamin Creme continues to carry out his task as messenger of this inspiring news. His books, nine at present, have been translated into many languages. He is also the editor of *Share International* magazine, which circulates in over 70 countries. He accepts no money for any of this work.

Benjamin Creme lives in London, is married, and has three children.